Understanding Emotion at Work

Stephen Fineman

SAGE Publications
London • Thousand Oaks • New Delhi

SAGE Publications Ltd
6 Bonhill Street
London EC2A 4PU

SAGE Publications Inc
2455 Teller Road
Thousand Oaks, California 91320

SAGE Publications India Pvt Ltd
B-42, Panchsheel Enclave
Post Box 4109
New Delhi - 100 017

British Library Cataloguing in Publication Data

A catalogue record for this book is available
from the British Library

ISBN 0 7619 4789 2
ISBN 0 7619 4790 6 (pbk)

Library of Congress Control Number available

Typeset by Photoprint, Torquay, Devon
Printed and bound in Great Britain by Athenaeum Press,
Gateshead

Contents

List of figures

Acknowledgements

In writing this book I am deeply grateful to the support and feedback of friends and colleagues. My special thanks to Tina Keifer, Sally Maitlis, Peter Frost, Jane Dutton and Yiannis Gabriel. Anna Fineman's comments were exceptionally helpful in giving a student's, and daughter's, eye view.

Introduction

THE EMOTIONAL ORGANIZATION

There are some bland portraits of organizations. They show organizational charts (boxes linked in hierarchical or mosaic form), formal job descriptions, lists of competencies and objectives, mission statements, inputs and outputs, production flow diagrams and measurement procedures applied to just about anything that is measurable. Over the years, organizational and management theorists have gone some way towards bringing people and life into such stiff images. But the kind of individuals they portray are also, typically, boxed and measured. They are human 'resources' or human 'capital', or 'variables', there to serve the bigger, 'more important', entities – the firm, the industry, production, profit.

The emotional organization overturns this picture. It does two things. First, it places people at the very centre of organization – they *constitute* the organization, what it is and what it can achieve. Second, it reveals emotion as the prime medium through which people act and interact. Organizational procedures and processes are shaped, negotiated, rejected, reformed, fought over or celebrated, because of feelings. Careers blossom or crash through feelings. Offices and departments grow, compete and change around the feelings that frame preferences, politics and ambitions. Who works hard, seems not to care, or rarely takes the initiative, is based on emotion. Organizations change or stagnate because of the emotions that energize or freeze people. All organizations are emotional arenas where feelings shape events, and events shape feelings.

When we enter the workplace we bring our loves, hates, anxieties, envies, excitement, disappointments and pride. We will meet and mix with others who have their own cares and concerns, their own emotional agendas. These are core influences on who we can collaborate with, how comfortable we feel, who we trust, how energized we become, what we can reveal and what we hide. They underpin, consciously or unconsciously, the coalitions, conflicts and negotiations that emerge. All this, in effect, makes 'the job' – what we do, what we produce, how we perform. Emotions are not an optional extra, or incidental to 'real' work. They are part of the warp and weft of work experiences and practices.

It is rare to hear people talk about their work as if it is a feeling-free zone. Confessions soon unroll the loves, disappointments, frustrations, envies and joys, such as in the following accounts:

> My career developed from general management to consultancy to Director-ship of a multinational oil company. I was Managing Director for 5 years. Success stories, high politics and intrigue. It was enormous fun which landed me fantastic bonuses as profits soared. I made the company a market leader. But the team spirit was broken up with the fragmentation of the company. Success breeds jealousy. (Managing Director of Oil Company)[1]

> Building a business can be boring. Heresy? Ask anyone who has been at the top of a company for more than a few years. The daily grind of business consists largely of taking care of thousands of tiny, laborious, details. Very little of what a company does ever sees the light of day, much less the camera lights of press conferences, photo shoots, or commercials. (Bill Marriott, Chief Executive of Marriott Hotels)[2]

> It's a relief when you get off the moving line. It's such a tremendous relief. I can't put it into words. When you're on the line it's on top of you all the time. You may feel ill, not one hundred percent, but that line will be one hundred percent. Being on sub-assembly is like getting off the roundabout. Y'know . . . day in, day out. . . . Never stopping. I still have nightmares about it. I couldn't go back on the line. Not for anything. (Ford Assembly-Line Worker)[3]

Inside such accounts are hints about what organizations and managerial practices can *do* to people emotionally. They can generate fun, pride and exhilaration. They can also make us bored, stressed, anxious and depressed. Our work organizations regulate our feelings – what we are able to express or display. Our emotions are fashioned by powerful social scripts where showing what you 'really' feel can sometimes be risky. It is often appearances that count. Familiar examples are management's desire for a cheery sales-force; the studied seriousness of the physician or lawyer; the sergeant's overblown anger in front of his platoon. When an organization gets a tight grip on what we can and cannot emotionally show or be, is this is a healthy state of affairs? What kind of control should an organization have over our emotions? Are some sectors of our economy becoming lifeless, with their robotized McDonald's or Disney smile?

For most of the time our work experiences are not saturated with the 'big', emotions, such as rage, anger or euphoria. Emotions are just 'there', mundane, barely discernible. Like much of life, being part of an organization is often dominated by everyday routines, such as ritualistic greetings to colleagues, corridor chats, lunchtime habits, periodic checking of e-mail, visiting the washroom, answering predicable phone requests, attending regular meetings and keeping things in their place. Such workaday episodes are, nevertheless, always brushed with feelings, however slight. They inject meaning into our working moments – positive, negative, mixed, conflicting or ambivalent. There is the ebb and flow of boredom, demoralization, self-consciousness, daydreaming, frustration, fun time, exhaustion, anxiety, attraction, play and absorption. Our emotionalities do not simply switch off; they tick over, quietly signalling how things are and how we are doing and what we want to do next.

THE PURPOSE OF THIS BOOK – AND WHO SHOULD READ IT

My aim in this book is to offer students of organizations and management an engaging, critical introduction to emotions in work life. What do organizational phenomena look like through an emotion lens and how might they be understood?

Emotion in organizations is a fascinating area to explore. Indeed, in recent years it has captured the imagination of a remarkable range of thinkers and scientists, from psychologists, sociologists and management theorists, to neuroscientists, biologists, philosophers, anthropologists and historians. In this book I have distilled some of their work. I have tried to bring to life the experiences of workplace emotion and, where appropriate, suggested implications, or questions, for the design or decision processes of an organization.

HOW THIS BOOK IS ORGANIZED

Chapter 2, *Where does emotion come from?*, tells the story, or more accurately the stories, of emotion in organizations. How can we understand emotional processes in organizations? What core perspectives mark the way, and what are the most productive insights? Is emotion biologically fixed? What is the role of early experiences? How is emotion socially shaped? These ideas will crop up in different ways in the chapters to come.

The rest of the book is then divided into two parts: *Organizing with emotion* and *Emotional injuries*.

Part I: organizing with emotion

Part I focuses on some key areas where emotion is directly used, or heavily implicated, in everyday workplace operations or management. It reveals the ways in which emotion is openly harnessed for profit and gain. It shows how emotion can make or break leadership, decision processes and different forms of organizational innovation or change.

Chapter 3, *Recruiting emotion*, explores the way displayed emotions have become appropriated and manipulated by employers. How is it done? What are the costs, benefits and consequences of making emotion a key product in commercial and professional transactions?

Chapter 4, *Being emotionally intelligent*, takes a critical look at the recent explosion of interest in emotional intelligence. Is emotional intelligence something that unlocks the potential for more effective, and more fulfilling, relationships at work? How cautious should we be about its claims?

Chapter 5, *Virtually emotion*, investigates our seduction with new information technologies at work: virtual organizations, computer-mediated work relationships, telecommuting. What happens to our emotions and personal relationships when virtuality penetrates our work lives? Do we end up emotionally impoverished, eyes fixed on screens instead of faces? Or does virtuality transform and enhance our ways of being and feeling?

Chapter 6, *Leading and following – with emotion*, examines leadership – as, quintessentially, an emotional process. Some leaders are skilled emotion managers. They 'move' their followers and their followers place their faith in them. The bond, and its tensions, is a curious one, where fear, love and anxiety can all work together. It is also fragile. The charismatic leader can suddenly lose his or her charm. In turning an emotion spotlight on leadership *and* 'followership', what new insights emerge for our understanding and practice?

Chapter 7, *Emotion and decisions*, focuses on decision making. Dispassionate decision making is taken as the hallmark of an effective manager. Through an emotion lens, however, decision making looks limp without emotions. We *need* emotions to make decisions, especially ethically sound ones. We often make important decisions for emotional reasons, and our moods and emotions – felt and displayed – are deeply implicated in how and what we negotiate. Emotions bind us to certain decisions, as well as blind us to some of their consequences.

Chapter 8, *Emotion and change*, observes organizational change through an emotion lens. Change often involves loss and anxiety. It can also be exciting: the promise of a better future. People often want change, but they are also fearful of it because it represents uncertainty, especially when imposed. Resistance is a common reaction. Some organizational changes try to manipulate group emotion. What are the ethical implications of this?

Part II: emotional injuries

For many people, work offers excitement, challenge and, periodically, joy. But it would misleading (albeit comforting) to present emotion in organizations exclusively in these terms. For every happy moment, there are unhappy ones. Indeed, we tend to talk, ruminate on and take home the emotional distress of work more than the fun moments. When these feelings are persistent and severe they expose the darker side of work – its pains, stresses and violence. This part of the book examines the essence of such injuries and the implications of seeing organizations from such a standpoint.

Chapter 9, *Stress as emotion and fashion*, looks at how stress at work has become a popular 'disease' and emotional 'problem'. What is stress and can it be avoided? What makes stressful feelings stressful? Why is it that some people cannot admit their work stresses, while others talk about stress openly and willingly? Should we look for roots of stress in the individual, the job, the management, the wider social conditions, or all of these?

Chapter 10 is about *Bullying and violence at work*. Such practices prey on fear, insecurity and humiliation. Who bullies and why? Who gets bullied? How do certain organizational cultures produce bullies, even celebrate them? There are workgroups, and even whole institutions, that can be violent. Why? What can be done?

Chapter 11 investigates *Sexual harassment*. Sexual harassment is a particularly pernicious form of violence, involving power and powerlessness. It can create considerable distress for the victim at, and away from, work. The perpetrators are usually, but not always, men – often individually, sometimes in groups. The norms of appropriate sexual conduct at work are neither fixed nor universal, so the boundaries of acceptable sexual conduct can sometime be unclear, and are certainly seen differently by victim and harasser. What are the deeper social and psychological roots of sexual harassment? How do organizations wittingly or unwittingly foster it? What are the organizational responses to complaints about harassment? Do they work?

Chapter 12, *Downsized*, explores the emotional wounds of downsizing on those who are left as 'unhappy stayers' and on those who execute the process. The dominance of downsizing as a fix for organizational ills is examined, as well as the lessons we can learn for the management of the process.

The book concludes with some reflections on the main themes and their implications.

HOW TO USE THIS BOOK

It is important, first, to read Chapter 2, *Where Does Emotion Come from?* This chapter provides the background to the rest of the book. Thereafter, choose any chapter that takes your interest. Some chapters have overlapping themes, and I have indicated where this occurs. There is a full list of references at the end of each chapter, and I have also selected a few sources that will be particularly helpful for further study.

REFERENCES

1   Fineman, S. (1983) *White Collar Unemployment*. Chichester: Wiley. p. 38.
2   Marriott, J.W. and Brown, K.A. (1997) *The Spirit to Serve*. New York: HarperCollins. p. 61.
3   Beynon, H. (1973) *Working for Ford*. London: Allen Lane. p. 128.

Where does emotion come from?

Where does emotion come from? What is it?

At first glance, these seem silly questions to ask. Experientially, emotions just happen . . .

- You can get up in the morning and feel gloomy – and simply not know why.
- You get criticized by your partner and then feel very irritable, even angry.
- You nervously open an envelope containing your examination results, heart pounding, and then feel elated – or devastated.
- You cuddle the family cat and feel warm and cosy (and so, it seems, does the cat).
- You walk through a strange city late at night and feel edgy at the sound of footsteps behind you – and automatically quicken your pace.
- You look attentive and interested as you sit through a long lecture, but actually feel extremely bored and distracted.
- You meet your cheery friends for a drink and instantly feel more cheery yourself.

• You're in love, and everything in the world is absolutely wonderful!

These events show how ubiquitous emotions are. They matter, both in an everyday sense, and with the big issues of life. John Elster captures the point well:

> Most simply, emotions matter because if we did not have them nothing else would matter. Creatures without emotion would have no reason for living nor, for that matter, for committing suicide . . . Emotions are the stuff of life. Emotions are the most important bond or glue that links us together.[1]

But how do they matter? A close look at the experiences above gives us some clues. What we privately feel and what we publicly show are sometimes very different. Displaying the 'right' emotion keeps an organization on track. The personal meaning of a social situation or event shapes emotion.

Emotion can spontaneously affect our body processes and behaviour. How we are evaluated, and how we evaluate others, triggers particular feelings. Some feelings can swamp our perceptions. We are often unaware of the reason for our feelings. We can 'catch' others' emotions.

Different perspectives on emotion, which have their roots in many different disciplines, try to make sense of these processes. But before looking at them, there are some definitional issues. We commonly talk about emotion, feeling and mood interchangeably, and so do some writers in the field. Although there is little consensus when it comes to definitions, some important distinctions can be made:

• There is the *subjective* element of emotions, what we *feel*. And there is the *displayed* feature of emotion, what we *show*. In this book I have, generally, distinguished between the two by using the term 'emotion' for the display, and 'feeling' for the subjective, private, experience.
• What we show of our feelings, our emotional performance, is heavily influenced by social conventions and the impressions we wish to convey to others. It is *socially constructed*.
• Feelings and emotions are usually short-term and attached to a particular object or occurrence: 'angry with Jane', 'jealous of John', 'delighted with the gift'. They come and go fairly quickly. Some are intense and hard driving (like rage, spite, terror), others more subdued. Many will be mixed, uncertain, ambivalent – love with hate, guilt with excitement, anger with embarrassment.
• *Moods* are feelings that linger (such as being in a sad mood, depressed mood, cheerful mood). They are not linked to any particular object or event; the cause or trigger is often obscure. They typically undulate gradually over time. We may feel gloomy all morning, but cheery by mid-afternoon, only to feel down again when we arrive home in the evening. Some people have fairly steady moods, while others are 'moody', experiencing more frequent shifts in feeling. Moods are often hard to disguise.

There is one further term mentioned by writers on emotion: *affect*. This is an all-encompassing expression for any emotional or emotionalized activity. It is sometimes used instead of 'feeling' or 'emotion'.

EMOTION PERSPECTIVES

Emotion perspectives divide roughly into four types: *emotion as biological*; *emotion as early experiences*; *emotion as cognitive appraisal*; *emotion as social*. All offer insights into the way feeling and emotion arise, and I have borrowed from each in the chapters that follow. However, I have particular regard for the social perspective, because it shows how much feeling and emotion are embedded in cultural learning and cultural practices, of which work organizations are inevitably a part. It also suggests routes for productive change in organizations. I shall return to this point later.

Emotion as biological: 'It's all in the genes'

> 'Gerry. It's not that I think just your analysis is faulty', barked Gerry's boss across the table. 'It's based on a complete, incompetent, misreading of the situation!'. He sat back and glared at Gerry.
>
> Gerry, normally a mild-mannered man, reddened. There was a tense silence. Then Gerry got up from his seat and made as if to leave the room. He suddenly stopped, spun round and exploded in rage: 'How dare you say that to me! Months of work with no help, scant reward, and virtually no interest from you. You can stuff your job! He then marched out of the room, slamming the door behind him.'

A biological perspective holds that many of our basic emotional responses are 'wired' into our body system through genetic heritage. In other words, we are preprogrammed to respond emotionally; and that is no accident. Emotional responses are, or certainly have been, very useful for our survival. When under threat, like Gerry, the reasoning of the heart, not the head, takes over. Fury and anger drive his action to restore some sense of here-and-now integrity, esteem and self-respect. The possible future consequences are not measured in such an instinctive response.

The perspective was fundamental to Charles Darwin's monumental work, *The Expression of the Emotions in Man and Animals* published in 1872.[2] Darwin concluded that many of our emotional reactions are rooted in prehistoric patterns of survival, the genetic residue of which is still with us. For instance, snarling, which developed from the action of biting, now simply shows as displeasure. Raising one's hands, open palm, now signals rejection, but it was once an act of direct physical repulsion – pushing another away.

Darwin was particularly interested in the universality of emotional expressions across different human cultures. Would, for instance, the expression of anger in the USA be recognized as anger by the natives of New Guinea, and vice versa? The more an emotional expression was recognized universally, the more likely it was to be part of our evolutionary inheritance. Darwin was convinced that there were universal emotions, and recent cross-cultural research tends to broadly support him, at least for a small cluster of emotions: fear, sadness, disgust and enjoyment.[3, 4] These can be read off the face and body with relative ease in most parts of the globe, despite our ability to fake or mask them. Others, such as guilt, humour and embarrassment, are not so easily recognizable; they depend on the culture and particular social conventions. Yet even these emotions may be considered derivations from the major emotions, rather like secondary from primary colours.[5] Astutely, Darwin separated subjective feeling from the observable display of emotion, as they can be very different. We may look angry, but feel content; we may look shocked, yet feel unfazed. The social and organizational *use* and *meaning* of emotion is complex, depending on what, and how, we want to communicate.

Darwin marked the way for subsequent biological approaches. He showed that extent to which we are all, in part, the genetic legacy of our distant ancestors. Comparatively, modern societies are a blip in the human evolutionary timescale, so it is not surprising that the civilization of our emotions is likely to be but a very thin veneer.

The emotional brain   Evolutionary psychologists have recently been intensely interested in building on Darwin's insights. Emotional reactions are seen as the result of neurological programmes that have developed over the ages to meet recurring demands on human survival. These include dealing with sexual infidelity, fighting, falling in love, finding food and responding to the death of a family member. Some feelings (for instance fear, envy, grief) set off a cascade of chemical and behavioural changes which help the individual survive – to live another day, to preserve an essential community or relationship.[6, 7]

Such primitive programming is said to be still very much with us in our work settings. It shapes the emphasis on hierarchies, male patterns of dominance, alliances, aggression, and even the kind of corporations that will, or will not, succeed.[8, 9] These claims have sparked fierce controversy, some critics accusing evolutionary psychologists of blind religious fervour.[10] Clearly, the assertion that we have a genetic destiny, regardless of the social systems we create, is not to be taken lightly – and is at variance with many of the social theories of emotion, as we shall discuss below.

One part of the human body that contains evolutionary secrets is the brain. It has long been believed that areas at the front of the brain, the prefrontal lobes, regulate people's moods. So much so that, up until the 1950s, it was fairly common to 'lobotomize' patients who suffered extreme anxiety or depression. This was a drastic surgical procedure, with mixed success. However, the prefrontal lobes are still regarded as playing a major role in controlling emotion (see Chapter 7, *Emotion and decisions*). In another area of the brain, there is a small, almond-shaped, structure called the *amygydala*. It identifies threat and danger, key to our self-preservation. It signals when anger, fear or aggression is called for. People who suffer damage to their amygydala, through disease or accident, fail to respond to danger with fear, anger or rage, or to recognize emotional faces.

But these physiological–emotional processes are not stand-alone. The thinking, or cognitive, parts of the brain are constantly conversing with the emotional parts. They need each other.[11–13] While some emotional responses may be 'hard-wired' into the brain, what makes us feel in a particular way is much affected by learning and experience. This is illustrated by attempts to find unique biochemical fingerprints for different emotions. For example, fear, excitement, feeling overwhelmed and sudden surprise are all different feelings, but, when measured for their physiological arousal, there is little to distinguish between them. Furthermore, being deliberately swamped with a fear-arousing chemical does not mean that that fear is necessarily felt.[14] Our psychological processes intervene. William James, an eminent nineteenth-century psychologist, exposed a further twist. Does emotional experience cause bodily changes, or is it the other way round? Do we automatically feel sad because we are crying? Are we afraid because we are shaking? He was convinced that the physical change stimulated the feeling. This logic fits with the way our own act of smiling can sometimes make us feel happier, and how we often feel sad on seeing someone else's tears of distress.[15]

As we learn more about the physiology and biology of emotion it becomes clear that the capacity to be emotional is fundamental to human existence. In this respect evolution has done us a remarkable favour. Emotions provide us with key signals on how to cope with crises, as well as with everyday demands and encounters. They help us adapt to our changing needs and circumstances and provide us with the capacity to create and share meanings. Our inherited emotional tendencies may also lend general shape to the way we organize our societal affairs. The broad backcloth is in place, but that takes us only so far. Human emotions are also embedded in a lifetime of accumulated experiences and learning. We need to look at other perspectives to unravel these influences.

Emotion as early experiences: the psychodynamic connection

> What is hurting this organization? How do I interpret what key people cite as their main problem? The pain may be literally what the informants say it is or it may be something more deep seated.[16]

Our feelings today can be shaped by events of yesterday and yesteryear. We can relive old experiences in the present – but often not know why, or even when, because the original feelings are so buried and deep seated. These are processes that intrigued Sigmund Freud. His psychodynamic approach to emotion is significant in understanding emotion and some of its organizational manifestations.

Freud was particularly influenced by Darwin's *The Expression of the Emotions in Man and Animals*, and it was to affect his practice as a physician in nineteenth-century Vienna. Freud, however, was no ordinary physician. His dominant concern was with the severe emotional problems of his patients, especially hysteria. Hysteria was characterized by excessive or uncontrollable fears, or other strong emotions. It was often accompanied by unusual physical symptoms, such as nervous ticks, stammering, even paralysis of limbs, all with no obvious physical-disease basis. Like Darwin, Freud reasoned that the past contained clues to present behaviour, and that once-functional responses can outlive their usefulness.

An emotional reaction to a painful event in childhood, such as a deep shock, fear or trauma, can become fixed in such a way that it disables a person in later life. The emotional response continues as if the object of the threat or pain still exists. Importantly, such emotional flooding is often beyond the consciousness of the patient. The emotional roots of the problem are lodged in the *unconscious*. Freud's therapeutic approach was to help his patients discharge the unconsciously held emotions attached to their symptoms. Unconscious conflicts would be brought into the open where they could be resolved through *catharsis*. Catharsis derives from the Greek *kathartikos*, to purify or purge, and is the basis of *psychoanalysis*, or the 'talking cure'.

According to Freud, most of personality is hidden, rather like an iceberg. He called this area the *id*, the seat of primitive desires that demand instant gratification. It is where our unacceptable passions are repressed: a reservoir for unconscious impulses. Our conscious awareness, the *ego*, is the smallest area, the part of the iceberg that we see on the surface. As our ego develops it helps us deal with real-world demands, balancing them with id urges; it is like an executive, policing our perceptions and actions. The *superego* is the voice of conscience. The superego matures as we internalize the values of our parents and culture. It interacts with the ego to shape what we do and what we feel in accord with the moral codes around us. Freud did not intend these categories to be literal, nor to correspond to physical parts of the brain or body. They are conceptual representations of psychological processes that are dynamic and interacting.

Freud's legacy has been far reaching. It has also been controversial as researchers test and question the validity of his assumptions.[17–19] We are left, however, with some strong images.

- First, that we are all, to an extent, prisoners of our past; our personal history, our childhood experiences, our relationships with parents and siblings, all mould our personalities and emotional sensitivities.

- Second, some of these events can be particularly traumatic, such as a death in the family, abuse, a marriage break-up, or failure at school. These can leave their emotional mark, painful feelings and anxieties that we try to shut out, or repress from consciousness.
- Third, by doing this, the pain does not simply vanish but can leak into, and transform, our everyday conduct. The precise outcome rather depends upon the psychological *defence mechanisms* we unwittingly deploy. Painful feelings may be *converted* into unusual physical reactions, such as Freud observed in his hysteric patients. Other defences include: *rationalization*, the elaborate justification of our actions; *projection*, attributing one's own feeling to others; *regression*, adopting patterns of behaviour that were comforting in childhood; *sublimation*, channelling 'unacceptable' urges into socially acceptable forms; and *reaction formation*, changing a feeling into its opposite.

Into organizations   Psychoanalysis has moved off the couch, so to speak, into organizations. Organizational psychoanalysts have used Freud's ideas to examine the functioning, and especially the ills, of organizational life. Through their eyes, we get a picture of organizations shaped by the unconscious desires of their members. The organization is a cauldron of repressed thoughts, fantasies and hopes. People behave according to concealed personal agendas, urges that are often at odds with the formal aims of the organization, but which contribute to the political buzz, plots and passions of work life. They also underpin the motives of key players in the organization, especially organizational leaders. Unconscious fears are seen to distort reality and undermine organizational 'rationality', efficiency and health.

Workgroups are similarly affected. From a psychoanalytic perspective, workgroups can raise feelings of vulnerability, embarrassment and fear among their members, corresponding to the tensions and dramas of early family life.[20–22] When there is a shared threat, such as facing new working methods, radical organizational change, or a shift in leadership, the group can regress to childlike behaviour. They may refuse to cooperate with management or become aggressive. These reactions are likely to be organizationally unhelpful, but they are comforting and bonding to group members, just as they might have been during childhood.

Groups may protect themselves in other ways, through *social defences*. Social defences are shared organizational regimes or states that protect people from primitive anxieties, such as about sexuality, death, or disaster. An example is the impersonal way of working by nurses in some hospitals, where patients are known by their bed number or disease type. Strict routines are adhered to – regardless of patient need – such as waking a patient to administer drugs, even when it is better for the patient to let them sleep.[23, 24] What appears bureaucratic or unfeeling is no accident of organization; it emerges to screen the nurses from the anxiety of death, physical intimacy with patients, and making difficult decisions about a patient's care.

In summary, the shadows of early-learning experiences are often faintly, sometimes sharply, present in the way our lives are emotionalized. Psychoanalysts offer a stark picture of the way personal histories matter. In our desire to feel in control – especially in 'rational', 'clear thinking', organizations – it is insightful, but disturbing, to be informed that our aspirations and choices are not always what they seem. Yet psychoanalysts are constrained by their preoccupation with one emotional area – anxiety. They also tend to overemphasize the grip of early-life experiences and underplay the important effects of the social and organizational structures of power and domination on our feelings. Moreover, their success at making organizations less anxious and more rational is limited.[25–27]

Emotion as cognitive appraisal

There was perfunctory knock on the door and Helen's supervisor walked in, looking stressed. It was 5.15 pm. Helen's heart sank as she saw a bundle of new invoices in her supervisor's hand – more work, more pressure . . .

A cognitive perspective, unlike a psychoanalytic approach, proposes that emotion is not 'there' in any meaningful psychological sense until we *appraise*, or try and make sense of, what we see or hear. Feeling and emotion follows the appraisal process. So the gloom and anxiety that Helen feels when her supervisor enters the room stems from the meaning that the event has for her. She knows that it is rare for her supervisor to visit, especially at that late hour, and it occurs only when she is going to be asked to take on extra work. Helen's cognitive processes – memory, knowledge of boss – come into play in evaluating, or appraising, the event. As it is seen as threatening, pushing her in a direction she would rather not go, anxiety follows (see also Chapter 9, *Stress as emotion and fashion*).

Richard Lazarus and his colleagues have been prominent in developing appraisal theory of emotion.[28–31] Lazarus identifies two forms of appraisal: *primary* and *secondary*. In primary appraisal, the individual is, in effect, asking of him or herself, '*Does this situation affect me personally? Am I in trouble or benefited in some way, now or in the future?*' Secondary appraisal raises different questions: '*What can I do about it? How can I cope?*' So, to return to Helen, we could sketch a very different scenario. Helen knows she has some good news to tell her boss as soon as he enters the room, as well as having a slack week ahead. She is pleased to see him, and happy to be able to assist him with the invoices. Importantly, she also knows that this will help her in the future when she needs some time off. Together, the processes of primary and secondary appraisal shape the quality and quantity of the emotional reaction.

The observation that 'headwork' precedes 'heartwork' has been a popular perspective in the understanding of emotion. It also seems intuitively plausible. For example, why fear a snake unless we believe that that snake can do us harm? Some interpretation of the meaning of the object or event is clearly an important part of the flow of feeling and emotion. Cognitive appraisal theory, however, does not address the way that appraisals *themselves* are often laced with feeling and body sensations, especially in complex social interactions.[32] In other words our appraisal processes are also likely to be emotional. In the psychological world, we cannot draw a neat separation between the two; thinking and feeling interpenetrate. We often go through multiple feelings/appraisals as events unfold – they get mixed and confused. Appraisal theory, moreover, tells us little about the *social* and *cultural* contexts of our appraisals and emotions, the nub of much organizational emotion. For enlightenment here, we turn to social theories.

Emotion as social

> What do you do when a policeman takes his trousers off in front of you? I was with this police superintendent in his small, well-ordered, office – a first meeting – conducting a research interview with him. He was in full uniform. He was a very formal man, and quite proper in his style. After about an hour and a half he invited me to go lunch with him at a local restaurant. I was pleased to accept. He said he would have to change out of his uniform, and made as if to go to another room. Instead, he stopped at a large wardrobe in the office, took out his civilian clothes, and slowly started to change in front of me, removing his trousers first of all. I was suddenly struck by the absurdity of it all. This sober, authoritarian man silently performing a fairly private act in front of a relative stranger – and in a work office. I felt embarrassed, but I did not want to show it. I stumbled for something to chat about, but I just couldn't continue the interview while he was standing there in his underpants. It felt like a sketch from Monty Python! I tried to hide my embarrassment (he wasn't the slightest bit ruffled) by getting up, talking about the weather, and then, strolling as casually as I could into an adjacent room – until he had finished changing.[33]

To say emotion is social is to spotlight the cultural settings in which emotions are learned and expressed. For the researcher in the above story, the emotion norms of the formal setting meant preserving decorum and seriousness. But the policeman's 'private' act, and ease about it, sent confusing signals. It confronted the researcher with a sight he felt he should not witness. He felt embarrassed, but could not show it without disturbing an important professional relationship. Saving his face, and his host's, was crucial.

Social learning is seen to transform, or overwrite, evolutionary impulses, as well as reshape our early-life experiences and interpretations. A social perspective emphasizes:

- the effects of different cultural experiences and everyday social expectations
- emotion roles and scripts
- language and interpretation.

These are the elements of the *social construction* of emotion. Social constructionists believe that we are neither stuck in the tramlines of evolution, nor with our past experiences or traumas. They also believe that the physiological changes that may accompany feelings do not tell us about the *meaning* of those feelings, emotion, because meaning is a cultural artefact, something that is peculiar to the personal, social and communicative setting. Take, for instance, sheep's eyeballs, a delicacy in some Arab cultures. Compare the different emotional and physical responses of a Western and Arab diner when presented with this 'delicacy'. Both will see, smell, and possibly touch, the dish. However, whether these sensations are felt as disgust, pleasure, excitement or apprehension depends on how eyeballs fit with the diners' beliefs about appropriate and acceptable food – something very much rooted in their own culture.

But the social link does not end there. What, for instance, should a disgusted diner *do*, emotionally? Grimace and groan to their companion? Throw up their hands in horror? Smile wanly? Look excited and appreciative? The display of emotion depends on the relationship between the parties, and how each wants to be seen in the social context. Are they old, trusting friends or new business contacts? Are they eating in a smart restaurant, a family house, or off a street stall? The social rules of emotional display will vary according to the circumstances, and how those circumstances are interpreted by each of parties. If the Westerner is an honoured guest in the Arab's home, then he may have to swallow, literally and metaphorically, his disgust.

There are occasions when a diet-rule is so passionately held and ideologically entrenched that it will overrule all other courtesies. A committed vegetarian or vegan would be prepared to risk offence to a host, rather than eat unacceptable food. It is not unknown for followers of a strict Kosher diet to become physically ill, and also feel profoundly guilty, if they discover they have accidentally consumed food forbidden by orthodox Judaism. The connection between feeling, body and social meaning, is especially powerful in such circumstances.

All words?   Emotion words and emotion talk are key ingredients of a social constructionist perspective. To love, hate, despise, fear, worry, cry, giggle, smile, smirk, enthuse and so forth, are descriptions that are all socially and politically loaded. That is, we tend to attribute some value to them, and that value and meaning can shift according to the context and culture in which they are used. For example, the very notion of being 'highly emotional' is itself a pejorative label in many managerial and professional circles, yet we will apply it more forgivingly to young children, actors and artists. Social anthropologists, who study the way very different communities behave and express their meanings, have revealed some dramatic differences in the way emotions are expressed and labelled. 'Wild pig behaviour' would not be used to describe a human emotional state in the West, but in the highlands of New Guinea, it is a sometimes-familiar sight. One writer explains:

> In the highlands of New Guinea, otherwise normal men in their mid-twenties may occasionally explode into patterns of 'wild pig behavior'. The

'wild pig' will break into local dwellings, loot, shoot arrows at bystanders, and generally make an abysmal nuisance of himself. After several days he will disappear into the forest where he destroys what he has taken . . . Afterwards, he again enters the village, unable to recall his actions and seldom reminded by the villagers.[34]

In this instance, translation into the terms of Western emotion is tricky. Is the man temporarily insane, over-excited, love-smitten, frustrated, sad, jealous? Without knowing the meaning of his behaviour in relationship to the community expectations and traditions, we cannot but guess, and even then, our own emotion words – and the values inherent in them – may do scant justice to the experience of the event.

The stories we tell   We often express our feelings in direct, discrete, terms: 'I feel really pissed off today'; 'I'm so happy to be here'. Sometimes, however, the words we use to convey our feelings are wrapped in a *story narrative*, a tale about 'what happened when . . .', 'I must tell you about . . .', 'have you heard what happened to . . .'. The stories we tell give substance, nuance, purpose and legitimacy to our feelings. Stories at work are a key mechanism to express what is bothering us, what excites us, what is oppressive, what we aspire to. Stories are intrinsically social in that that they are shaped for a particular audience, place and time, and often involve other characters, apart from ourselves. They are also mobile and mutable. We often adjust and embellish the narrative of our story about, for example, 'how the boss treated me when he called me into his office last week', according to whether we are talking to our colleague, the departmental secretary, the office cleaner, a best friend or our partner. The story is not a measure of objective truth of an event, but is a fine indicator of our feelings and how we wish to present them – and influence different people.

Stories are of different types.[35-37] Some have an epic quality, where pride and enthusiasm attend the heroic exploits of the teller (such as standing up to an overbearing boss). There are comic stories where laughter and amusement is at the expense of a disliked person. Tragic stories stress fear and compassion, where someone is suffering in an uncaring organization. Finally, there are romantic stories where love, nostalgia and affection feature, such as with acts of kindness in the organization, or romantic attachments. For psychoanalysts, organizational stories are ripe for interpretation of hidden meanings – wishes, fantasies, desires. They are an emotional coding of the work culture of an organization. Social constructionists tend to take a different slant: stories do more than represent individual emotions, they actually *constitute* the emotional form of work life. They are alive in social interactions, moulded by the cultural language and conventions of organization.

Emotion conventions   Emotion conventions are embedded in social etiquette. They are socially transmitted principles of 'correct' emotional display. Occasionally, as in the opening story in this section, we stumble because we are not sure what is appropriate – when we are in a strange situation, a foreign country, or unfamiliar culture. Nods, winks, smiles, tears and tantrums can vary considerably in emotional nuance within a culture. Across nations, the permutations of meaning are myriad. Emotion conventions, often referred to as 'emotion rules', signal the appropriate emotional display for the situation, event or happening. They help to sustain relationships and organizational order. They reinforce status divisions, deference patterns, belonging and collaboration. They keep us in our place. Knowing when it is acceptable to express anger, affection, love, fear, derision, sexual attraction or pleasure – regardless of what is privately felt – is fundamental to the making and maintenance of relationships and organizations.

Emotion conventions control what we outwardly express to particular audiences. A teenager's grunts to his or her perplexed parents transforms to a babble of excitement with a close friend, and to a polite smile with a teacher. Displays of grief are expected at funerals in some of parts of the world, but laughter is in order in other regions. We are usually expected to appear serious, respectful and attentive before a lecturer or a judge, but when partying and clubbing it is fun-time, and extravagant displays of pleasure are in order.

Master passions   Mostly, we conform to conventional rules of emotional behaviour because of special, learned, social-control emotions. *Shame* and *embarrassment* are particularly important. Both are uncomfortable and are to be avoided if possible. Shame is felt when we contravene a moral code. Embarrassment occurs when we break a local norm, such as the expectations of a work relationship or workgroup. It would be shameful deliberately to exploit someone else's personal weakness or vulnerability in a work team-meeting, but it would be embarrassing to forget to prepare the agenda for that meeting. Knowing that something we might do could be shameful or embarrassing often restrains that behaviour. The expected feelings act as a self-policing process that is crucial for maintaining social order – it stops us, most of the time, from stepping out of line. This is most apparent in our efforts to deal with people who seem not to experience shame or embarrassment in conventional ways – the 'oddball', eccentric, or persistent anti-conformist.

Yet to *be* shamed is not always a quiet, private, affair. Public shaming for an errant soul can happen in gangs, village communities or nationally (a favoured role of the media). In highly competitive organizations, exposing 'poor' performers publicly, such as in performance league tables, has the effect of celebrating winners at the price of the losers' shame. The ritual helps to reinforce a particular set of corporate values. But to be shamed in a way that is felt unjust can spark powerful retributive emotions, such as rage, revenge, or bitter resentment. History is replete with battles, literal and in courts-of-law, fought to retrieve a reputation or honour after being 'wrongly' shamed.[38, 39] There are, however, important national–cultural nuances. For example, in Japan, compared to the UK or USA, shame holds a strong grip on the disciplining of social conduct; it is a 'shame culture'. The USA, in contrast, has been described as a 'guilt culture'.[40]

The idea that a few major feelings can shape major changes, or directions, in a society and organizations, is intriguing. Shame and embarrassment are not the only ones. Fear and insecurity in a population, for instance, have helped many a dictator rise to power. Love and trust of a national leader have energized social movements (see Chapter 6). Resistance, rebellion and subjugation, such as in worker lockouts and strikes, can be traced to feelings – especially fear and pride – stemming from a loss or gain of power, control or status.[41, 42] Recent writers have reflected on the way many of our major institutions and organizations have arisen to serve the 'master passions' that seep into our lives and grip us, particularly ambition, envy, jealousy and rage.[43] Such feelings can drive corporate takeovers, leadership battles, and internecine wars amongst directors or departmental heads.

Feeling-rules   Compared to the public world of emotions, our private feelings are in a quiet preserve, where social courtesies and protocols cannot intrude. Or so it seems. For social constructionists, this perception is a myth. As well as rules for the display of emotion, we internalize *feeling-rules* on what we ought, privately, to feel in particular circumstances or settings: celebrations, love, loss, achievement, winning, failing, on holiday, on the birth of a child, facing conflict, and so forth. The 'correct' feelings will, like emotion display-rules, be culturally specific. For example, beating an opponent in a competition should result in feelings of pride in many Western settings, but humility in some Asian cultures. The socially correct feeling is further reinforced when others remind us what we 'ought' to be experiencing in a particular circumstance – 'You surely must feel so . . . (happy, sad, and so forth)'.

Of course, we do not always feel what we are supposed to feel because our feelings connect with our own personal interpretation of events. But others can influence those interpretations. It is not uncommon to persuade, or argue, people 'out' of their feelings, to put them back 'on track'. Finally passing a tough examination, after months of preparation, may leave you feeling flat and exhausted: it is an anticlimax. You confide this to your best friend, who protests: 'Wow, how can you feel that way? You've finally cracked it; that's fantastic! You really ought to feel great; it's a huge achievement, let's celebrate!' And you begin to believe him or her and, indeed, start to feel different, excited and a little proud.

If we are persuaded to put on a happy face in a situation where happiness is expected (at a party, a wedding, getting a new job, passing an examination) then we may actually begin to *feel* happy. This is most evident when feelings are *socially contagious*, the 'picking up' of others' fun, laughter, sympathy, aggression, fervour or sadness. It can operate subtlety as people note the tiny body cues (tone of voice, posture, facial expression) of another's mood and automatically mimic them. Doing this can help sustain a relationship or bond. At other times, contagion transmits urgent emotional messages, spreading them rapidly from person to person, such as joy at the safety of a loved one, or fear because of the threat of layoffs.

Emotional contagion also unites groups, helping individuals to feel psychologically bigger, more secure and energized. Football crowds, pop concerts, evangelistic religious gatherings, political conferences and civil riots, are prime examples. Work organizations have borrowed this principle when they organize grand events to motivate their employees, such as celebrating 'salesperson of the year', a new product launch, or organizational growth.[44] A heady mix of rousing music, fine wine, high-quality food and stirring speeches creates a seductive emotional aura for delegates to feel good about themselves and their company.

Emotion scripts   Emotion and feeling rules are social products that have their 'scripts'. 'Scripts', because they are ways of expressing our feelings that are already inscribed into the language and stories that make up a culture. Emotion scripts define the ways people are able to talk about their feelings, within the social rules that govern those feelings.

For example, an emotion rule for a man may be, *You never reveal how vulnerable you feel.* To the observation 'you're looking upset', the scripted response could be a curt denial, '*Oh' I'm fine*', or a reversal, '*Am I? That's funny, I'm really enjoying this job*', or a deflection, '*Not as miserable as you look!*' The scripts are designed to reinforce the emotion rule. They are rarely original, having been heard or used before, although perhaps adapted by the user. They are consistent with what a 'man' can say about his feelings, and the appearances he has to maintain. Emotion scripts, therefore, are gendered.[45] For a woman, a script for the rule *Hide your aggression and anger* might be '*Please can we talk about that a bit more?*' or '*I'm feeling a bit uneasy about that*'. Scripts also reflect status, power and occupation: how royalty, chief executives, janitors, police officers and physicians are differently able to describe how they feel – in public, in private, or to themselves.

Conflicting scripts: the importance of hypocrisy   We are all emotional hypocrites. This is not meant in a pejorative sense, but in the spirit of its Greek derivation, *hypokrisis* – playing a part on stage. Without such hypocrisy it would be very difficult, if not impossible, to achieve a viable working order, either for everyday social communication and relationships, or for producing the goods and services that we have come to appreciate. So, we become skilled at faking, masking, dissembling; not always showing what we feel, and not always feeling what we show.

To achieve this we engage in *emotion work*, a term coined by American sociologist Arlie Hochschild.[46, 47] Emotion work is the effort we put into presenting and re-presenting our feelings; scripting them to be fit for external consumption. It is also the effort we put into feeling what we ought to feel. Emotion work can be hard work, even stressful, especially when we feel we are 'battling with ourselves' to disguise our feelings. Hochschild was particularly interested in what happened when an employer appropriated emotion work, when emotion work turned into *emotional labour*.

Emotional labourers hold jobs where an employer is, in effect, purchasing their emotional display: the smile, the cool demeanour, the cheery disposition, the firmness. Emotional labour has replaced traditional physical labour, or brawn, as one of the crucial requirements of many jobs, especially in the service sector: the flight attendant, the hamburger salesperson, the call-centre operator. Hochschild was concerned about the difficulties such people experienced when their emotional display and private feelings have to follow corporate rules and scripts; when an employer, in effect, hijacks emotional hypocrisy. She describes the *surface acting* and the *deep acting* that is involved. Surface acting is simulating emotions not actually felt. Deep acting involves suppressing what you privately feel, to come into line with what the employer wants you to feel. Thus surface acting changes outward behaviour; deep acting changes experienced feeling. Surface acting, of course, is not just the prerogative of the service giver. It is also for the customer to do emotion work (a little or a lot) to reciprocate the 'smile', or to deal with their pique or anger at not receiving the kind of smile and 'warmth' they have come to expect.

The concept of emotional labour has been highly influential on our thinking about how emotion at work is socially affected (see Chapter 3 for a more extensive discussion). There have been important debates on the ethical and psychological implications of emotional labour, such as whether emotional labour is oppressive and exploitative. Do emotional labourers suffer, or do they find creative ways of coping? It has also raised questions about occupations or professions that have long internalized emotional labour, such as nurses, counsellors, social workers and physicians.[48-50]

Being authentic?   Another matter raised in discussions on emotional labour, concerns authenticity. When are we being authentic, or real? A common answer is: the authentic 'me' is my private, inner, feelings; my public display of emotion is a far less reliable indicator, as shown in Figure 2.1. However, social constructionists are not entirely at ease with this picture. They will point out that private feelings are shaped by social and cultural influences, just like public displays of emotion, so what makes them any more authentic? Moreover, we do not necessarily have one fixed notion of our selves, but carry different identities depending on where we are and whom we are with. Life is a montage of identities. The basis for feeling authentic or genuine can be different when we are out with our friends, working at the office, being with our family or playing a sport.[51, 52] The idea of *a* core centre of authenticity, revealed by stripping away the surface layers of 'falsehood', begins to melt away.

But are there not some feelings that are so special, so intimate, that their authenticity shines through, such as being in love? Expressions of love are not all that they appear.[53, 54] For a start, romantic love is a *discourse*, a

FIGURE 2.1
Being authentic?

My real feelings;
the authentic me

⟶

My public face;
the false me

particular way of talking about and expressing feeling, which itself defines that feeling. It often has a number of sub-discourses, such as on eroticism, friendship and possession. All these are cultural products, expressed in films, novels, plays, popular magazines, TV soap operas, newspapers and advertisements. Our exposure to them, and related influences, gives us a 'love' package to draw upon when we are searching to give meaning to feeling. Wetherall puts it thus:

> . . . it is not the case that every woman and man in love magically find themselves uttering, creating and discovering afresh, for the first time, these words as the mirror or reflection of their experience, although they may well feel they are doing just that. The words instead are second-hand, already in circulation, already in there, waiting for the moment of appropriation.[55]

This view rightly deromanticizes our uniqueness, but it also exaggerates the power of ready-made social scripts. We are often 'lost for words' when experiencing feelings such as love, so we improvise and invent. The love script, in particular, is remarkable for its mutability and multiplicity over the ages, as our playwrights and poets constantly reveal. A puzzle is why the belief in 'being real' persists. In Western Europe and the USA, especially, there is a huge self-help, self-discovery, industry which extols the benefits of discovering the 'authentic you', your 'inner self', 'true feelings', 'hidden passions'. All this feeds the popular belief that seeking authenticity is a worthy venture. It reflects what some psychoanalysts and philosophers tell us: we yearn to escape a sense of rootlessness, nothingness or artifice. The invention of a place where real feelings can be found and liberated is a step along the way.

Perhaps, also, it stems from the existential moments that seem beyond the touch of feeling-rules or social determinism. There is the special *flow* of feeling when, for example, listening to music we love; engrossed in the beauty of a fine work of art; marvelling at a stunning natural landscape; comforted by someone we trust. Flow is being totally, and positively, absorbed in what one is doing; a deep sense of rightness, goodness, engagement or being. Potentially, it could happen in any job, but it is often reported by artistic and high-skilled workers, such as dancers, potters, designers, writers, surgeons, computer programmers and mathematicians. Is a sense of flow the most real of real feelings?[56-58]

CONCLUSION

The emotion field is rich in ideas and perspectives. It has intrigued philosophers, psychologists and sociologists, as well as biological scientists. We learn that feelings and emotions are central to just about everything we do. They have genetic components, which have been crucial for human survival. However, their mystery cannot be unravelled without knowing something about (a) the personal background of the individual, (b) the meaning of situations to the individual, and (c) the cultural and organizational context that shapes the way emotion is expressed and controlled.

All these processes carry over into our workplaces. Here, a psychodynamic perspective tells us that we are not emotionally empty vessels when we get anxious about change, fearful about a new leader, infatuated with a colleague, envious of someone's promotion or aggressively ambitious. We are acting-out some of the desires and distresses that we have been carrying from our early-life experiences, and will probably continue to do so. Getting to know more of the individual background of our colleagues, leaders or subordinates is one way to appreciate their emotional reactions and gain access to how they interpret their demands and pressures.

However, it is the social construction of emotion that provides especially revealing understandings, as well as the prospect of change. Change is closed to the biological determinist, and hard to realize for psychodynamic theorists. Emotions are not all our own, although we like to think they are. They are borrowed from our national and organizational culture, and we return them in sometimes modified form. This is how the norms of appropriate feelings and emotions change over time. The culture of the organization helps create and reinforce the dominant emotions of control in the workplace, such as guilt, fear, shame, anxiety or 'looking happy'. We have to learn what emotional 'face' is appropriate, and when. We are subject to influences from our boss, workgroup and colleagues on how and what to feel, or pretend to feel – to keep the social atmosphere cool, to be suitably deferent, to be the right kind of male, female, manager, accountant or personnel specialist. We have roles to play at work, and those roles have emotional scripts attached to them. Hypocrisy is part of the act. How these, and other processes, contribute to emotionalizing organizations, and what we can do about them, is discussed in the chapters to come.

FURTHER READING

Fineman, S. (1995) 'Emotion and organizing', in S. Clegg, C. Hardy and W. Nord (eds), *Handbook of Organization Studies*. London: Sage.
Gabriel, Y. (1999) *Organizations in Depth: The Psychoanalysis of Organizations*. London: Sage.
Lazarus, R.S. and Lazarus, B.N. (1996) *Passion and Reason: Making Sense of our Emotions*. New York: Oxford University Press.
Parkinson, B. (1995) *Ideas and Realities of Emotion*. London: Routledge.

REFERENCES

1   Elster, J. (1999) *Alchemies of the Mind*. Cambridge: Cambridge University Press. p. 403.
2   Darwin, C. (1872) *The Expression of the Emotions in Man and Animals*. London: Murray.
3   Ekman, P. (ed.) (1998) *Introduction and Afterward to the Third Edition of Darwin's Expression of the Emotions in Man and Animals*. London: HarperCollins.
4   Ekman, P. (1984) 'Expression and the nature of emotion', in K.R. Scherer and P. Ekman (eds), *Approaches to Emotion*. Hillside, NJ: Erlbaum.
5   Plutchik, R. (1980) *Emotion, a Psychoevolutionary Synthesis*. New York: Harper & Row.
6   Cosmides, L. and Tooby, J. (2000) 'Evolutionary psychology and the emotions', in M. Lewis and J.M. Haviland-Jones (eds), *Handbook of Emotions, 2nd Edition*. New York: The Guilford Press.
7   Badcock, C. (2000) *Evolutionary Psychology*. Cambridge: Polity Press.
8   Nicholson, N. (2000) *Executive Instinct*. New York: Crown Business.
9   Trivers, R.L. (1985) *Social Evolution*. Menlo Park, California: Lexington Books.
10 Rose, H. and Rose, S. (eds) (2000) *Alas, Poor Darwin*. London: Jonathon Cape.
11 Damasio, A.R. (1994) *Descartes' Error*. New York: G.P. Putman's Sons.

12 Damasio, A.R. (2000) *The Feeling of What Happens*. London: Heinemann.

13 LeDoux (1988) *The Emotional Brain*. London: Weidenfeld and Nicolson.

14 Schachter, S. and Singer, J.E. (1984) 'Cognitive, social, and physiological determinants of emotional state', in C. Calhoun and R.C. Solomon (eds), *What is an Emotion?* New York: Oxford University Press.

15 Dachler, K. and Ekman, P. (2000) 'Facial expression of emotion', in M Lewis and J.M. Haviland-Jones (eds), *Handbook of Emotions*. New York: The Guildford Press.

16 Levinson, H. (1991) 'Diagnosing organizations sytematically', in M.F.R. Kets de Vries (ed.), *Organizations on the Couch*. San Francisco: Jossey Bass. p. 61.

17 Myers, D.G. (1995) *Psychology*. New York: Worth.

18 Stevens, A. (1990) *On Jung*. London: Routledge.

19 Klein, M. (1963) *Our Adult World and Other Essays*. London: Heinemann Medical Books.

20 Rycroft, C.A. (1968) *A Critical Dictionary of Psychoanalysis*. New York: Penguin Books.

21 Weinberg, R.B. and Mauksch, L.B. (1991) 'Examining family-of-origin influences in life at work', *Journal of Marital and Family Therapy*, 17233–42.

22 Bion, W.R. (1959) *Experiences in Groups*. New York: Basic Books.

23 Menzies-Lythe, I. (1988) *Containing Anxiety in Institutions. Selected Essays*. London: Free Association Books.

24 Hinshelwood, R.D. (1987) *What Happens in Groups*. London: Free Association Books.

25 Fineman, S. (1995) 'Emotion and organizing', in S. Clegg, C. Hardy and W. Nord (eds), *Handbook of Organization Studies*. London: Sage.

26 Gould, L.J. (1991) 'Using psychoanalytic frameworks for organizational analysis', in M.F.R. de Vries (ed.), *Organizations on the Couch: Clinical Perspectives on Organizational Behaviour*. San Francisco: Jossey Bass.

27 Kersten, A. (2001) 'Organizing for the powerless: a critical perspective on psychodymanics and dysfunctionality', *Journal of Organizational Change Management*, 14 (5): 452–67.

28 Lazarus, R.S. (1991) *Emotion and Adaptation*. New York: Oxford University Press.

29 Lazarus, R.S. and Cohen-Charash, Y. (2001) 'Discrete emotions in organizational life', in R.L. Payne and C. Cooper (eds), *Emotions at Work*. Chichester: Wiley.

30 Lazarus, R.S. (1991) 'Cognition and motivation in emotion', *American Psychologist*, 46 (4): 352–67.

31 Lazarus, R.S. and Lazarus, B.N. (1996) *Passion and Reason: Making Sense of our Emotions*. New York: Oxford University Press.

32 Parkinson, B. (1995) *Ideas and Realities of Emotion*. London: Routledge.

33 Gabriel, Y., Fineman, S. and Sims, D. (2000) *Organizing and Organizations: An Introduction, 2nd Edition*. London: Sage. p. 167.

34 Gergen, K. (1999) *An Invitation to Social Construction*. London: Sage. p. 109.

35 Gabriel, Y. (1999) *Organizations in Depth: The Psychoanalysis of Organizations*. London: Sage.

36 Boyce, M.E. (1996) 'Organizational story and storytelling: a critical review', *Journal of Organizational Change Management*, 9 (5): 5–26.

37 Gabriel, Y. (2000) *Organizational Storytelling: Facts, Fictions, Fantasies*. Oxford: Oxford University Press.

38 Scheff, T.J. (1988) 'Shame and conformity: the deference-emotion system', *American Sociological Review*, (53): 395–406.

39 Sabini, J. and Silver, M. (1998) *Emotion, Character, and Responsibility*. New York: Oxford University Press.

40 McVeigh, B. (1997) *Life in a Japanese Women's College: Learning to be Ladylike*. London: Routledge.

41 Barbalet, J.M. (1995) 'Climates of fear and socio-political change', *Journal for the Theory of Social Behaviour*, 25 (1): 15–33.

42 Kemper, T.D. (1990) 'Foundations of social relational determinants of emotions', in T.D. Kemper (ed.), *Research Agendas in the Sociology of Emotions*. New York: SUNY Press.

43 Moldoveanu, M. and Nohria, N. (2002) *Master Passions: Emotions, Narrative and the Development of Culture*. Cambridge, MA: MIT.

44 Kelly, J.R. and Barsade, S.G. (2001) 'Mood and emotions in small groups and work teams', *Organizational Behavior and Human Decision Processes*, 86 (1): 99–130.

45 Shields, S.A. (2002) *Speaking From the Heart: Gender and the Social Meaning of Emotion*. Cambridge: Cambridge University Press.

46 Hochschild, A. (1983) *The Managed Heart*. Berkeley: University of California.

47 Hochschild, A. (1979) 'Emotion work, feeling rules, and social structure', *American Journal of Sociology*, 39 (Dec): 551–75.

48 Morris, J.A. and Feldman, D.C. (1996) 'The dimensions, antecedents, and consequences of emotional labor', *Academy of Management Review*, 21 (4): 986–1010.

49 Steinberg, R. (1999) 'Emotional labor in job evaluation: redesigning compensation packages', *The Annals of the American Academy of Political and Social Science*, 561 (January): 143–76.

50 Wharton, A. (1999) 'The psychosocial consequences of emotional labor.' *The Annals of the American Academy of Political and Social Science*, 561 (Jan): 158–75.

51 Erickson, R.J. (1995) 'The importance of authenticity for self and society', *Symbolic Interaction*, (18): 121–44.

52 Gergen, K. (1991) *The Saturated Self*. New York: Basic Books.

53 Stearns, C.Z. and Stearns, P.N. (1988) *Emotion and Social Change: Toward a New Psychohistory*. New York: Holmes & Meier.

54 Jaggar, A.M. (1989) 'Love and knowledge: Emotion in feminist epistemology', in A.M. Jaggar and S.R. Bordo (eds), *Gender/Body/Knowledge*. New Brunswick, NJ: Rutgers University Press, pp. 145–71.

55 Wetherall, M. (1966) 'Romantic discourse and feminist analysis: interrogating investment, power and desire', in S. Wilkinson and C. Kitzinger (eds), *Feminism and Discourse: Psychological Perspectives*. London: Sage. p. 134.

56 Czikszentmihalyi, M. (1977) *Beyond Boredom and Freedom*. San Francisco: Jossey Bass.

57 Sandelands, L.E. and Buckner, G.C. (1989) 'Of art and work: aesthetic experience and the psychology of work feelings', *Research in Organizational Behaviour*, (11).

58 Sandelands, L.E. and Boudens, C.J. (2000) 'Feeling at Work', in S. Fineman (ed.), *Emotion in Organizations, 2nd Edition*. London: Sage.

PART ONE
Organizing with emotion

Emotions permeate all organizational processes. Part I includes some practices selected to demonstrate this. The first is where emotion has been deliberately used, taken by corporations as a selling point, or essential recipe, for success: the harnessing of emotional labour and emotional intelligence (Chapters 3 and 4). The second is where a technological innovation overturns established ways of knowing and communicating emotion – such as in virtual organizations (Chapter 5). Finally, there are central, recurring, organizational activities that generate or engage emotions: leadership, decision making and organizational change (Chapters 6–8).

Recruiting emotion

LEARNING OBJECTIVES

This chapter goes behind the scenes of the service-with-a-smile industry. It looks at workplaces where expressed emotion and suppressed feeling has become essential to how the job is designed, and how the work is done. It highlights:

- The way front-line service jobs, professional and non-professional, use emotion
- The emotion work and emotional labour that are required, and their psychological effects
- The new exploitation of emotion in jobs
- The nature of the socio-emotional economy – its use and abuse.

Appearances matter. How to look 'right' in public is drummed into many a child by his or her parents – the correct clothes, the right manners, the appropriate smile, posture, expression. In commercial exchanges, the rule-of-appearances is especially applicable. A sale can be lost or won on the back of smile, sigh or frown. An over-enthusiastic salesperson can put off a customer. An indifferent one can be equally repelling. Over the years, prudent sales-people have discovered these principles for themselves and have infused them with their own personalities and styles, whether they are working in a street market, on the doorstep or in a high-street shop. A sincere belief in the product can shine through, and the building of trust is a precious ingredient in the transaction.

What has changed? While the above scenarios are still recognizable, they are being fast eroded. In their place are surrogate processes, created by large corporations. The following account of a training seminar for telephone-salespeople makes the point:

New staff are initially subjected to 12 hours of service training to invoke positive feelings from customers – *'making it easy for them to say "yes"'* [training course title]. Here, certain common words or expressions such as 'sorry', 'no problem' and 'premium' are considered to have negative connotations – the wrong emotional tone. They are replaced by a range of positive, up-beat sounding, or 'sexy' words such as 'certainly', 'rest assured', 'immediate' and 'great' which are to be used in all areas of work – *and even at home* – to avoid getting 'out of the habit'. This new language is not simply another rigid telephone sales script, but a new 'empowering' vocabulary and dialogue structure developed partly in order to allow a measure of choice. It is, however, monitored through random eavesdropping of the salesperson's telephone calls. The aim is to leave customers with the impression that the salesperson was 'genuine' and 'natural' and, of course, to secure a sale.[1]

The trainers, in this instance, carefully script workers' emotional performances. What might look spontaneous is not. What appears as genuine feeling is carefully counterfeited. Trainees who cannot achieve the required mood are exhorted to 'imagine good things', such as a 'thirty-second holiday' to induce a pleasant disposition. If all else fails, they should pretend until the good feeling comes – *'fake it 'til you make it'*.

PRESCRIBING EMOTION

Corporate emotion-prescriptions can, as is evident, be very explicit. They are aimed at standardizing emotional performance and, sometimes, private feeling. For example, in the 1980s, employees of Marshall Figure Salons in the USA were instructed to use a 'personalized' script that would make them appear exuberant and flattering to clients: *'Mary, I love your suit. I really admire how professional you dress ... where do you buy your clothes?'*[2] At the 'Disney University', the theme park 'cast' are taught The Disney Way, described by one dazzled recruit as leaving him convinced that Walt himself was still alive and well: 'We call it getting doused with pixie dust.'[3] Emotional indoctrination is fine-tuned through written rules, some containing taboos, such as:

Never embarrass a guest.
Never improvise with scripts.

And there are other uncompromising prescriptions: *always make eye contact and smile; greet and welcome each and every guest; say 'thank you' to each and every guest; demonstrate patience and honesty in handling complaints.* The Disney look extends to body appearance, such as hair length and style, make-up, deodorant, nail polish and fingernails that 'should not exceed one-forth of an inch beyond the fingertip'.[4]

Now switch the scene to a McDonald's restaurant. A young, ebullient, assistant-manager bounces up to Sal, during a pause in her hamburger selling:[5]

<u>Manager</u>:	Morning Sal! How you feeling today?
<u>Sal</u>:	Fine.
<u>Manager</u>:	Now look, when I say how you feeling, I want you to say 'outstanding!'
<u>Sal</u>:	OK. [*She looks bewildered.*]
<u>Manager</u>:	So how you feeling today!?
<u>Sal</u>:	Outstanding.
<u>Manager</u>:	OK. Really get motivation. I'm telling all the crew today, when I ask them how they feel I want them to say 'outstanding!' Go like that with your arms. [*He throws his arms outwards.*]
<u>Sal</u>:	OK.
<u>Manager</u>:	So how you feeling today!?
<u>Sal</u>:	Outstanding! [*She mimics him with obvious feigned enthusiasm.*]

'When you're smiling . . .'

Here, as with Disney, we see the corporate engineering of emotion on a grand scale. The manager in McDonald's was dutifully transferring the emotion script he had practised, and used on himself, during his own intensive training at McDonald's 'Hamburger University'. It represents a growing 'smile industry' where the control of employees' emotions radically replaces the spontaneity and variability once attached to the service encounter. Rather like Frederick Taylor's streamlining of the physical movements of labourers in the early 1900s, organizational control is now exerted over the mass production of emotion movements.

This is not without reason, the principal one being economic. If employees are able to 'give' customers a momentary 'nice day', make them feel welcome and comfortable, then they may repeat their visit and purchase. So, the more of the 'right' emotions the better – at least in terms of the managerial interests of the firm.[6,7] It is deeply embedded in the folklore of effective salesmanship that the smile is a key feature of 'good' employee attitude and customer retention. It is backed-up by customer surveys that suggest that customers are less likely to return to organizations where they are not made to feel special.[8] Indeed, by way of illustration, a British Airways advertisement for customer service agents portrays a smiling face with a caption: *When you're smiling, the whole world smiles with you.* The infectious smile is regarded as source of competitive advantage. Smiles beget smiles and can also, albeit fleetingly, create good feelings for the customer, especially if the smile is believed. Customers begin to expect service to be smiling.

As a consequence, what was once put down to 'personality' or 'chemistry' among service providers is now regarded as an emotional competency to be taught to sales staff. Face-to-face encounters in banks, supermarkets, airlines, holiday firms, utility services, hotels, fast-food outlets and themed entertainments, are harmonized with their respective emotion scripts. Telephone salespeople cultivate a 'telephone smile', a warm, enthusiastic voice (it is no coincidence that 'resting' professional actors often fill such positions).

Managerial control over emotional performance is exercised through surveillance, such as 'mystery shoppers' (smile police who pose as customers); spy cameras; the random monitoring of phone calls; and customer-satisfaction questionnaires. Those who drop the mask risk punishment, such as being allocated menial tasks.[9]

'Leave your problems at home'

Such close control may, of course, bring unintended consequences, creating fear, mistrust and, ultimately, defiance among employees. So, paradoxically, some forms of surveillance are dressed up as rewarding for employees. For example, an American supermarket has offered gifts, ranging from $25 to a new car, to clerks 'caught' being friendly to a mystery shopper. Bonuses are given to managers when a high percentage of their clerks have been greeting, and smiling at, customers.[10, 11]

Jennifer Talwar describes how McDonald's and Burger King managers in New York invent ways of stimulating employees' moods, so that negative feelings are suppressed.[12] They constantly remind employees to 'leave your problems at home' and to report to work in a 'good mood'. Some managers exploit the extra leverage that comes from building personal ties with staff – such as by offering them loans from their own pockets to cover the costs of subway tokens, utility or medical bills. Whispering jokes is another tack:

> Well, like myself, they like to hear rude things. So I will go to their ears and tell them something about their boyfriends. That is the only way I get them to smile.[13]

Or, in more confrontational mode:

> I'll go up to their faces and I go, 'What is wrong?' They look at me and they don't; know what I am doing. 'What is wrong with your face?' 'I am smiling. You don't know what it is like? You have to smile right?'[14]

THE (SOUR) FRUITS OF EMOTIONAL LABOUR

> When you wake up in the morning, turn your smile on. Don't turn it back off again until you go to sleep. (Pietro, Head Waiter of a cruise ship).[15]

The shaping of emotion for commercial ends is now pervasive. It has been regarded as a trend towards the 'Disneyization', or 'McDonaldization', of organizations.[16, 17] In other words, in producing the exacting standards of the Dreamland Experience or the Big Mac, these commercial giants also produce emotion in their staff. They shape the way that emotion is to be performed, as well as the labour that goes into making it look good, the *emotional* labour. The idea of emotional labour captures the intrapsychic (within-the-person) and interpersonal work that people have to do to create the prescribed demeanour: the ever-present smile, the cheery voice, the politeness when under pressure, the enthusiasm for the task or product, the suppression of annoyance or fatigue, the willingness to please (see also the discussion in Chapter 2).

Smiling and numb

Many of those who take on the 'happy' mantle are remarkably acquiescent. They incorporate emotional labour into their work-lives; it is something that they 'just do' and it begins to feel natural.[18] Others will submit for a different reason: it pays them to do so – in commission, bonuses and prizes.[19] But these responses disguise another image – numbness. For example, John Van Maanen, an organizational anthropologist, creates a sombre picture of Disney workers:

> Much of the numbness is, of course, beyond the knowledge of supervisors and guests because most employees have little trouble appearing as if they are present even when they are not. It is, in a sense, a passive form of resistance that suggests there still is a sacred preserve of individuality left among employees in the park.[20]

Other emotional labourers have even greater difficulties in sustaining their act:

> Some days I just can't do it. There's only so much you can smile and put on a phoney face. Sometimes I'm actually too tired or bored or pissed off at the world to pretend I am happy, but my jobs require that I am happy all the time.[21]

> A young businessman said to a flight attendant, 'Why aren't you smiling?' She put her tray back on the food cart and said, 'I'll tell you what. You smile first, then I'll smile.' The businessman smiled at her. 'Good,' she replied. 'Now freeze and hold that for fifteen hours.'[22]

Such reactions suggest that all is not well among emotional labourers. Emotional labour can be onerous. Exhaustion and stress can crack the mask when less-acceptable private feelings can leak out. The relentless pressure to perform can feed cynicism. Sociologist, Arlie Hochschild, has revealed how costly emotional labour can be for flight attendants. In her landmark book, *The Managed Heart*, she describes the 'feeling-rules' that flight attendants are expected to follow in one major airline.[23] They had to live up to seductive, '*Fly me, you'll like it*', advertisements, designed to attract and titilate new customers. The warmth and smiles had to be 'inside out' ones: really felt and meant. The turmoil of passenger service, the time pressures, the spillages, the provocative customers, the angry customers, the sexualized remarks, all had to be received with understanding and a smile.

For some this was tough, emotional hard-labour. They strove through 'deep acting', working hard within themselves to take the company's message to heart, to 'really feel' what they were presenting. Our identities are very much emotional – how comfortable, anxious or perplexed we feel about who we are, and about how others see us. The more the flight attendants were consumed by their work role, the more confused they became about their identity, especially their sexuality. Others took the job to be all about 'surface acting', putting on a show, looking right, but no more. They resisted the company's attempts at deeper programming. The smile, the laughter, the sympathy, could be switched on and off as and when necessary. The act, though, could still collapse under pressure, when their anger, irritation or rebellion would break through.

Culture clashes

Unlike some flight attendants, most fast-food workers have little self-investment in their work. It is not that kind of job. Labour turnover is very high and it is one of the few jobs available to low-skilled workers. Many are recent immigrants who have little to smile about when they arrive at work. They often have financial burdens, language difficulties, and have to face the challenge of adapting to an alien culture in a low-status, stigmatized, job.[24]

Switching on the all-American smile demands all the resources of surface acting, and the ingenuity of corporate cultural programming to hold the act in place. Some of this work is a little eased in restaurants in ethnic communities. McDonald's, for example, have moved away from their early insistence that all outlets should be identical, by adding Chinese or Spanish motifs to the décor and menu of their restaurants in the Chinese and Spanish communities of New York. The smile however, has not been compromised, which can be difficult for people whose social–cultural backgrounds do not support smiling in commercial exchanges. It can produce some bizarre episodes. A manager in Talwar's study explains:

> If you are smiling to them [Chinese customers], first they think what is it you want since you are smiling? Every day you are smiling to them [customers] and he or she is trying to smile with you but the first time you are smiling at them they are so shocked. They [the customers] are thinking, why is this lady smiling? I receive a lot of letters. One letter asked why are they [employees] smiling here?[25]

Emotional labour is not restricted to low-skilled service work. It is an implicit feature of many other occupations where there is interpersonal contact, such as physicians, psychiatrists, counsellors, managers, teachers, nurses, police officers, professional carers, professors and lawyers. Many professional workers are, in effect, expected to be skilled at emotion management, but that expectation is largely tacit, unwritten. The emotion-rules are implicit to the professionals' disciplines and training that, typically, emphasize rationality, objectivity and detachment. Professionals, mostly, are to look serious, understanding, controlled, cool, or empathetic with their clients or patients, whatever they might privately feel. Their jobs require a greater range, and intensity, of emotional performances than the typical customer-service agent. This is one way that professional image and mystique is maintained.

If the mask is allowed to slip, the trust between professional and client is jeopardized. It is a fate that befalls the manager who openly curses his staff, the nurse who is scathing to a patient, the physician who weeps during a consultation, the social worker who mocks a client, the lawyer who is over-casual at the reading of a will, the police officer who screams in frustration at, or ridicules, a motorist. The relationship is irreparably fractured if the professional reveals certain 'inappropriate' emotions, such as personal attraction or lust for a client or customer. When emotional labour fails, so does the professional.

REDUCING THE COSTS OF EMOTIONAL LABOUR

Hochschild's research points-up the psychological damage to the worker that can follow emotional labour. Because of this, some regard its very existence as pernicious. It is something to be reduced, designed out of jobs or, at the very least, met with special compensation or reward. However, it would be wrong to portray all emotional labourers as oppressed by their emotional lot. There are ways that they can knowingly exert some control over their destiny. They can make emotional labour a *game*; they can *shift zones*; or they can *resist*.

'It's a game'

The service, or professional, encounter can be treated as a game, a theatrical episode where the reward, the fun, is pulling-off a good performance. It is riding the role. Stepping into the spotlight of the aircraft cabin, the restaurant lounge, the shop floor, the client's office or the consulting room, is an opportunity to 'perform'.[26] It is faking, but 'faking in good faith'.[27] Neither server nor served, professional nor client, necessarily believes the genuineness of the feelings that other person is portraying, but they need each other to play their respective roles – with humour, flattery, innuendo. In this way the emotion-script can be unofficially lightened or improvised. For instance, in one study checkout clerks joked with customers, offered personal advice, even prayed for them in times of trouble. It reduced the onerousness of their emotional labour and gave them a sense of ownership of their emotional act.[28]

Shift zones

Organizations can be regarded as a mosaic of *emotionalized zones*. Some zones will be formally demarcated. They are designed by the organization for relaxation, escape or leisure, such as coffee rooms, lounges, designated smoking areas and exercise spaces. Others will be informal, invented through everyday social interactions, such as certain corridors, carparks, lobby areas, washrooms and out of site corners of rooms.[29]

Retreating to a less-demanding emotionalized zone can reduce the personal costs of emotional labour. The prescribed performances can stop, and the public mask be lifted, or at least exchanged temporarily for an alternative one. For example, the galley of an aircraft is a place where flight attendants can relax their 'be nice to customer' face. Behind the curtains, in low voice and by body language, they can reveal their feelings about their passengers ('that dreadful man in seat 37D'), the management ('always get the number of vegetarian meals wrong'), or whatever. Similar processes occur in school staffrooms, restaurant kitchens, police cars, the back of shops, and in hospital staff washrooms. They all offer workers an amnesty from their normal emotional labours, more freedom to express subversive feelings about the people to whom they would normally have to be nice and polite.

Resistance

Resistance is a way of expressing defiance: 'I'm not like that; I don't like what you are making me do; I feel uncomfortable, pushed too far'. It helps assert an identity of one's own, separate from the constraints of the organization. Cynicism (as well as sarcasm and humour) is one way of achieving this. Cynics psychologically distance themselves from the prescriptions of their role, while going through the 'motions'. Cynics look with a jaundiced eye on what they do, acknowledging that the game that they are playing is a hollow one.[30] A UK flight attendant explains:

> Your try saying 'hello' to 300 people and sound as though you mean it towards the end. Most of us make a game of it. Someone – probably a manager – said 'This business is all about interpersonal transactions'. He was wrong. It's all about bullshit. If life is a cabaret, this is a bloody circus.[31]

Collective resistance to unreasonable or oppressive working conditions is another way of declaring one's difference and distress. A newspaper story tells of a Californian supermarket where unionized, female, shop workers actively resisted being forced to make eye-contact with customers and to smile at them. They claimed it increased their exposure to sexual harassment from customers.[32] In another report, hotel desk clerks went on a 'smile strike'. They were angry at being monitored secretly by managerially 'planted' customers.[33] In the fast-food industry, much of which is non-unionized, collective opposition is more difficult. Resistance, where it occurs, appears to be indirect – such as cooking too much food near closing time, because any leftover food is officially allowed to be taken home by staff. Jennifer Talwar reports how front-line staff mock, and spread unflattering rumours about, managers who have 'bought into Burger King land'.[34]

GIVING AND RECEIVING EMOTION

Emotions are given and received. The organizational setting determines the kinds of emotions appropriate to the transaction, and what might be achieved. For instance, a restaurant waitress may playfully flirt with a male customer, with an enhanced tip in mind. A nurse may cautiously sexualize her interactions with a patient in order to build rapport. A local shopkeeper might tell a regular customer about some of her work worries in order to cement customer loyalty. There can also be pecking order in emotional presentation and labour: who can say/display what to whom. A company director can get openly angry with peers who challenge his professionalism, while his junior staff are likely have to swallow their pride when he criticizes them. In class, a university professor can show her displeasure about one of her student's conduct. It is much more difficult for the student to publicly remonstrate about the professor's lecturing style.

One study examined the way emotions were controlled by hospital staff as they dealt with cancer.[35] Who discloses what to whom? How do the relatives of a victim get informed? The study revealed that the various parties – consultants, senior doctors, junior staff, nurses, voluntary carers – all direct and control each other's emotions, and each take their place in what they hold back and what they reveal. Emotional labour is tougher for some than for others, depending on their level of involvement with, and personal closeness to, the cancer victim. This, in effect, helps spread the emotional load and permits the various workers to create safe space for what, ideally, they can do best.

The socioemotional economy

The give and take of emotions has been called the *socioemotional economy*.[36] It is the exchange of sympathy, compassion, love, appreciation, liking, and so forth, which reinforces social bonds and sustains organizational relationships. The 'economy' means the emotions are 'spent' and 'saved' differently. Because some are rarer, or more precious, than others, they require more emotion work to produce, especially when there is no clear social script to follow.

Sometimes we are prepared to do this work for free, without expectation of return. The emotion is a willing gift, such as love to one's child, praise or liking to a friend, gratitude to someone we appreciate, or compassion to a distressed colleague. At work it can be offered in quiet areas of the organization with a hand on the shoulder, a hug or embrace.[37-39] At times, delivering the gift is not easy. For instance, in gynaecological units there are nurses who have to prepare women for feelings of loss and grief following termination of pregnancy due to foetal abnormalities. They will mask their feelings of abhorrence or ambivalence about the appearance of the baby, but in doing so offer more than the detached face of the professional carer. In Sharon Bolton's words, they 'carry out hard emotion work and offer a gift to grieving parents by forcing themselves to visualize the baby on the parent's terms – as a beautiful lost child'. The work is regarded as giving the patient something that they deserve, regardless of the cost to the carer. It is an act of compassion. One nurse in Bolton's research study explains:

> If the mother wants to hold and see the baby that's the first thing you do, so you take the baby back into them. We dress the baby and try to cover the worst of the abnormalities. If that's what the mother wants then we have to help them through it. If she's going to breathe easier, because she's had all this, then it's worth it . . .They've had to make an awful decision and it helps them to know it was the right decision in the end . . . The baby is part of them and to them it's beautiful and of course it is, every child is.[40]

Humour can lighten the load – when it is appropriate, well timed and well meaning. One ward sister in Bolton's study was remembered, with fondness, for her 'ice-cream, sweeties!' cry as she wheeled the drugs' trolley into the ward, followed by her one-woman comedy act. It was seen as appropriate and timely by the patients, and helpful for their recovery. This was not the case in a different neonatal-care unit:

> One night . . . we had a baby that very nearly died. It was a close thing. After we got the baby stabilized, we called the mother, and she came hurrying in. This was about 6 or 7 a.m., and she was running down the hall to reach the [unit], when her pediatrician hailed her with the comment: 'So you're the mother of the baby who had that out-of-body experience last night?' Now this lady did not yet know that her baby was going to be all right, she'd had nothing but the news that the child had almost died but was stable. But this doctor didn't even think of that, he just wanted to be funny. And he wasn't.[41]

Stealing the gift?

Emotional gifts are characteristically spontaneous, self-authored and beyond the normal, formal, emotion protocols of the job. When they are appreciated they can result in a significant positive-shift in another's feeling or mood. When and how the gift is given is normally entirely at the discretion of the individual worker. But consider the tale below:

CASE STUDY

Not long ago, a room service waiter at one of our hotels in the west delivered a dinner to a guest. When he knocked on the door, he found the woman inside sobbing and distraught. He learned that her sister had just died of cancer.

On his own initiative, this associate went to the hotel gift shop, bought a sympathy card and had every member of the staff sign it.

Then he collected a dollar from every employee, bought her flowers, delivered them and said, 'we just wanted you to know you're not among strangers here.'

That guest's room may be our product, but our associate's caring attitude is our value. We can't measure it with statistics, and we can't manufacture it. We can deliver that value only if we can attract, retain and inspire the best people – with what we call 'The Spirit To Serve'.

This story was related by J.W. Marriott, Chairman and Chief Executive of Marriott Hotels, in a formal speech entitled, 'Our competitive strength: human capital'.[42] It can be read in two ways. First, as an account of a sensitive gift of compassion from a junior employee, well beyond the expected labour associated with his job, humanizing what is normally a cursory, staged, social interaction. Second, as a chief executive making public-relations capital from someone else's spontaneous emotional act. He is appropriating the gift for wider political purposes and, indirectly, putting pressure on other employees to be 'best' people like the room-service waiter. The gift is stolen.

In search of competitive advantage, companies ranging from hotels to car-rental, typically exhort their employees to go 'that extra mile' to meet their customers' particular needs, crises, or convenience. The danger is in exploiting the precious, discretionary part of an employee's emotional gift-economy. It can rob them of an emotional form that should be no one's business but their own. Wiser, perhaps, to acknowledge and appreciate an employee's compassion, or other spontaneous emotion acts, in private – in incidental meetings or informal communications. This reinforces the organizational value of such acts and adds a quiet thread of support to others who may *choose* to behave in this way.

CONCLUSIONS

Using people's emotions and feelings as a means to someone else's end raises questions about the morality of such endeavours, and about the very notion of an organization managing an employee's emotions. Although emotional labour is not inevitably damaging to health, or necessarily exploitative, it sometimes is. This is especially so in rapidly expanding, low-skilled, occupations where employees have little discretion over 'the smile'. Also in professions, where competence is as much to do with emotion self-management as with technical skills.

Stealing the gift is clearly an area of concern, but to what extent should emotional spontaneity be suppressed in the service of the 'product'? In jobs where there is implicit emotional labour, how much of it gets in the way of more effective, honest, relationships with customers or clients? When emotional labour is so extreme that the nurse, doctor or social worker burns-out, then we might rightly question the nature of the job rather than the person who holds the job.

The cultural *insensitivity* is a further point to ponder. In Japan, in the face of several thousand years of inscrutability, management consultants have been hired to teach native Japanese businessmen to smile – to help them with international business deals. It conflicts dramatically with traditional Japanese ways, where the instant smile is something of a cultural insult.[43, 44] In Moscow, McDonald's has insisted that its staff should serve Big Macs with a smile, despite the wider cultural predilection to greet customers with a grimace or blank stare.[45] Inuit sales staff of the Greenlandic Co-operative supermarket chain have no cultural tradition of smiling, or greeting others with a 'hi' or 'hello', but are subjected to smiling training by their employer.[46]

The employees who carry the brand, the bearers of smiles, have to play their part according to similar emotion rules, wherever they happen to be. In practice, this usually means that the same techniques of emotion control, derived mostly from American corporate ideas and values, are implanted in places as far flung as Paris, London, Moscow, Beijing, Sydney and Deli. They can be in tension with the host culture but, emotionally, it is something of an unequal contest – the ubiquitous smile wins.[47]

Should we feel comforted by this, or worried? Perhaps an honest grimace or grunt is better than a contrived smile? Corporate profits, customer satisfaction and employees might all benefit in the end if employees took charge of their own sales demeanour. The task of management, then, is to produce jobs that stimulate important feelings and emotions rather than flatten them in anticipation of a ready-made graft. In other words, the opportunity for discretion, participation and creativity is designed into the core of jobs, whatever their nature, not relegated to the trivial edges of the corporate script. Even writers such as Albrecht and Zemke, high priests of the American way of service, were uneasy about the signs some two decades ago:

> By all means, let's use training . . . But let's not insult our employees with smile training or 'be nice' training. Let's treat them like adults.[48]

FURTHER READING

Hochschild, A. (1983) *The Managed Heart*. Berkeley: University of California.

Matsumoto, D. (1996) *Umasking Japan: Myths and Realities About Emotions of the Japanese.* Stanford: Stanford University Press.

Talwar, J.T. (2002) *Fast Food, Fast Track.* Boulder, Colorado: Westview Press.

Wasko, J. (2001) *Understanding Disney: The Manufacture of Fantasy.* Malden, MA: Blackwell.

REFERENCES

1   Sturdy, A. and Fineman, S. (2001) 'Struggles for the control of affect-resistance as politics and emotion', in A. Sturdy, I. Grugulis and H. Willmott (eds), *Customer Service: Empowerment and Entrapment.* Houndmills, Basingstoke: Palgrave. p. 140.

2   Lally-Benedetto, C. (1985) 'Women and the tone of the body: an analysis of a figure salon'. Midwest Sociological Society, St Louis, MO. p. 8.

3   Zibart, E. (1997) *The Unofficial Disney Companion.* New York: Macmillan. p. 177.

4   Wasko, J. (2001) *Understanding Disney: The Manufacture of Fantasy.* Malden, MA: Blackwell. p. 94.

5   Extracted from a BBC Channel 2 television film on 'empowerment', for the Open University, 1988.

6   Rafaeli, A. and Sutton, R.I. (1987) 'Expression of emotion as part of the work role', *Academy of Management Review,* 12 (1): 23–37.

7   Rafaeli, A. and Sutton, R.I. (1989) 'The expression of emotion in organizational life', *Research in Organizational Behaviour,* 111–42.

8   Medley, L. (2002) The customer comes second, <http://customernet.org.uk/order/dbase/html>.

9   Talwar, J.T. (2002) *Fast Food, Fast Track.* Boulder, Colorado: Westview Press. p. 113.

10 Rafaeli, A. and Sutton, R.I. (1989) 'Expression of emotion as part of the work role', *Academy of Management Review,* 12 (1): 23–37.

11 Rafaeli, A. and Sutton, R.I. (1989) 'The expression of emotion in organizational life', *Research in Organizational Behaviour,* 111–42.

12 Talwar, J.T. (2002) *Fast Food, Fast Track.* Boulder, Colorado: Westview Press. p. 113.

13 Talwar, J.T. (2002) *Fast Food, Fast Track.* Boulder, Colorado: Westview Press. p. 114.

14 Talwar, J.T. (2002) *Fast Food, Fast Track.* Boulder, Colorado: Westview Press. p. 114.

15 Tracy, S.J. (2000) 'Becoming a character for commerce: emotion labor, self-subordination, and discursive construction of identity in a total

institution', *Communication Quarterly*, 14 (1): 90–128, especially p. 91.

16 Ritzer, G. (1993) *The McDonaldization of Society*. Thousand Oaks, California: Pine Forge Press.

17 Bryman, A. (1999) 'The Disneyization of society', *The Sociological Review*, 47 (1): 25–47.

18 Bryman, A. (1999) 'The Disneyization of society', *The Sociological Review*, 47 (1): 25–47.

19 Leidner, R. (1991) 'Serving hamburgers and selling insurance: gender, work and identity in interactive service jobs', *Gender and Society*, 5 (2): 154–77.

20 Van Maanen, J. (1991) 'The smile factory: work at Disneyland', in P.J. Frost, L.F. Moore, M.R. Louis, C.C. Lundberg and J. Martin (eds), *Reframing Organizational Culture*. Newbury Park: Sage. p. 75.

21 Pinder, C.C. (1988) *Work Motivation in Organizational Behavior*. New Jersey: Prentice Hall. p. 111.

22 Hochschild, A. (1983) *The Managed Heart*. Berkeley: University of California. p. 127.

23 Hochschild, A. (1983) *The Managed Heart*. Berkeley: University of California. p. 127.

24 Talwar, J.T. (2002) *Fast Food, Fast Track*. Boulder, Colorado: Westview Press. p. 113.

25 Talwar, J.T. (2002) *Fast Food, Fast Track*. Boulder, Colorado: Westview Press. p. 103.

26 Wouters, C. (1989) 'The sociology of emotions and flight attendants: Hochschild's "Managed Heart"', *Theory, Culture and Society*, 6 (1): 95–123.

27 Adelman, P.K. (1995) 'Emotional labor as a potential source of job stress', in S.L. Sauster and M.L.R (eds), *Organizational Risk Factors for Job Stress*. Washington, DC: American Psychological Association.

28 Tolich, M.B. (1993) 'Alienating and liberating emotions at work', *Journal of Contemporary Ethnography*, 22 (3): 361–81.

29 Fineman, S. (1999) 'Emotion and organizing', in S. Clegg, C. Hardy and W. Nord (eds), *Studying Organizations*. London: Sage.

30 Sturdy, A. and Fineman, S. (2001) 'Struggles for the control of affect-resistance as politics and emotion', in A. Sturdy, I. Grugulis and H. Willmott (eds), *Customer Service: Empowerment and Entrapment*. Houndmills, Basingstoke: Palgrave. p. 140.

31 Hopfl, H. (1991) 'Nice jumper Jim!: dissonance and emotional labour in a management development programme'. *5th European Congress – The Psychology of Work and Organizations*, Rouen. pp. 5–6.

32 Zeidler, S. (1988) 'Don't have a nice day – workers protest smile rule', Reuters, Los Angeles.

33 Fuller, L. and Smith, V. (1991) 'Consumers' reports: management by customers in a changing economy', *Work, Employment and Society*, 5 (1): 1–16.

34 Talwar, J.T. (2002) *Fast Food, Fast Track*. Boulder, Colorado: Westview Press. p. 113.

35 James, N. (1993) 'Divisions of emotional labour: disclosure and cancer', in S. Fineman (ed.), *Emotion in Organizations*. London: Sage.

36 Clark, C. (1990) 'Emotions and micropolitics in everyday life: some patterns and paradoxes of "place"', in T.D. Kemper (ed.), *Research Agendas in the Sociology of Emotions*. Albany: State University of New York Press.

37 Hochschild, A. (1983) *The Managed Heart*. Berkeley: University of California. p. 127.

38 Titmus, R. (1970) *The Gift Relationship*. London: Allen and Unwin.

39 Frost, P.J., Dutton, J.E., Worline, M.C. and Wilson, A. (2000) 'Narratives of compassion in organizations', in S. Fineman (ed.), *Emotion in Organizations, 2nd Edition*. London: Sage. pp. 25–45.

40 Bolton, S. (2000) 'Who cares? Offering emotion work as a "gift" in the nursing labour process', *Journal of Advanced Nursing*, 32 (3): 580–6, especially pp. 584–5.

41 Francis, L., Monahan, K. and Berger, C. (1999) 'A laughing matter? The use of humor in medical interactions', *Motivation and Emotion*, 23 (2): especially pp. 168–9.

42 Marriott, J.W. and Brown, K.A. (1997) *The Spirit to Serve*. New York: HarperCollins.

43 Raz, A. (1999) *Riding the Black Ship: Japan and Tokyo Disneyland*. Cambridge, MA: Harvard University Press.

44 Matsumoto, D. (1996) *Umasking Japan: Myths and Realities About Emotions of the Japanese*. Stanford: Stanford University Press.

45 O'Conner, J. (2000) 'Have a nice day, comrade', *The Observer*, London, 19 November: 6–7.

46 Jones, L. (1999) 'Smiling lessons end service with a scowl in Greenland', *The Guardian*, London, 23 October: 21.

47 Talwar, J.T. (2002) *Fast Food, Fast Track*. Boulder, Colorado: Westview Press. p. 113.

48 Albrecht, K. and Zemke, R. (1985) *Service America!* New York: Warner Book. pp. 181–2.

4

Being emotionally intelligent

LEARNING OBJECTIVES

Emotional intelligence has caught the attention of managers in many organizations – as a recipe for success. This chapter will cast a critical eye over the claims for emotional intelligence. In particular:

- How it has been presented, popularized and measured
- Its historical roots and close relatives
- The assertion that it can be altered
- Its questionable assumptions.

Bringing together 'emotion' and 'intelligence' looks odd, like trying to fuse chalk with cheese. What does emotional intelligence mean and why should it be important? Does it live up to its claims? For some writers, there is little doubt that emotional intelligence should be at the heart of an organization's development plans. Robert Cooper and Ayman Sawaf, for example, write:

> Modern science is proving everyday that it is emotional intelligence, not IQ or raw brain power alone that underpins the best decisions, the most dynamic organizations and the most satisfying and successful lives.[1]

Emotional intelligence is the most recent 'take' on an ancient philosophical debate about the place of emotion and reason in human affairs. Emotions do not simply fire-off without rhyme or reason (although they sometimes feel as though they do); they shape our thoughts and directions and, without them, our thoughts would have no shape or direction. Emotional intelligence grasps this connection to explore how emotions can be used 'intelligently' in daily life and work settings. It is relatively easy, for instance, to get annoyed with people. It is less easy to know how to express annoyance, in the right manner at the right time for the right purpose.

THE APPEAL

In the past eight years, emotional intelligence has gained considerable attention. In 1996 Daniel Goleman, a science journalist, wrote a best-selling book called *Emotional Intelligence*, based on a liberal interpretation of a range of academic studies on intelligence and emotion [2] In it he claimed that emotionally intelligent people have abilities in five main domains:

- They know their emotions.
- They manage their emotions.
- They motivate themselves.
- They recognize emotions in others.
- They can handle relationships.

This is what helps them to be stars in their occupation or calling. In a follow-up book, Goleman asserts that 'twenty-five years' worth of empirical studies that tell us with a previously unknown precision just how much emotional intelligence matters for success'.[3] Goleman talks of a *tipping point*, or critical mass, when emotional intelligence makes that extra difference to performance, over and above one's normal professional skills or knowledge.

The appeal of emotional intelligence was immediate and wide. Feature articles appeared in publications as diverse as *American Nurseryman, Parents, Mademoiselle* ('Never lose it at work again'), *Better Homes and Gardens, Newsweek, Cosmopolitan* ('The lowdown on high EQ'), and *HRMagazine* ('The smarts that count'). In the UK, emotional intelligence is, according to *The Times' Higher Educational Supplement*, 'reshaping business school research programmes'. The national Sunday newspaper, *The Observer*, takes a similar upbeat line, proposing emotional intelligence as the 'final frontier' for performance improvement in companies.

Emotional intelligence has been applied to US presidents, everyday health, ('should be right up there with diet and exercise');[4] even to evaluations of beer advertisements:

> The new campaign for Coors Light [is] a light beer not in touch with its emotional intelligence. Or to put it another way, a campaign that is no smarter than the average beer commercial.[5]

And just as a beer can lose out to its smarter competitors, so can those who lack emotional intelligence. They have, according to Ann Beatty of the *St. Louis Business Journal* a 'fatal flaw'.[6] Instant emotional quotient (EQ) advice, however, is readily available, even in in-flight magazines. For example, British Airways passengers are given the following '10 ways to spot a person with high EQ':[7]

- You get warmth and respect from them
- You feel warmth and respect for them
- They don't play power games
- They are good at networking
- They know what they want and can communicate it clearly
- They know how to be firm and challenging without spoiling relationships
- They remember small, personal details about you
- They don't see mistakes as failure, just information
- They are open to opportunities and are optimistic about the outcome
- They look for win-win solutions

Making it attractive

The image of the emotionally intelligent person is highly seductive. It holds promise of a breakthrough, a 'missing ingredient' in our understanding about managerial effectiveness. It clearly gives new impetus and respectability to emotion in organizational life. Its packaging has been crucial to its acceptability. The skilful use of rhetoric is an essential tool of the trade for management and organizational consultants: crafting words, arguments, and image to persuade the client to take the product. Consultants' own books perform part of the job, with catchy titles such as:

- *Hidden Dynamics: How Emotions Affect Business Performance and How You Can Harness Their Power for Positive Results*[8]
- *Executive EQ: Emotional Intelligence in Leadership and Organizations*[9]
- *From Chaos to Coherence: Advancing Emotional and Organizational Intelligence through Inner Quality Management*[10]

In different ways, these books say they offer what employers want, especially what will be profitable for their businesses.

The considerable claims for emotional intelligence raise two important issues. What can we learn from academic analyses of emotional intelligence? Does it deserve its popular acclaim?

ROOTS AND APPLICATIONS

Traditionally, intelligence has been kept separate from emotion. Intelligence deals with the capacity to carry out abstract reasoning, thinking skills. Measures of intelligence typically contain questions that involve verbal reasoning, quantitative skills, abstract patterns and memory. Although the cognitive, 'getting the right answer', view of intelligence, has dominated the way intelligence has been viewed and used, there is a long history of social intelligence, the precursor to emotional intelligence. As early as the 1920s there were discussions about intelligence needing to go beyond academic-performance IQ, to include the ability to deal with other people, and the capacity to judge the moods and feelings of others.[11, 12]

Other challenges to traditional IQ have come from the notions of *practical* and *successful* intelligence. These refer to aspects of self-knowledge, such as recognition of one's strengths and weaknesses, and the facility to shape or change one's environment.[13, 14] The idea of *multiple intelligences*, by Howard Gardner, further helped to put social intelligence firmly on the map.[15, 16] Gardner claims that we possess at least eight intelligences. As well as the linguistic and logical ones that are valued at school, we have social and interpersonal intelligences, which are the basic ingredients of *emotional sensitivity.*

In the 1990s, emotional intelligence began to emerge from the background of social intelligence, stimulated by new findings from brain sciences on the role of emotion in thinking[17] (see Chapter 7, *Emotion and Decisions*). In a series of articles by John Mayer and Peter Salovey,[18–20] a theory of emotional intelligence was proposed. It claimed that:

> . . . individuals differ in how skilled they are at perceiving, understanding, and utilizing . . . emotional information, and that a person's level of 'emotional intelligence' contributes substantially to his or her intellectual and emotional well-being and growth.[21]

Accordingly, they define emotional intelligence as, the ability to perceive and express emotions, to understand and use them, and to manage emotions so as to foster personal growth.[22]

From here on, however, ideas on emotional intelligence divide. Different authors take different directions or emphases. For example, Bar-On speaks of 'an array of non-cognitive capabilities, competencies, and skills that influence one's ability to succeed in coping with environmental demands and pressures'.[23] For Cooper and Sawaf, emotional intelligence is 'the ability to sense, understand, and effectively apply the power and acumen of emotions as a source of human energy, information, connection, and influence'.[24] A pithier definition is suggested by Davies et al – 'the ability to perceive emotional information in visual and auditory stimuli'.[25] The picture is further confused by discussions of emotional intelligence which refer to just about any feature of social competence, such as 'the ability to integrate thinking, feeling, and behaviour to achieve social tasks and outcomes valued in the host context and culture'.[26]

We get a sense of something emotional and something practical from all these views, but murkiness on specifics. If we view emotional intelligence as a *skill* or *competency*, it promises to be learnable, and considerably attractive to practitioners and training specialists. An alternative view is that emotional intelligence is pretty much formed by adulthood and will be resistant to further change.

MEASURING EMOTIONAL INTELLIGENCE

The spectrum of definitions is matched by a growing range of measures that claim to tap emotional intelligence.[27] Some are of the quick-and-easy type. For example, on one website Goleman presents a multiple-choice, 10-item, EQ scale.[28] One of the items reads:

> You and your life partner have gotten into an argument that has escalated into a shouting match: you're both upset and, in the heat of anger, making personal attacks you don't really mean. What's the best thing to do?
>
> a. Take a 20-minute break and then continue the discussion.
> b. Just stop the argument – go silent, no matter what your partner says.
> c. Say you're sorry and ask your partner to apologize too.
> d. Stop for a moment, collect your thoughts, then state your side of the case as precisely as you can.

Goleman says choice (a) is the only emotionally intelligent response, because the break permits a cooling-down of the anger that distorts perceptions. This is, perhaps, plausible, but it would worry psychometricians, people who specialize in psychological measurement. They look for validation samples and a precise idea of what exactly each item shows, as has been the case with IQ tests. There is no such information provided for this particular measure. It is an approach that has drawn some acerbic criticism, such as 'slickly packaged junk science perpetrated by unscrupulous consultants on ignorant customers'.[29] Such a harsh judgement reflects a tension between those who want to promote an attractive-looking concept rapidly, and those who wish to refine it first (see later discussion).

Greater technical sophistication can be found in other instruments. For example:

- Bar-On's *Emotional Quotient Inventory* is a 60-item self-report instrument that scores for intrapersonal skills, interpersonal skills, stress management, adaptability and general mood.[30]
- The *Trait Meta-Mood Scale* is a 30-item self-report questionnaire focussing on clarity of feelings and mood.[31]
- The *Mayer-Salovey-Caruso Emotional Intelligence Test* claims to measure four branches of emotional intelligence: how well we identify emotions in others and oneself; how we use emotion to solve problems; how we understand complex emotions; how well emotions are managed in self and others.[32]
- Robert Cooper's *EQ-Map* divides emotional intelligence into five attributes: current environment; emotional literary; EQ competence; EQ values and attitudes; EQ outcomes.[33]
- The *Emotional Competence Inventory* of Boyatzis, Goleman and Rhee, focuses on four main areas: self-awareness, self-management, social awareness and social skills.[34]

As the emotional intelligence canvas has unfolded, so have the number of attributes associated with it. They include self-actualization, independence, flexibility, stress tolerance, impulse control, optimism, happiness, self-awareness, interpersonal connections, achievement drive and conscientiousness. The credibility of emotional intelligence is strained as each new attribute, and each new measure, is added. Those who wish to assess emotional intelligence need to ask themselves which particular version of emotional intelligence, and which measure, they prefer.[35, 36]

INCREASING EMOTIONAL INTELLIGENCE

As a social intelligence, rooted in early life experiences, significant changes in emotional intelligence would not normally be expected. But many organizational consultants and training specialists take a different view. Here are some illustrations:

> American Express Financial Advisors prides itself on helping clients develop financial plans that include the purchase of life insurance. But in 1991, the senior vice-president in charge of the life insurance and American Express Financial Advisors . . . noticed that something was wrong. Seventy-three percent of clients with plans never followed through with the purchase of life insurance . . . [T]he vice-president's process of inquiry led, a year later, to a novel solution – [they] would train its financial advisors and their managers in 'emotional competence' . . . to help advisors cope with the emotional reactions they have to selling life insurance.
>
> [They] learn about the impact of emotions on human behaviour, and how to identify and manage their own emotional reactions. The findings suggest that advisors who receive the training generate more sales revenue than the advisors who did not get training.[37]

The training required participants to learn, amongst other things, to stop and focus on their feelings, aided by a list of feeling words. They were encouraged to become aware of the 'self-talk' that led to 'disruptive' feelings, such as self-doubt and shame. They were to replace them with 'more accurate, constructive, self-talk' (see also Chapter 9). Self-talk is based on the ideas of psychotherapist Albert Ellis. How we 'talk' to ourselves (either literally or in our thoughts) creates our feelings. So when you insult me, it is not *you* who hurt me, but how I take the insult, how it fits with my image of myself. Shift that self-image, change how I think about myself, and the feelings should change.[38] It is consistent with a cognitive appraisal view emotion (see Chapter 2).

In another case, consultants applied emotional intelligence to an e-commerce team facing difficulties. The consultants describe the situation:

> An e-commerce team was floundering. There was little enthusiasm for the project, with a lot of energy being expended in blaming others for the lack

of progress. The team leader [Janet] was not the cause of the problems, but, clearly, it was going to be up to Janet to turn the situation around.[39]

On an emotional intelligence test, Janet scored poorly on 'using emotions'. The key to Janet's improvement was 'to have her accept the results . . . Focus on how her low score may impact on her performance; leverage her strengths to improve how she uses emotions'. Through counselling and discussion, she was encouraged to overcome her negative feelings and build on positive, 'using', emotions. The authors claim considerable success, in that Janet managed to do an 'amazing job' achieving 'meaningful outcomes' for her organization, and was much praised by her managers.

In a third report, Richard Boyatzis introduced emotional intelligence training into an MBA programme.[40] According to Boyatzis, there was strong evidence of improvement in the emotional intelligence competencies assessed, a change that was sustained for two years after graduation.

Raised emotional intelligence is seen to improve one's promotability and leadership effectiveness.[41, 42] But, it seems, we need to be reasonably emotionally intelligent (and therefore more receptive to training) to become even more emotionally intelligent; not everyone's level can be elevated.[43] Most of these findings are drawn from studies that fail to meet field-experimental standards for assessing change, and the results are often talked-up by their protagonists who have a vested interest in demonstrating improvements, using their particular perspective on emotional intelligence.

CONCLUSION: WHITHER EMOTIONAL INTELLIGENCE?

Emotional intelligence has catapulted into popularity in recent years. For the itchy journalist and results-hungry practitioner, the cautious caveats of academics are unhelpful. They do not make for quick applications or a newsy story. This, in turn, can irritate academics. Mayer and his colleagues, who have been at the forefront of the academic development of emotional intelligence, exemplify the tension:

> The scientist says, 'Here is what I've been working on recently . . .'. The journalist replies, 'This is really important,' and then jazzes up the story in a way that seems close to lunacy: 'EI is twice as important as IQ!' This often-made, often-repeated, claim, cannot be substantiated . . .[44]

The two different worlds – the scientist's and the journalist/consultant's – mostly follow their independent paths. The consultant looks for here-and-now usage, while the academic says, 'hang on, not quite yet'. Hence, the popularizing of emotional intelligence entails turning a bind eye to some contradictory evidence: reshaping, or simplifying, the complexities. It becomes oversold, oversimplified and, therefore, makes some claims that are bound to disappoint. It remains to be seen whether further refinement can come from the academic and practitioner communities, reducing confusion in a field that is in its early period of development.

Other reasons that restrict the scope of emotional intelligence lie deeper in its assumptions, particularly the *values* it represents and promotes, and its belief in our capacity to *control* our emotions.

Values bias

The management literature on emotional intelligence is heavily slanted towards certain notions of good and bad emotions, successful and unsuccessful ones. For example, bad feelings or states for Goleman include impulsiveness, abrasiveness and arrogance. Good feelings or states include enthusiasm, optimism, hope, composure and self-assurance, all ingredients of an Americanized, male, 'positive mental attitude'. Jealousy, rage, envy, fear, guilt, boredom, disgust and hurt are not specifically addressed, despite being intrinsic to the political flow of many organizations.

If and when they recognize them, can emotionally intelligent managers simply turn away from such impulses? And should they? There have been many commercially successful organizations built on 'less-desirable', even 'nasty', emotions. In this respect, it can sometimes be emotionally intelligent to be uncompromising, inflexible, grim, stringent, and even ruthless, to achieve 'good' organizational outcomes. Some military or crisis-conditions can demand such behaviours. Also, current renditions of emotional intelligence are insensitive to gender, social class and national culture. What might be regarded as an emotionally intelligent response in a mid-western US business could be radically different in a downtown store in Kowloon or Karachi. History is littered with failures to find universal personal qualities for managerial success, and emotional competencies are no exception.

Illusion of control

Thinking and feeling interpenetrate; that is, they cannot easily be separated. Applying our intelligence, our thinking, to our emotions is not nearly as straightforward as some emotional intelligence theorists imply, even after special regimes of training. Often our feelings are ambiguous or ambivalent, impossible to identify with any degree of clarity. The psychoanalytic reality, moreover, tells us that we often do not know what feelings are impelling us, partly because they are unconscious and partly because we build elaborate defences so that we do not have to acknowledge them (see Chapter 2). The promise of 'intelligently' controlling our emotions is over-optimistic.

Emotional intelligence or emotional sensitivity?

Emotional intelligence has clearly caught the mood of the times. It is *about* emotion, but not celebrating emotion just for emotion's sake, so it is attractive to organizations. It brings emotion out of the closet, but under sufficient control to appear to seem useful to the organization's goals. This is noteworthy because it shifts attention to the credibility of emotion in organizational affairs. On the other hand, when emotional intelligence is taken predominately as a device to lever more performance or profit out of people, it offers a highly restrictive view of the emotionality of relationships in organizations. Much of the value of social and emotional *sensitivity* lies in what it contributes to the quality of life in organizations, not just to the bottom line.

Organizations may do better to turn to ways of broadening the emotional sensitivity of its employees through processes of feminisation, emotionally responsive leadership styles, valuing intuition, and tolerance for a wide range of emotional expression and candour. Easier to say, perhaps, than do. In some organizations, where emotional hypocrisy is fine-tuned and emotional literacy muted, there is a tough cultural barrier to overcome to achieve such shifts. A senior, female, manager in a British bank expresses the position:[45]

> . . . being emotional in this particular work environment – financial services – gets you nowhere. You have to be incredibly strong and at times extraordinarily thick skinned.

And another reflects on the emotional display conventions of high office:

> When you get higher in terms of the hierarchy, you might show the elations but not the negatives. So you probably watch yourself and be a bit more guarded about what you do and don't do.

Arguably, both these managers are responding emotionally intelligently to the political contexts in which they find themselves. But they are also reproducing a culture of emotional stringency, wariness and deception. Creating different, more sensitive, emotional climates means taking risks, and that requires support from the very top of the organization.

FURTHER READING

Fineman, S. (2000) 'Commodifying the emotionally intelligent', in S. Fineman, (ed.), *Emotion in Organizations, 2nd Edition*. London: Sage. pp. 101–15.

Goleman, D. (1966) *Emotional Intelligence*. London: Bloomsbury.

Mayer, J.D. and Salovey, P. (1997) 'What is emotional intelligence?' in P. Salovey and D.J. Sluyter (eds), *Emotional Development and Emotional Intelligence*. New York: Basic Books.

Sternberg, R.J. (2001) 'Measuring the intelligence of an idea: how intelligent is the idea of emotional intelligence?' in J. Ciarrochi, J.P. Forgas and J.D. Mayer (eds), *Emotional Intelligence in Everyday Life*. Philadelphia: Psychology Press.

REFERENCES

1   Cooper, R.A. and Sawaf, A. (1977) *Executive EQ*. London: Orion Business. p. xii.
2   Goleman, D. (1996) *Emotional Intelligence*. London: Bloomsbury. p. 43.
3   Goleman, D. (1988) *Working With Emotional Intelligence*. London: Bloomsbury. p. 6.
4   Webb, J. (2001) 'Emotional rescue', *Better Nutrition*, 63 (2): 6.
5   Lippert, B. (2001) 'Bad news beer', *Adweek*, 42 (28): 24–6, especially p. 24.
6   Beatty, A. (1996) 'Emotion quotient – a different kind of smart', *St Louis Business Journal*, 16 (April): 43–4.
7   Pickles, H. (2000) 'I feel therefore I am', *Business Life* (July/August): 37–41, especially p. 38.
8   Ralston, F. (1995) *Hidden Dynamics: How Emotions Affect Business Performance and How You Can Harness Their Power for Positive Results*. New York: American Management Association.
9   Cooper, R. and Sawaf, A. (1997) *Executive EQ*. London: Orion Business.
10 Childre, D. and Cryer, B. (1998) *From Chaos to Coherence: Advancing Emotional and Organizational Intelligence Through Inner Quality Management*. Burlington, MA: Butterworth Heinemann.
11 Hunt, T. (1928) 'The measurement of social intelligence', *Journal of Applied Psychology*, 12: 317–34.
12 Wedeck, J. (1947) 'The relationship between personality and psychological ability', *British Journal of Psychology*, 36: 133–51.
13 Sternberg, R.J. (1997) *Successful Intelligence*. New York: Cambridge University Press.
14 Sternberg, R.J., Forsyth, G.B., Hedlund, J., Horvath, J.A., Wagner, R.K., Willams, W.M., Snook, S. and Grigorenko, E.L. (2000) *Practical Intelligence in Everyday Life*. New York: Cambridge University Press.
15 Gardner, H. (1993) *Multiple Intelligences*. New York: Basic Books.
16 Gardner, H. (1999) 'Who owns intelligence?', *The Atlantic Monthly*, 283: 67–76.
17 LeDoux (1988) *The Emotional Brain*. London: Weidenfeld and Nicolson.
18 Mayer, J.D. and Salovey, P. (1993) 'The intelligence of emotional intelligence', *Intelligence*, 27 (4): 433–42.
19 Salovey, P. and Mayer, J.D. (1990) 'Emotional Intelligence', *Imagination, Cognition and Personality*, 9 (3): 185–211.
20 Mayer, J.D., DiPaolo, M.T. and Salovey, P. (1990) 'Perceiving affective content in ambiguous stimuli: a component of emotional intelligence', *Journal of Personality Assessment*, 54: 772–81.

21 Salovey, P., Bedell, B.T., Detweiler, J.B. and Mayer, J.D. (2000) 'Current directions in emotional intelligence research', in M. Lewis and J.M. Haviland-Jones (eds), *Handbook of Emotions*. New York: The Guilford Press.

22 Salovey, P., Bedell, B.T., Detweiler, J.B. and Mayer, J.D. (2000) 'Current directions in emotional intelligence research', in M. Lewis and J.M. Haviland-Jones (eds), *Handbook of Emotions*. New York: The Guilford Press. p. 506.

23 Bar-On, R. (1997) *The Emotional Quotient Inventory (EQi): A test of Emotional Intelligence*. Toronto, Canada: Multi-Health Systems. p. 14.

24 Cooper, R.A. and Sawaf, A. (1977) *Executive EQ*. London: Orion Business. p. xiii.

25 Davies, M., Stankov, L. and Roberts, R.D. (1998) 'Emotional intelligence: in search of an elusive construct', *Journal of Personality and Social Psychology*, (75): 989–1015, especially p. 1001.

26 Topping, K., Bremner, W. and Holmes, E.A. (2000) 'Social competence', in R. Bar-On and J.D.A. Parker (eds), *The Handbook of Emotional Intelligence*. San-Francisco: Jossey Bass. p. 32.

27 Gowing, M.K. (2001) 'Measurement of individual emotional competence', in C. Cherniss and D. Goleman (eds), *The Emotionally Intelligent Workplace*. San Francisco: Jossey-Bass.

28 Goleman, D. (1995) What's your EQ? The Utne Lens, Utne Reader [On-Line]. <http://www.utne.com/>.

29 Barrett, G.V. (2000) 'Emotional intelligence: the Madison Avenue approach to professional practice', *15th annual meeting of the Society for Industrial and Organizational Psychology, April*, New Orleans.

30 Bar-On, R. and Parker, J.D.A. (eds) (2000) *The Handbook of Emotional Intelligence*. San Francisco: Jossey-Bass.

31 Salovey, P., Mayer, J.D., Goldman, S.L., Turvey, C. and Palfai, T.P. (1995) 'Emotional attention, clarity, and repair: exploring emotional intelligence using the Trait Meta-Mood Scale', in J.W. Pennebaker (ed.), *Emotion, Disclosure and Health*. Washington, DC: American Psychological Association.

32 Mayer, J.D. and Salovey, P. (1997) 'What is emotional intelligence?' in P. Salovey and D.J. Sluyter (eds), *Emotional Development and Emotional Intelligence*. New York: Basic Books.

33 Cooper, R.K. (1996/1997) *EQ Map*. San Francisco: AIT and Essi Systems.

34 Boyatzis, R.E., Goleman, D. and Rhee, K.S. (2000) 'Clustering competence in emotional intelligence', in R. Bar-On and J.D.A. Parker (eds), *The Handbook of Emotional Intelligence*. San Francisco: Jossey-Bass.

35 Sternberg, R.J. (2001) 'Measuring the intelligence of an idea: how intelligent is the idea of emotional intelligence?' in J. Ciarrochi, J.P. Forgas and J.D. Mayer (eds), *Emotional Intelligence in Everyday Life*. Philadelphia: Psychology Press.

36 Pfeiffer, S. (2001) 'Emotional intelligence: popular but elusive construct', *Roeper Review*, 23 (3): 138–42.

37 Cherniss, C. and Caplan, R.D. (2001) 'Implementing emotional intelligence programs in organizations', in C. Cherniss and D. Goleman (eds), *The Emotionally Intelligent Workplace*. San Francisco: Jossey-Bass. pp. 286–7.

38 Ellis, A. and Whitley, J.M. (eds) (1979) *Theoretical and Empirical Foundations of Rational–Emotional Therapy*. Monterey, California: Brooks-Cole.

39 Caruso, D.R. and Wolfe, C.J. (2001) 'Emotional intelligence in the workplace', in J. Ciarrochi, J.P. Forgas and J.D. Mayer (eds), *Emotional Intelligence in Everyday Life*. Philadelphia: Psychology Press. p. 150.

40 Boyatzis, R.E. (2001) 'How and why individuals are able to develop emotional intelligence', in C. Cherniss and D. Goleman (eds), *The Emotionally Intelligent Workplace*. San Francisco: Jossey Bass. p. 236.

41 Dulewicz, V. and Higgs, M. (1988) 'Emotional intelligence: can it be measured reliably and validly using competency data?', *Competency*, 6 (1): 28–37.

42 Goleman, D. (2001) 'An EI-based theory of performance', in C. Cherniss and D. Goleman (eds), *The Emotionally Intelligent Workplace*. San Francisco: Jossey-Bass.

43 Kram, K.E. and Cherniss, C. (2001) 'Developing emotional competence through relationships at work', in C. Cherniss and D. Goleman (eds), *The Emotionally Intelligent Workplace*. San Francisco: Jossey-Bass.

44 Mayer, J.D., Ciarrochi, J. and Forgas, J.P. (2001) 'Emotional intelligence in everyday life: an introduction', in J. Ciarrochi, J.P. Forgas and J.D. Mayer (eds), *Emotional Intelligence in Everyday Life*. Philadelphia: Psychology Press. p. xiii.

45 My thanks to Caroline Moore of Cranfield University for permission to use these quotes from her PhD research.

5
Virtually emotion

LEARNING OBJECTIVES

Virtual technologies have transformed how, where, when and with whom we work. This chapter examines the emotional implications of the virtual revolution and asks:

- Does virtual communication change the way feeling can be expressed?
- How do we create 'real' impressions of others and ourselves in the virtual world?
- What is missed and gained when the 'human moment' is lost?
- What is the emotional subtext of telecommuting?
- How do virtual teams and negotiators work together to create trust?

The development of information technologies has been dramatic. Personal and laptop computers, mobile (cellular) phones, videoconferencing, e-mail, the Internet and fax have transformed how, when and what we communicate. Distance and time zones have shrunk, making global transactions no more than a click away.

In work settings, information technologies were initially used as enhancements to traditional working methods, such as speeding up typing (the word processor), increasing the efficiency and quality of manufacturing (robots), and rapid changes to the design of objects, such as furniture, freeways and buildings (computer-aided design). Now, however, information technologies have begun to influence the whole nature and meaning of work, the very experience of 'working'. Traditional workspaces and places are beginning to be superseded by work arrangements and management systems and communications that are shaped, root and branch, by the power and promise of the computer. We see the emergence of *virtual organizations*, which take emotion into uncharted waters. A virtual organization transforms many of the face to face, interpersonal, means by which feeling is formed and expressed. It reorganizes feeling. How are such feelings shared, shaped or exploited?

CYBERSPACE AND EMOTION

Virtual organizations are 'virtual' because the have no obvious physical existence. Virtual organizations have a fuzzy, indefinite structure compared to the clear shape of the traditional, hierarchical organization. They are typically flexible and dynamic, made to *appear* tangible through information technology and software – e-mail, telework, groupware, teleconferencing, e-cash, the Internet, intranets, extranets, Electronic Data Interchange.

To work in a 'pure' virtual organization means that we cannot see, touch, feel or bump into our colleagues, customers or clients. We cannot leave daily for our office downtown (as there is no office there). We cannot meet fellow workers at the water cooler, coffee room or canteen, or stroll down the corridor to chat to our boss (these places do not exist). We cannot casually joke, flirt or grumble, face to face. We cannot smell the grease of the machines or our associate's after-shave or perfume. We cannot seal a contract with a firm handshake and feel good from the ritual. The customary emotion work, emotional labour and feeling rules-of-engagement are displaced or rendered redundant.

Where we do meet, however, is in cyberspace. Cyberspace is an illusion of a place where actual people meet, chat, do business. It is where they live out their own life dramas – loves and hates, ambitions and anxieties. William Gibson, in seductive prose, describes cyberspace as a

> consensual hallucination experienced daily by billions of legitimate operators, in every nation . . . A graphic representation of data abstracted from the banks of every computer in the human system. Unthinkable complexity. Lines of light ranged in the nonspace of the mind, clusters and constellations of data. Like city lights, receding.[1]

Getting lost in such cyberspace, an electronic universe without boundaries, is an awesome prospect, well fantasized in some Hollywood films. In practice, we avoid this outcome by creating an imaginary niche for ourselves, replete with familiar props and everyday assumptions. It then feels more comfortable and secure. The personalized home page on the Internet is one way of doing this, where the virtual 'you' can appear warm, intimate and homely (or some other identity). It is an example of *impression formation*, creating a public impression of three-dimensional, 'real', feeling people through a medium that has none of those qualities.

Impression formation is part of doing business virtually. When we telephone a domestic company, or customer-service advisor, we have traditionally assumed that the person we are speaking to is in their organization, seated at their usual workstation. But, in the virtual world, that person could be at a desk in their living room, in their car, or in another country. An inquiry from Britain to a call centre can be routed to Singapore or India. Pantelli describes instances where business calls have been received on mobile phones from unusual places, but without revealing as much to the caller.[2] In one case, the chief executive of a UK management consultancy was on holiday in France, but was updated by faxes to her hotel on a particularly complex deal. She then proceeded to negotiate between the parties over her mobile phone from a local cemetery – where reception was good and which had useful flat surfaces. In a second illustration, an elderly, retired salesman set up a housing development business in Cyprus to keep him busy during his retirement. His permanent work-base was, in fact, his mobile phone, and no more. One customer called the number while the salesman was on holiday in Greece. This did not rattle him as he coolly arranged a viewing of a property in Cyprus for the following day.

The 'feeling' customer in the machine

An important point in the tales above is that the technology enables the impression to be created that the virtual space is real, bounded and somewhere it is not. It is a *socially constructed* place, based on mix of deception by one party and blind faith, or suspension of disbelief, by the other. This is precisely the formula adopted by some banks, a sector that has been at the forefront of virtualization. In search of competitive efficiencies and economies, many have closed their high-street branches and replaced them with a telephone and/or Internet service, coordinated from call centres. In the main, call centres are large, open-plan buildings with rows of desks, staffed by operators trained to take customers' telephone queries. As 'customer-care' staff, they are able to perform basic banking operations over the phone, aided by a computerized screen-display, containing the account details of every customer. The flesh-and-blood, feeling, customer is never seen, and no customer enters the call centre. Transactions are virtual.[3]

One obvious consequence of this approach is the loss of the personal, face-to-face 'touch'. Unsurprisingly, there are customers who are uncomfortable about this. They prefer to talk to *their* local bank and to someone they know, and who knows them, and to create a 'feeling' connection. In response, some banks have created an illusion that the call is being taken locally when, in fact, it is not. The personalization process is further enhanced by self-introductions of the sort, 'Good morning Mr Jones; my name is Irene, how can I help you?'. Irene knows it is Mr Jones without asking him, because his name is automatically flagged on her computer screen when he dials in, using his personal identification number. Irene has also been trained to be friendly and 'smile down the telephone'. In a study of a virtual bank, Hughes and his colleagues saw stickers reminding workers to: *smile, your next customer may be the mystery shopper* (managerial surveillance), and *a complaint is a sales opportunity* (see also Chapter 3).

Employees learnt scripts to deal with complaining customers, to be expressed with tolerance and warmth such as the following two examples:

> I'm sorry that you're disappointed with our service – if I can be of any further help . . .

> I will pass on your comments to my manager . . . it's not so personal as in a branch . . . I'm sorry about that . . . if I can be of any assistance . . .[4]

But, for many people, no amount of virtual friendliness, or cleverly personalized websites, can substitute for face-to-face relationship. It is missed by some bank customers. It can be a problem for bank staff too. For example, many Internet banks are now expected to 'cross-sell', promoting services and goods well beyond the traditional bank account or loan. They include anything from motor, household and holiday insurance, to 'fantastic offers' on television sets, mobile phones and even Barbie dolls. But it can be difficult to sell to the customer-in-the-machine, with whom the employee has no personalized 'feeling' or knowledge. A manager in Hughes et al's study makes the point:

> I'm actually seeing very, very few of my own . . . customers. So then we've got to say 'where are the rest of them?' because I can produce a printout that says I've got fourteen thousand customers . . . Some of them have credit balances of twenty, thirty thousand pounds. And we never see them. We've never heard of them . . .[5]

TYPES OF VIRTUAL WORK

Virtual work varies in form and scope. It can be found in corporations, government departments, hospitals, libraries, schools and universities. A common denominator is that information technology takes some, or all, of the work to the workers, rather than workers going to the source of the work. It reverses the employment logic that has been in place since the Industrial Revolution, where going *to* work, 'to the factory, to the office' has been taken for granted. It also challenges the traditional belief that home and work are separate, and that commuting, often considerable distances, is a necessary part of working life.

Tele (from the Greek, 'far off') is the prefix that characterizes the different kinds of virtual work. *Telecommuting* is working from home, or from a variety of remote stations. There are now some 10 million teleworkers in Europe and over 11 million in the USA.[6] Some people telecommute for approximately a day a week for supplementary income, the remaining work time spent in conventional employment. There are mobile teleworkers who work both from home and an established office, but spend a fair part of their week away on business trips. They keep in touch through portable modems and mobile phones. Yet others telecommute from tele-centres or telecottages. These are local centres, often in remote rural areas, that provide fixed-site information technology for neighbourhood use, as and when required.[7] *Teleconferences* link participants in different places.

In *telemedicine* there is virtual communication between healthcare professionals and their patients, incorporating *telesurgery* and *telecare*. *Telemarketing* promotes products and services to potential customers by telephone. In the political sphere, *teledemocracy* gives citizens greater voice through the Internet, radio, television and satellite communications. *Tele-ducation*, or distance learning, delivers education to students wherever they happen to be, using television and the Internet. A prime example of teleducation is the UK's Open University. With over 200,000 students, the Open University reaches out to students in their homes through dedicated television and radio programmes, and telephone contact with tutors. Recently, this provision has been has been enhanced with videoconferencing, e-mail and mobile phones.

All forms of telework lack direct, eye-to-eye contact and therefore miss the commonly understood cues of feeling and emotion. For some teleworkers this is no impediment. They can still create an emotionally rewarding lifestyle. For others, though, the picture is less rosy.

Telecommuting: the emotional upside

There are people for whom telecommuting is a joy. It liberates them from the daily trip to the office and gives them more freedom to organize their own lives and work patterns. Tammy, a US real-estate manager, is one of those people. She telecommutes three days a week:

> I really have established myself at home as I would in the office. I see it a privilege to telecommute, so I try very hard to make it work. I usually end up working nine hours a day instead of seven or eight. I do a lot less socializing and instead of taking an hour for lunch, I'll go fix lunch and get back to work. It helps my morale. The biggest bonus is the elimination of a 44-mile round trip to the office. In the summer I can go out and start my gardening right after work. I think it's the greatest thing.[8]

Even more enthusiastic is Sid, a Californian technical writer, who describes himself as an 'extreme' telecommuter:

> Welcome to the office odyssey! Jack in, wire up, drop out! The Internet is all about freedom – freedom from soft-walled cubicles, freedom from bad coffee, freedom from rules that just don't apply anymore. Why do you need to be in a corporate business park when there's a whole wide, wired world out there?
>
> The short answer is that you don't. Two years ago, I cast off my office-bound shackles, packed my life into a backpack and a laptop computer and hit the road. Since then, I've been a digital nomad, travelling around Europe and North America while working my regular job as a technical writer for a software company back in California. So, yes, I'm still in the rat race. It's just that where I'm at, there aren't any other rats.[9]

Telework, in these circumstances, provides significant opportunities for people to re-balance their work and non-work lives and realize desires that were eclipsed by the routines of conventional employment. They are energized and excited by the new possibilities that telework offers.

Telecommuting: the emotional downside

Fear of losing career momentum when out of the usual networks, as well as feeling lonely, are clear disincentives to certain people. When only some people in an organization telecommute, their apparent freedom can be resented by those tied to the office.[10] At home, children can become rancorous if parents shut themselves away, a slave to the e–mail 'ping'. Teleworking can put a strain on household relationships as family members compete for space and attention. The emotional toll from feeling out of control, isolated and overloaded, with 'instant' child-care demands, can lead to stress and depression.[11]

Home has traditionally been a place to escape to, away from the stresses of work, an emotional bolthole. It is less of a haven when it doubles as a workplace. Consider the following tale reported in a Canadian newspaper. It is entitled 'Deadlines and Diapers':

> How to juggle the stress of running a business with the vocal demands of a toddler who knows perfectly well it's time to play . . . True, he needs me in a way that no company ever will, but I've yet to work anywhere else where the schedule revolves around naptime, a favourite TV show and a trip to the park (with a baby-sitter). So why am I doing this, feeding the fax machine with one hand while I dump the diaper pail with the other? I wanted flexible hours, freedom from the company's strictures and most of all lots of time for my son . . . Sure, you can spend time with your child when you want to . . . But there are plenty of times when I really don't want to crawl over the furniture or sing the latest hits of Sharon, Lois & Bram . . . I've even finished off a piece or two bouncing Alex on one knee, turned as far from my desk as I can, while picking with one finger at the keyboard, pushed to the outer limits in the opposite direction.[12]

Love and sex   When the traditional worker becomes a home-based telecommuter the rules of domestic love and sex conflate with those of work. Furthermore, sexuality is now highly focused, usually on just one person. This is rarely discussed in accounts of teleworking, other than in oblique comments about 'relationship issues'.

In traditional work settings, sexual desires are typically revealed in banter, jokes, sexual teasing between and across the sexes and rumoured office romances. It is where sexual fantasies are expressed or repressed. Sexual playfulness can be exciting, brightening up the day and making dull work more fun.[13] Crucially, it is something that most people leave behind when they leave their workplace. The home-based teleworker has none of these opportunities. A case account by Pauline Hodgson[14] gives us some clues as to what can happen:

CASE STUDY

David and Christine are both professional workers and have been married for fifteen years. They are generally contented and secure. Their children are at school all day and Christine already works from home. David decides to give up his regular job and telework from home. Things start well, very well. They revel in a new intimacy, 'drifting upstairs during the afternoon to make love'. They enjoy more time together chatting, and David appreciates Christine's visits to his work room. He does not feel alone and is delightfully free from office politics and commuting. After three months the agreeable periods fade as David becomes progressively busier. By the time six-months has passed there are no more romantic interludes as David works round the clock, alone in his room. Christine feels excluded, 'resentful and angry and very jealous about the seductress [David's virtual work contacts] behind the closed door'. For his part, David is angry and perplexed about this hostile and suspicious woman. Why is she so interested in his work, given she has never been before? Why doesn't she simply get on with her own work? And what, they both think, has happened to their love life?

With a psychoanalytic eye, Hodgson observes that the shift from David's social relationships at work to virtual ones 'upstairs', were clearly problematic for his wife. The former relationships were separate, invisible, something David did at the office. But his virtual ones, ironically, were more real, far more present and threatening. They came between them and shut her out. The teleworking arrangements raised old emotional ghosts for Christine, linked to her childhood when her parents sent her to bed, shut her out. For David, his wife was now resonant of his own mother, someone who was persistently intrusive and critical and would not leave him alone to live his own life. He withdrew from her and became secretive, as he now did with Christine.

This is an example of how a new, technologically shaped work structure can have unexpected emotional consequences. What initially appears liberating can become enslaving. Love relationships become more complex as the old boundaries between work and home dissolve. Privacy becomes reconfigured, along with its emotional expectations. Getting the best of both worlds – the work advantages of home teleworking and the physical and psychological space to nourish intimacy – requires careful negotiation and frequent review.

Loneliness on the move?   For the mobile teleworker, often away from home, virtual technology has been promoted as a way of counteracting isolation, and a more-than-adequate surrogate for an absent parent or partner. A UK television advertisement for mobile phones portrays a busy, happy executive walking down a street, telling a bedtime story to her eager child at home – over her mobile phone. Some psychotherapists advise teleworkers not to feel guilty about this, because 'ten minutes on the phone is more quality time than the average parent at home'.[15]

Such images give telework an undeserved gloss. Jill Fraser, in her book *White Collar Sweatshop*, notes the stress, exhaustion and despair among a growing number of corporate Americans, who are literally wired into a highly competitive, global business culture.[16] The virtual window never closes. Regular checking of e-mail from outside the office has become a tacit requirement of many jobs. Physical commuting time has become conflated with telecommuting time as laptops are snapped open on the train or plane. Mobile phones ring incessantly, with little respect for time or place, or the irritated looks of bystanders. The trap closes on the worker when it becomes apparent that they cannot meet their employer's demands without being accessible anywhere, anytime. This, in turn, becomes an expectation that is internalized, taken for granted, by the worker. It becomes 'normal work', to the exclusion of other life activities and relationships.

As the technology of virtuality proliferates, each new communication gadget gets rapidly transformed into an essential, everyday tool of the trade. It is promoted as better than the previous one: faster, lighter, more efficient, more portable, more flexible. Some are advertised as important fashion accessories – the 'beautiful' *iMac* or the 'ultra elegant', latest model of mobile phone. Virtual technology is big business and it is well know by marketing specialists that a new product can appeal for reasons of vanity, image and identity as much as, if not more than, its utility value. The circle is constantly self-reinforcing. The more business becomes virtual, the more it needs equipment that promises to make that virtuality even better.

In the frenzy, the emotional consequences are overlooked, taken for granted or framed to look far brighter than they really are. There is typically a lag between the adoption of new work technologies and an appreciation of their human consequences. Virtuality is no exception to this. Not only have we to learn what the buttons, icons and touch-screens can do, but also how to take care of the personal relationships that are disrupted and/or newly connected through such devices.

VIRTUAL TEAMS

Teamwork is familiar to many organizations. Now virtual teams are complementing, and in many cases replacing, face-to-face teams. Like 'real' teams, virtual teams bring together groups of people, often with different skills, who work together on a common task. Beyond this the similarity ends.

Virtual teams never, or hardly ever, meet face to face. Team members are not located in the same place, and contacts are not restricted to specific times. Computers, e-mailing and videoconferencing create the connections. Some virtual teams are temporary, such as *e-lancers*, short-lived networks of electronically connected freelancers selling goods and services. When the job is finished the network dissolves. Temporary arrangements such as these are attractive to some employers as they promise flexibility, responsiveness, lower costs and improved resource utilization. Other virtual teams have a longer life span. For example, the British Council employs 6000 people in 109 countries who, after a series of initial workshops, will not meet each other again in the flesh for up to two years.

To create a capable face-to-face team requires a fair amount of emotion work: mutual understanding, listening and negotiation. Different team members bring different desires, fears, insecurities, hidden concerns and vulnerabilities. The leader who cultivates trust appreciates the team's social and emotional dynamics as much as the task in hand.[17] Without trust we are suspicious of others' intentions or promises. We are wary about what we say or reveal, because we may be taken advantage of, or exploited. When we watch people's eyes, interpret their smiles, listen to the tone of their voice, we sense whom we can trust and those who seem untrustworthy.[18] So how do virtual teams cope? Can they exchange their feelings virtually, with any significance or depth? How can trust be formed, and what is the leader's role in the process?

Swift trust

If intimacy, touch and co-location are crucial for making and repairing trust, then virtual teams are doomed. There are some writers who are inclined to this view. Charles Handy, for example, argues that computer-based communications eliminate the cues that people use to convey warmth, trust, attentiveness and other interpersonal communications: they are emotionally void.[19] But the 'touch trust' perspective is not necessarily the best way of conceptualizing the nature of community in cyberspace. It was developed before computer-mediated communication. We now need to think differently about how bonds are created.[20-22] For example, many common prejudices and social stereotypes are no longer barriers to trust when team members cannot see each other. People cannot judge one another on the basis of age, physical handicap, skin colour or clothing.

Debra Meyerson and her colleagues found that temporary, virtual teams could develop *swift trust* – in the first few keystrokes of communication.[23] This was a critical period for trust to be established. In other words, unless they developed trust speedily, they may never trust at all. The important signals, or cues, were fast actions and an enthusiastic, generative, approach. The receiver of the message made clear his or her excitement, commitment and optimism. The more of this, the greater the trust. Those who developed swift trust described their team members as considerate of each other's feelings, friendly, and as people they could rely on. In another study of swift trust, virtual teams of students from business programmes around the world were given projects that required international collaboration. High-trust teams exchanged messages rapidly and frequently. They displayed (on the screen) optimism, excitement and clear orientation to project's goals. They shared leadership, volunteered for assignments, and even found ways of communicating over weekends. Low-trust teams had infrequent and non-committal communicators.[24]

Managerial dilemmas

> If you have 10 people in 10 different places and they are not all sure that they know what they're doing, chaos breaks out. It is critical they establish a relationship and trust each other.[25]

Managers of virtual teams have their own particular quandary: how to manage people they do not see in the flesh? Trust, once again, becomes highly relevant when traditional methods of control no longer apply. Managers (and the managed) of virtual teams are now reliant on others' good faith, goodwill and feelings of cooperativeness – which can feel strange and disempowering if they are accustomed to direct, face-to-face, contact and control.[26-28] They also have to learn ways of conveying and sustaining trust and personal relationships through web-camera images, the types of questions they ask, how they interpret on-line responses, and how they organize and schedule their time.

Virtual management requires particular supervisory routines. Fostering social chat on-line appears to be helpful, as is the stating of clear purposes and goals. Virtual 'management-by-walking-around' is another approach. The manager is periodically 'present' and supportive through phone, fax e-mail or videoconference, encouraging connections and trust across the team. There is software designed to facilitate this, such as 'groupware' that helps people work collectively while located remotely. Groupware includes shared database access, calendar sharing, collective writing and electronic meetings. It can also help in picking up cues of *telestress* in people's communication styles. Telestress is the stress, anxiety and despair that can come from long periods on-line with little contact with others. It is some-times revealed in compulsive logging in during the day and night, and excessive irritation when the system is inaccessible.

FEELING AND FLAMING THROUGH THE MACHINE

Feeling

We can begin to think of telework, not as an emotionally impoverished medium, but one where people find different ways of expressing feeling – just as they did through handwritten letters, the telegraph and the telephone. The new communication technologies may limit the kind of emotionality that 'real' contact brings, but this is a rather misleading comparison. Emotionality becomes reframed and renormed as users explore the capabilities of the different information technologies and invent new protocols for emotion.

Mobile telephones, for example, have thrust the private expression of feeling into new, unexpected, places. Display-rules have begun to shift as mobile phone users talk openly and loudly about personal and business confidences, within earshot of strangers. It is now common to overhear someone's happy or sad news, and other intimacies, in corridors, restaurants, buses, trains or streets. Hands-free equipment adds the spectacle of people apparently talking to themselves and emoting (once taken as a sign of mental instability). A new emotional zone has been created where the convenience and mobility of the phone is valued above the old protocols of emotional privacy, and where the unintended listeners to conversations now mask their embarrassment, irritation or curiosity.[29, 30]

'Netiquette' norms for emotion are another example. A word in capital letters is taken as an expression of shouting or anger, edging on rudeness. Body-language words can be added to the text, such as 'grin', 'frown', 'smile', 'smirk'. Shorthands for emotion have been invented, *emoticons*, like 'smilies' ☺☹☺, or quick keyboard notations such as:

: -)	a smile to inflect a sarcastic or joking statement
; -)	a smile with a wink to signal a flirtatious remark
: - (	a frown; upset, depressed
>; - >	a very lewd remark
: ' – (	crying
: D	laughter
: [	real downer

For the novice or the perplexed, there are now 'smile dictionaries' placed, appropriately, on the Internet.

Virtual communication on the Internet has immediate emotional advantage to some people. As noted earlier, they can communicate free of some of the common prejudices attached to physical appearance. It is less influenced by status and social games. Gender, social class and ethnic differences are not apparent, nor are physical or psychological disabilities. Shy individuals do not have to fight their way in.[31] The medium, furthermore, encourages boldness or 'disinhibition', where people become less concerned about self-presentation and the judgement of others. Web logs ('Blogs'), for example, are confessional websites where people revel in the process of instant sharing of some of their innermost feelings, to a virtual community of like-minded diarists. Love, sex and despair are given voice, with therapeutic/self-discovery effect. The immediacy of distribution and feedback is exciting and seductive. Amber, for example, bares her soul on one such site:[32]

> But I'm not unhappy; not really. There are moments where I sink back into bottomless depressions, times when I realize I've forgotten my Prozac or

I've not gotten enough sleep and have to make a concerted effort to keep from reverting to slicing my arms up with fingernail scissors . . . But really, that's not who I am. I may not know myself as well as I once did, but I do know that I've come leaps and bounds from 1999, and I don't plan on looking back.

Flaming

Web interactions can also lead to extreme emotional displays, such as 'flaming'. Here, an initially sober exchange of e-views can explode into vitriolic retorts, even a flame war, the text littered with capitals, exclamation marks and open expressions of negative feeling. Typically, the flames are fanned by each new contributor to the argument, to then die out as quickly as they had arisen.[33] Flame war aficionados suggest that a battle usually has a 'flame master', someone who takes the moral high ground, leads the attack and has probably survived, unscathed, previous campaigns. Once started, the cause of the conflict is often lost in the exchange of insults and shifts in loyalties. The clash is fuelled by patronising remarks ('You are an idiot. You take snippets out of context, so I'm going to take you thru, step by step'), contempt ('I refuse to have a battle of wits with an unarmed person'), and other undermining assertions.[34]

Flaming can get serious, but its harm often melts away in the welter of scorn and outrage. But there is the darker side to disinhibition on the net. For example, there are pornographic sites that target women or children, and ones that incite violence towards racial or religious groups. Disinhibition is a two-edged sword, freeing up the repressed or oppressed, but also licensing hostility and violence.[35, 36]

Illusions of safety

The demarcation between private and public is less clearly drawn on the Internet and e-mail. It can feel an emotionally safe environment to disclose distress and enlist others' support, as is evidenced by the many different self-help groups on the Internet. In this way computer-mediated communication supports strong, multiple, ties and fosters social and emotional connections – precisely the stuff of community, but virtual community. Its psychological safety, however, is far from perfect, at times illusory, as the pitfalls of disinhibition show. Moreover, the success of hackers has compromised the confidentiality of transactions, and some institutions are able to monitor the content of their employees' e-mails. Embarrassment is extreme when a confidential message is inadvertently circulated to the wrong person, sometimes at the accidental press of a 'Forward' icon. There is the tale of one of the most famous, mistakenly routed, e-mails, sent to tens of thousands of readers. It began:

Darling, at last we have a way to send messages that is completely private.

E-negotiation and the schmooze

Face-to-face negotiations are steadily giving way to virtual negotiation. Like any negotiation, some friction is almost inevitable, given that each party is defending their own interests. And where there is friction, flames are not far off. E-mail negotiation, over considerable distances with strangers, misses the traditional social lubricants: getting to know your opponent, breaking the ice, small talk, background chats, rapport building. Michael Morris and his colleagues call this the 'schmooze' factor.[37]

E-mail communications have little room for schmooze, although they have plenty of capacity for detail – such as setting out the full content of a negotiator's position and desires. Statements in e-mails can come across more harshly than intended without the feedback of facial expressions or gestures that provide cues to the richness of meaning. Cyber-humour can be taken as an insult and brevity as curtness.[38] Knowing how an offer is being made or received, or what clarifications are necessary, can be lost in the context-vacuum of the interaction and the absence of voice and body emotion. Much hinges on the impressions gained in the first moments of a communication where swift trust is, or is not, established. That rapport, good or ill, carries through the ups and downs of the negotiation process.

But can swift trust and negotiation outcomes be enhanced with *some* schmoozing? This question intrigued Morris et al., so they decided to put it to the test. They compared e-negotiators who had a prior, just five-minute, phone call to chat about themselves (but not about the actual negotiation) with negotiators who were communicating exclusively by e-mail. The 'schmoozers' developed more realistic goals, generated a bigger range of outcomes and were less likely to conflict and flame. A little schmoozing, it seems, can go a long way.

CONCLUSIONS: VIRTUAL FUTURES

The shift to remote, virtual, working is relatively recent. This contrasts with the long period during which people have adapted to working away from home in a factory, shop or office. In these settings there have been reasonably clear boundaries between home and work. Such an assumption no longer holds as virtual working reshapes and, in many instances replaces, conventional organizations. There will be continuing issues about the way people adapt to such changes. Feelings and emotions – trust, alienation, bonding, loneliness, stress, love, intimacy and self-identity – are on the line, in a both a virtual and metaphorical sense.

Like all new technologies, virtual communications are neither intrinsically good nor bad. However, the way they are exploited can lead to consequences that are socially and psychologically helpful or harmful, organizationally healthy or unhealthy. Organizational managers often lack approaches to anticipate, and respond to, such outcomes. Virtual technologies are adopted mainly because of their promise of greater efficiency (some of which spectacularly fail) and/or their fashionableness, not their emotional effects. But efficiency and emotions interact. Each new virtual form challenges the way people at work

- relate
- trust
- develop long-term relationships
- express their contentment and discontent
- feel powerful or powerless
- feel lonely and overwhelmed with information
- feel 'real' and engaged in their organizational world.

Virtual communications certainly liberate some people, adding meaning to their work lives and making transactions quicker and easier. Many people are able to make new emotional capital from the virtual process, creating different ways of relating meaningfully to others. But not all feel that way, especially those who have not been brought up in the cyber generation. Still others find it hard to substitute the human moment with virtual ones, and can feel isolated and misunderstood.[39] The trick, it seems, is not to be seduced by the runaway developments of virtual communication, but to combine their clear virtues with the even clearer ones of face-to-face relationships.

FURTHER READING

Fraser, J.A. (2001) *White Collar Sweatshop: The Deterioration of Work and Its Rewards in Corporate America*. New York: Norton.

Gackenbach, J. (ed.) (1998) *Psychology and the Internet*. San Diego: Academic Press.

Handy, C.B. (1995) 'Trust and the virtual organization', *Harvard Business Review*, 73 (3): 40–50.

Sheehy, N. and Gallager, T. (1996) 'Can virtual organizations be made real?' *The Psychologist*, (April): 159–62.

REFERENCES

1 Quoted in Kollock, P. and Smith, M.A. (1999) 'Communities in cyberspace', in M.A. Smith and P. Kollock (eds), *Communities in Cyberspace*. London: Routledge. p. 17.

2 Panteli, N. (2001) 'Impressions and boundaries within virtual work spaces'. The 17th EGOS Colloquium, *The Odyssey of Organizing*, Lyon, France, 5–7 July.

3 Abbott, A. (1990) 'Positivism and interpretation in sociology: lessons for sociologists form the history of stress research', *Sociological Forum*, 5435–58.

4 Hughes, J.A., O'Brien, J., Randall, D., Rouncefield, M. and Peter, T. (2001) 'Some "real" problems of "virtual organization"', *New Technology, Work and Employment*, 16 (1): 49–64, especially p. 59.

5 Hughes, J.A., O'Brien, J., Randall, D., Rouncefield, M. and Peter, T. (2001) 'Some "real" problems of "virtual organization"', *New Technology, Work and Employment*, 16 (1): 49–64, especially p. 61.

6 Johnson, P. and Nolan, J. (2000) 'eWork 2000: Status Report on New Ways to Work in the Information Society'. European Commission, Brussels.

7 Daniels, K., Lamond, D.A. and Standen, P. (2001) 'Teleworking: framework for organizational research', *Journal of Management Studies*, 38 (8): 1151–85.

8 Henson, B. (1997) 'Remote working: marvellous, perilous or both?', University Corporation for Atmospheric Research. <http://www.ucar.edu/communications/staffnotes/9704/telecommuting.html>, Colorado. p. 4.

9 Sid and Kristine (2000) 'Extreme telecommuting - and office odyssey with Sid and Kristine', <http://www.officeodyssey.com/index.htm>.

10 Bredin, A. (1996) *The Virtual Office Survival Handbook*. New York: Wiley.

11 Bredin, A. (1996) *The Virtual Office Survival Handbook*. New York: Wiley.

12 Anonymous (June 1995) 'Deadlines and diapers'. *The Globe and Mail*: C1–C6.

13 Gabriel, Y., Fineman, S. and Sims, D. (2000) *Organizing and Organizations: An Introduction, 2nd Edition*. London: Sage.

14 Hodson, P. (1996) 'Love and the teleworker', *Distans*, (February).

15 Bredin, A. (1996) *The Virtual Office Survival Handbook*. New York: Wiley. pp. 67–8.

16 Fraser, J.A. (2001) *White Collar Sweatshop: The Deterioration of Work and Its Rewards in Corporate America*. New York: Norton.

17 Hackman, J.R. (2002) *Leading Teams*. Harvard: Harvard University Press.

18 Jarvenpaa, S.L. and Leidner, D.E. (1999) 'Communication and trust in global virtual teams', *Organization Science*, 10 (6): 791–815.

19 Handy, C.B. (1995) 'Trust and the virtual organization', *Harvard Business Review*, 73 (3): 40–50.

20 Kollock, P. and Smith, M.A. (1999) 'Communities in cyberspace', in
    M.A. Smith and P. Kollock (eds), *Communities in Cyberspace*. London:
    Routledge.

21 Jorge, A.d.L. (2001) 'Social networks in education'. *Social Geographies
    of Educational Change: Contexts, Networks and Generalizability*,
    Barcelona, 11–14 March.

22 Sheehy, N. and Gallager, T. (1996) 'Can virtual organizations be made
    real', *The Psychologist*, (April): 159–62.

23 Meyerson, D., Weick, K.E. and Kramer, R.M. (1966) 'Swift trust and
    temporary groups', in R.M. Kramer and T.R. Tyler (eds), *Trust in
    Organizations: Frontiers of Theory and Research*. Thousand Oaks,
    California: Sage.

24 Jarvenpaa, S.L. and Leidner, D.E. (1999) 'Communication and trust in
    global virtual teams', *Organization Science*, 10 (6): 791–815.

25 Daniels, K., Lamond, D.A. and Standen, P. (eds) (2000) *Managing
    Telework: Perspective from Human Resource Management and Work
    Psychology*. London: Business Press. p. 169.

26 Daniels, K., Lamond, D.A. and Standen, P. (eds) (2000) *Managing
    Telework: Perspective from Human Resource Management and Work
    Psychology*. London: Business Press. p. 169.

27 Dwelly, T. (2000) *Living at Work*. York: Joseph Rowntree
    Foundation.

28 Weisenfeld, B.M., Raghuram, S. and Garud, R. (1999) 'Communication
    patterns as determinants of organizational identfication in a virtual
    organization', *Organization Science*, 10 (6): 777–90.

29 Fineman, S. (1996) 'Emotion and organizing', in S. Clegg, C. Hardy and
    W. Nord (eds), *Handbook of Organization Studies*. London: Sage.

30 Scherer, K.R. (2001) 'Emotional experience is subject to social and
    technological change: extrapolating to the future', *Social Science
    Information*, 40 (1): 125–51.

31 Daniels, K., Lamond, D.A. and Standen, P. (eds) (2000) *Managing
    Telework: Perspective from Human Resource Management and Work
    Psychology*. London: Business Press. p. 169.

32 <http://www.timeformetofly.com/mt/>.

33 Gackenbach, J. (ed.) (1998) *Psychology and the Internet*. San Diego:
    Academic Press.

34 <http://www.heenan.net/flame>.

35 Reid, E. (1999) 'Hierarchy and power: social control in cyberspace', in
    M.A. Smith and P. Kollock (eds), *Communities in Cyberspace*. London:
    Routledge.

36 Reid, E. (1998) 'The self and the internet: variations on the illusion of
    one self', in J. Gackenbach (ed.), *Psychology and the Internet*. San
    Diego: Academic Press.

37 Morris, M., Nadler, J., Kurtzberg, T. and Thompson, L. (2000) 'Schmooze or lose: social friction in e-mail negotiations'. Graduate School of Business, Stanford University, Stanford.

38 Collinson, D. (2002) 'Managing humour', *Human Relations*, 39 (3): 269–88.

39 Hallowell, E.M. (1999) 'The human moment at work', *Harvard Business Review*, (Jan–Feb): 58–66.

Leading and following – with emotion

Interviewer:	But there's a part of you, Al, I mean – you know, even today, there's a part – you like the confrontation. You like the competition. You like the battle. That's part of what gets your juices flowing. Isn't that right?
Al Dunlap:	Well, I'm a very competitive person. I like to take on the situations that no one else will take on.
Interviewer:	But most people would not like to walk into a board room unaccompanied and look at an eleven-member executive committee and say, 'You two I'm keeping. The rest of you are fired. Goodbye'. That is not typical behavior from leaders. What is it? I mean, why do you like to do that? What – what is it that – that – that turns you on and – and – and that makes it work for you?
Al Dunlap:	I don't know that you'd say, 'You like to do that.' But, when you go into a company that's failing miserably, it all starts at the top. And, when you go in, you know these are the people that created the problem, so you're gonna have very little empathy for those people. They're the people that have created the problem for the workers in the factory, and so you get rid of those people. As long

as they're there, you're not gonna be able to improve the company. Now, most people don't do that because the minute you do that you create controversy.[1]

Al, 'Corporate Rambo', Dunlap was Chief Executive Officer of the Sunbeam Corporation until he was fired in 1998. When it happened the announcement was, allegedly, met with cheers from the many thousands of laid off workers he had ousted through the years.

The very idea of leadership is imbued with emotion and is central to organizing processes. In most cultures, organizational leadership is prized, a mark of high office and power. It invites a mixture of awe, envy, fear and suspicion. For some followers, a new leader can symbolize a fresh start, the exciting prospect of righting old wrongs, of finally realizing their dreams. They are energized and hopeful. For others, of more sceptical disposition, the new leader will be just one of many who disappoints, who fails to deliver on promises. And indeed, one inevitable tension of a leader's own role is that, in meeting the needs of some, he or she is bound to displease others. There is a thin dividing-line between leader as hero and leader as villain.

In examining the emotional core of leadership we must also consider 'followership'. They belong together. Leaders and followers need each other to play out the dramas and dances of power and control, persuasion and resistance. It is a process of mutual influence. They bring their desires, fantasies and frailties to the leadership situation, through which differences in status deference and dependence are expressed.

WHY FOLLOW A LEADER?

This is perhaps one the profoundest questions we can ask. We follow, readily or reluctantly, the direction or inclinations of our leaders – be they supervisors, managers, chief executives, presidents or prime ministers. We talk about them a lot. We soon dissect their shortcomings. They dominate our media. Why? What emotional undercurrents create such attention?

To some observers, there is one dominant emotion responsible for leadership – fear. A chief or leader in a community is essential for survival of the human species, the most efficient way of ensuring sufficient discipline in order to meet threats, to reproduce and protect offspring.[2] Respect for, or fear of, the leader reduces the likelihood of chaos in the community. Threats from outsiders can be more successfully resisted. So leadership here is 'natural', to the greater good of the community. Primates will always jostle for a place in a hierarchy of dominance, a pyramid of fear.

But different social and economic systems locate their leaders differently, and have different emotional priorities. For the pygmies and Bantu of central Africa, for instance, leadership is mostly non-hierarchical and participative in an agricultural economy. Consensus building is more important than rule by fear. The complexities of widespread industrialization have produced their own, often contrasting, leadership structures. Some are steeply hierarchical, others are flatter arrangements. In 'matrix organizations' a person can have more than one boss. There are followers who are closely supervised, while others are left more to their own devices. But circuits of emotion – fear, respect, deference or trust – underpin each leader–follower format. There is always someone to turn to who acts as controller or guide, consoler or critic, punisher or rewarder.

Emotional roots

Yet the desire to follow has even deeper emotional roots. Psychoanalysts suggest that, just as an infant craves care and attention from a parent or parental figure, so does an adult. Similar emotional needs are linked together over time, forever. Even a weak, flawed, or downright evil leader can provide a sense of identity and purpose. Sigmund Freud spoke of the leader as the 'primal father', a person who taps into our buried impulse to be controlled and directed, released from the existential anxiety about who we are and where we are going.

By accepting a leader, people feel strong, protected, secure, supplied with explanations and simplifications in a complex world. The leader provides a framework of meaning. Religious leaders, particularly, can fill this role.[3, 4] Some leaders attract chronic followers, people who move from group to group, leader to leader, in the hope of finding 'the' answer. Some followers are captivated by the apparent strength or power of the leader; others by the leader's unusual ideas or spirituality.[5] Underpinning such strivings is the search for meaning, something or someone to fill the frightening abyss of purposelessness.

The wondrous leader

The adulation, and god-like image, of the leader is common in sects and totalitarian regimes. But corporate leaders and managers can also be seen as wondrous figures, endowed with superhuman abilities and secret knowledge. Merely being acknowledged by the leader can be a blissful occurrence, cementing a fantasy about someone who cares, and knows you personally. Yiannis Gabriel reports the excitement of a young intern in a publishing company as she anticipates meeting her boss for the first time.

> I was becoming even more obsessed with the idea that I had to talk with her and ask her to reveal to me all the secrets that had guided her to her success. Finally, one afternoon she was free and pleased to talk to me. I wanted to find out about everything. Was this feasible? The discussion continued for a long time . . . My satisfaction from listening to my manager talk about these issues was indescribable. All the theories I had seen applied in our department with great success, were now reconfirmed to me by my manager, a person whom I respect and admire enormously. I hope that one

day I will have the chance to practice all that I have learned and I am still learning, becoming a successful manager.[6]

Here, the follower makes the leader, and the creation is a perfect one because perfection is what the intern wants to see. There is an inevitable imbalance in this process as many leaders are, in practice, likely to be faced with a blur of faces, not a series of special people. The follower recalls a unique experience; for the leader it is just one of many encounters. But for the follower who bathes in the aura of someone they *need* to respect and admire, this fact counts for little. So the friendly smile from the managing director, the kiss from a pop idol, the handshake from the politician, the glance from the Queen or the Emperor, is a rapturous moment. Kapuscinki's vivid account of the influence of Ethiopia's once Emperor, Hallie Selassie, on his subjects, illustrates an extreme of such adoration:

> A crowd awaited the Emperor . . . We gathered early so as not to miss the Emperor's arrival, because that moment has special significance for us . . . One wanted the smallest, second-rate sort of attention, nothing that burdened the Emperor, nothing that burdened the Emperor with any obligations. A passing notice, a fraction of a second, yet the sort of notice that later would make one tremble inside and overwhelm one with the triumphal thought – 'I have been noticed.' What strength it gave afterward! What unlimited possibilities it created![7]

Yet some emperors, parents, and parental figures, can disappoint us. They can fail to live up to our aspirations, or fantasies. They are not always as invulnerable, wise or powerful as we had expected. This can be a profound shock, such as when the 'wondrous', 'whiz kid' chief executive turns out to be untrustworthy, even a cheat or thief. Like the Wizard of Oz, once stripped of his bold façade, he is revealed to be a rather sad and diminished figure. Bhagwan Shree Rajneesh, for instance, was an Indian spiritual leader who created a following of over 15,000 members. His creed was mix of Eastern mysticism, individual devotion and sexual freedom. In 1985 he was deported from the USA for immigration fraud. His movement was under investigation for arson, attempted murder, drug smuggling and vote fraud. Rajneesh himself had amassed a vast personal wealth. Under these circumstances, followers are left exposed to their own vulnerability, damaged pride and the full force of their dependency on the leader. When followers identify very closely with leaders, they rise and fall with them. The wise follower keeps his or her distance.

THE CRAFTING OF CHARISMA

The emotionalities of leader–follower relationships are especially evident in the notion of charisma. Charismatic leaders are generally viewed as having an intangible, intriguing, power or resource; a personal magnetism that attracts people. They are able to make irresistible emotional connections with their followers. Followers feel pleasure and pride in identifying with them, inspired by all that they say and do. High profile, charismatic, leaders in the political and social field include Martin Luther King, Mother Theresa, Mahatma Gandhi, Adolf Hitler, Winston Churchill, Fidel Castro and John F. Kennedy. Among the ranks of industrialists cited for their charisma are Alfred P. Sloan of General Motors, Lee Iacocca of Chrysler, Jan Carlzon of Scandinavian Airlines, Anita Roddick of The Body Shop, and Mary Kay Ash of Mary Kay Cosmetics. Mary Kay devotees have reported meeting her as '. . . quite an experience. You could just feel the power. It was a very unusual experience. You can just feel the powerful vibes and charisma'.[8]

The charisma-spotlight invariably rests on the 'great' leaders of our time, symbolizing their cultural value. However, charisma can equally be applied to the corner-shop owner beloved by her staff and customers, the effervescent middle manager in a small engineering factory, or the school head who is deeply admired by staff and pupils. But what, exactly, constitutes charisma and its emotion magic? Is it a mysterious, intrinsic attribute of the leader? Or is it a learned skill, carefully crafted words and mannerisms? Or, as our discussion of 'followership' suggests, has it more to do with the needs and desires of followers?

Moving moments

Of the various analyses of charisma, there is agreement on two things. First, that charismatic leaders engender extraordinary passion among their followers. Followers are stirred by the leader's passion about particular ideals, visions or images. Charisma underpins *transformational* or *servant* leaders in organizations, who aim to alter the moods and desires of their subordinates – towards devotion, piety, love, exuberance, or excitement.[9–12] They are said to inspire their followers to transcend their own self-interests for the good of the organization or some broader social cause. They are able to think inspirationally, 'out of the box'.[13] Energized emotions can move followers to shift their commitments and allegiances, help them re-evaluate their priorities, as well as hold them in line once they are committed. The charismatic leader has a rich feeling-field in which to operate.

The second point of agreement is that charismatic leadership is most likely to flourish in times of social distress or crisis. When there is need for help or rescue, the potential for dependency on a leader is greatest: 'We're finished, desperate; just look at our faces; please give us some hope'. We are willing to *attribute* charisma to a leader who gives voice to our pains and provides us with hope.[14, 15] In the economically troubled times of the 1930s, Hitler put it thus to the German people:

> That is the mightiest mission of our Movement, namely, to give the searching and bewildered masses a new, firm belief, a belief that we will not abandon them in these days of chaos, which they will swear and abide by,

so that at least somewhere they will find a place where their hearts can be at rest.[16]

Moving hearts was also Jan Carlzon's aim in 1978. As president of Sweden's ailing domestic airline, he made a stirring speech in a huge aircraft hangar to his assembled staff. It was an oration that signalled a turning point in his company's fortunes. Standing on a tall ladder he opened his speech 'This company is not doing well . . .', . . . and closed with 'I have some ideas of my own, and we'll probably be able to use them. But most important, you are the ones who must help me, not the other way round'.[17] The charismatic bond it reinforced by gestures that demonstrate that the leader shares some of the suffering of his or her followers. Mahatma Gandhi lived in poverty, while Lee Iacocca, chief executive of Chrysler, elected to take a salary of $1 during the worst of times.[18]

Charisma originates from the Greek *kharis*, 'the gift of grace'. For Plato it was a divine attribute, a favour from god. Religious and cult evangelists, to whom the emotionally distressed are often attracted, frequently claim links to the divine. Charismatic leaders, of course, have their own emotional biographies. Many have had childhoods marked by isolation and loneliness. Churchill, for example, spent much of his time alone and Mussolini was twice expelled from school for stabbing fellow students. Gardner observes:

> Future leaders have often lost fathers at an early age. According to one study, over 60 percent of major British political leaders lost a parent in childhood, more often the father . . . Their precocious dependence on themselves may place them in a favourable position for directing others.[19]

The ruthlessness of some famous leaders has been associated with childhood wounds and confusing or conflicting parental relations. Former British prime minister, Margaret Thatcher, reports having 'nothing more to say' to her mother after her 15th birthday, yet she adored her father.[20] Stalin, Lenin, Hitler and Gandhi all shared ambivalent feelings about authority, feeling close to one parent, but alienated from the other. As a child, Stalin was beaten savagely by his drunken father, but his mother loved him dearly.[21] Wielding power is one way of resolving the anxiety of such tensions, a defensive shield that provides the comfort of control and predictability.[22] Recent leaders, such as former US president, Bill Clinton, fall into this mould:

> President Bill Clinton's childhood was rife with parental tensions: he never knew his biological father, he did not get along at all with his violent stepfather, and he was called on increasingly to mediate among adults in his household. He reportedly first began to consider a career in politics when he discovered, as a schoolchild, that he was able to resolve conflicts among his peers.[23]

The dark side of charisma

Mixing characters such as Stalin and Hitler with Mother Teresa and Gandhi reveals one of the crucial features of charisma – it can be employed to very different ends, good or evil, ethical or unethical. Such valuations are, of course, subjective and relative. Most leaders will claim the moral high ground, whatever their cause. As I write, Slobodan Milosevic, the former, persuasive, president of Yugoslavia, protests his innocence of genocide in his trial at the Hague international court. He does this indirectly and skilfully by accusing his accusers:

> Genocide is a method your colonial powers use. North and South, in Africa and Asia, all the colonial powers used genocide. And today our part of Europe is also a target of colonial powers who want to take back what they have lost.[24]

In this manner, the leader's responsibility for individual suffering and appalling misery gets obscured in the trading and contestation of ideologies.

Involvement in activities that many would judge as evil or perverse also requires the inhibition of certain emotional responses. Feelings for the victim, empathy, and anticipated shame or guilt for one's actions, are normally potent emotions of social control and care. They check behaviours that may do harm to others. Their absence or suspension in powerful leaders can be especially dangerous.[25] This is compounded by other emotions, especially contempt – for an ethnic group, for blacks, Jews, women, the working class, the aristocracy, the uneducated, managers. Contempt spurs and welds prejudice. It provides an emotional justification for discrimination or, more catastrophically, for genocide.[26, 27]

Mis-leading is the dark side of charisma, where entire groups become influenced by the delusional ideas of the leader. Howell distinguishes two types of charismatic leadership: the *socialized* and the *personalized*. Socialized leaders foster autonomy amongst their followers, a condition that outlives the leader's tenure in the organization. Personalized leaders, on the other hand, exhibit personally dominant and authoritarian behaviour. They bond followers to themselves for their own personal ambitions and needs. They evoke feelings of obedience and loyalty, which creates dependency and conformity. Their influence rarely continues after they have left the setting that initially nourished them.[28]

In business organizations, personalized charismatic leaders often have a skewed vision of the future, deeply coloured by their own ambitions. They are likely to be blind to marketplace realities, deaf to critical feedback, impulsive and autocratic. The demise of UK retailer Marks and Spencer in the 1990s reflected just such a scenario. Its once successful and admired chairman clung to his personal formula for operating, and highly directive style, even though customers were fast deserting the company. In military settings, the effectiveness of the personalized, charismatic leader is also suspect. The eccentric, 'tough but loved' general or commanding officer, is the stuff of legend, and certainly of Hollywood. Keithly and Tritten cast a cool eye over this image:

> The record for charismatic combat leaders is in fact dubious, their actual contributions have been prodigiously inflated with the passage of time . . .

If anything, the evidence indicates that charismatic leaders are more trouble than they are worth.[29]

In support of their claim, they note how charismatic leaders are difficult to deal with in a military culture that prides itself on its rational/legal authority. Also, studies of the effective combat battalions indicate that it is technical competence and a high degree of training that marks out their commanders, not charisma.

Manufacturing charisma

What it is that leaders *do* to become labelled as charismatic? We here shift attention from the psychodynamics of charisma, to its *performance*. Leaders who inspire others, who 'move' their audiences, use words, mannerisms, labels and slogans in a particular way. They have a dramatic flair to communicate emotions and *engage* their followers. Is there a special language of inspiration that anyone can learn? Consider the following two speeches:

> We wanted to start a company that had a lot to do with education and in particular higher education, colleges and universities. So our vision is that there's a revolution in software going on now on college and university campuses. And it has to do with providing two types of breakthrough software . . . I think we can make a real difference in the way the learning experience happens in the next five years. And that's what we're trying to do . . . [and] one of my largest wishes is that we build Next from the heart. And that people that are thinking about coming to work for us, or buying our products or who want to sell us things, feel that we're doing this because we have a passion about it. We're doing this because we really care about the higher education process, not because we want to make a buck, you know, because we want to do it.

> Good morning and welcome to our sixth annual management meeting. As in the past, the purpose of the meeting is to review and discuss the overall objectives for 1985. I am certain 1985 will be another successful year . . . As in the past, our principal objectives will be to accomplish our sales goal while limiting the price of promotional activity . . . Last week we presented the operating and capital budgets to the corporate staff for approval. I am pleased to report that the budgets were generally approved and the corporation has made available up to $39 million of capital to support the growth and improve the profitability of the Beverage Division . . . Incremental and profitable case sales are expected where development capital is invested. Each manager will be responsible for generating a 20 percent return on all development capital invested.

The first quotation is from Steve Jobs, Chief Executive of Apple Computers. He is explaining to staff his thoughts about his new computer company, NEXT. The second is a senior executive addressing his staff at an annual management meeting.[30] The implied tone, language and images used are very different. The first is visionary, aspirational and personalized. The second is dry, anonymous, mechanical and largely empty of expressed feeling. Statistical summaries are often felt to be uninformative, abstract and colourless compared to the vividness of 'face' talk, values and ideals.

Frame alignment   Inspirational leadership is often framed around some grand purpose that chimes with followers' yearnings. The skilful leader reads the audience carefully to then, also carefully, choose his or her words. Hence Martin Luther King's evocative 'dream' of freedom. In the more mundane world of business leadership, computers can be linked with care for higher education; cosmetics with equal rights for women:

> My objective was just to help women. It was not to make a tremendous amount of sales. I want women to earn money commensurate with men. I want them to be paid on the basis of what they have between their ears and their brains, not because they are male or female. (Mary Kay Ash)[31]

In this manner, leaders align the expression of their own values with what they believe their employees desire. It is a *frame alignment*. Frame alignment and *frame breaking* often go hand in hand. For example, some leaders use of the word 'not' as a frame breaker, 'it's not this but it's that' shifts the frame in the direction that the leader desires, once the audience's attention is caught. On his successful election to US presidency, John F. Kennedy said, '. . . observe today not as victory for the party but a celebration of freedom . . .'. Fiol and her colleagues explored the use of 'not' through the archived speeches of past US presidents. They found it significantly distinguished charismatic from non-charismatic presidents.[32]

Language and staging   There is an intimate link between the use of language and charismatic, inspirational, leadership. The more utopian the strategic vision and the more expressively it is described, the stronger the charismatic 'glue'. The bond is only weakened when the vision becomes unbelievable and no longer provides the followers with a deeper sense of purpose. This much the leading gurus of new management ideas know, the purveyors of management 'fixes'. They will support their new techniques by appealing to hard-to-deny 'goods', grand ideals such as such as fetching good out of evil, trust, caring, humanness and comradeship.[33]

The language of charisma is also the language of the body and the physical setting. Charismatic leaders have an ability to manage their followers' impressions of themselves by framing, as mentioned; but also by the way they *stage* their oratory. Convincing theatricality is fundamental to this, and there is no theatricality without emotion.[24] The awesome, minutely orchestrated, rallies of Hitler, the public speeches of Mussolini, Martin Luther King on the steps of the Washington Lincoln Memorial, and religious-evangelist assemblies, are prime examples. Outwardly they appear fluid and animated. While some emotion from the leader may be spontaneous, what is hidden is the careful scripting, the rehearsed gestures, the choice of metaphors, the practised cadences, the pauses and the rants. The charismatic leader is an emotional labourer *par excellence*, showing just the 'right' emotions at the 'right' time. Wardrobe, grooming, position on the rostrum, lighting, all attest to the mood-manager's art.

The engineering of such transcendental states is not confined to the world of politics and religion. Corporate sales rallies, training events and major celebrations can be designed to feature the leader's centrality, moving employees through emotional experiences towards the 'soul' of the enterprise. Heather Hopfl and Steve Linstead report one manager's experience of such an event – a training rally for employees of a perfume company:

> It was a magnificent set with two huge silver pyramids at the front. There was dry ice everywhere and then, suddenly, he [the founder] came out from between the pyramids and everyone went wild. He raised his arms and said, 'Manna from heaven' and hundreds of balloons were released onto the audience. It was amazing.[35]

Sincere acts   The stage-managing of charisma raises the question of the sincerity of the leader. Does the leader's expressed feeling correspond to his or her private belief? And does it matter, especially if the outcome is regarded as good and effective by the followers? Given that we all practice a degree of deceit, or emotional hypocrisy, are we not better to judge charismatic leaders by their results, rather than the 'genuineness' of their expressions? (See Chapter 2.)

Some are critical of the charismatic leader who is a mere performer of scripts, scripts often penned by others. It is bogus or pseudo, a media creation where the leader, surrounded by advisors, has every move carefully choreographed.[36] A convincing performance may be a necessary condition for charisma, it is suggested, but it is insufficient. It is the actual values, or mission, of the leader that provide moral backbone to charisma. These should shine through, providing depth and conviction to the leader's performance, spontaneity and passion, regardless of the 'lines' of the day.

Amichai Hamburger is especially scathing of what he calls 'mathematical vision' in leadership. This is where a leader's vision is not his or her own, but statistically derived from market-research techniques, consumer polling and focus groups. The 'vision' is then constructed from these data, repackaged and sold back to the audience, unbeknown to them. They are told exactly what they want to hear. As charisma feeds on crisis, using the same methodology, the leader (or the leader's advisers) can also manufacture a crisis. It is a common approach in modern-day national politics, and is especially attractive to leaders whose ambitions are dominantly power-centred and personalized. After being elected, the vision often dissolves, or is carefully obfuscated, as the leader pursues other agendas.[37]

There is nothing inherently unworthy about crafting one's emotional display for an audience. *Feeling* inspired as a leader, and *feeling* an important mission or message, is worth little if it cannot be communicated with flair and focus. On the other hand, we would expect the leader's values and passion, at least through a crisis period, to be more enduring if the leader owns them and they are not simply borrowed. Yet, it is often hard to tell. Management trainers have now invaded the charisma field, reducing charisma to a sequence of learnable behavioural/body skills.[38] Skilled acting can fool most of the people much of the time. Ronald Reagan, for example, US president in the 1980s, was dubbed 'the great communicator'. It was no coincidence that he had been a Hollywood actor, and is now ranked alongside former US presidents John F. Kennedy and Franklin D. Roosevelt for his charismatic appeal.[39]

A more recent example is the response of different political leaders to the untimely death of Princess Diana in 1997. Compare the speech of the then British prime minister, Tony Blair, with that of John Howard, the Australian premier:[40]

Tony Blair

We are a nation in a state of shock, in mourning, in grieving that is so deeply painful for us. She was a wonderful and warm human being. Though her own life was often, sadly, touched by tragedy she touched the lives of so many others in Britain. You know how difficult things were for her from time to time, I am sure we can only guess, but the people everywhere, not just here in Britain, everywhere . . . kept faith with Princess Diana. They liked her – they loved her. They regarded her as one of the people. She was the People's Princess. And that is how she will stay, how she will remain in our hearts and memories forever.

John Howard

I know that Australians will be both saddened and shocked at the tragic death of Diana, Princess of Wales. It removes . . . a special fascination for things around the world.

There are many Australians who will remember Diana's visits to this country over the years. The last of those visits was in 1996 in aid of the esteemed Victor Chang Memorial Foundation.

On behalf of the Australian Government and the Australian people, I want to extend my very deep sympathy, particularly to her two young sons who have suffered the trauma of a marriage break up and had now lost their mother at the very young age of 36. And to other members of the royal family it is a horrible and tragic accident and it will sadden many people around the world.

Blair's speech was delivered in a hushed, seemingly heartfelt, manner. Graham Little adds: '. . . the tone was hopeful rather than devastated. It sounded impromptu, though it probably wasn't, and managed to be light and grave at the same time . . . Well chosen words were interspersed with pauses that allowed a huge audience to feel they were part of what was being said'.[41] John Howard, who read from a prepared speech, presents a stiff, perfunctory, message. Diana is not directly addressed and her sons are reminded of their misfortune rather than comforted. The connection with the feelings of grieving Australians is largely missed. And here is the nub of the matter. Leaders, national or corporate, represent us emotionally. They turn private feeling within our community, organization or group, into public emotion. They are expected to say what we feel, or would like to feel, but find hard to express.

The leader and follower's emotions are intimately interconnected. Influential leaders can be suggestive of emotions, the 'right' ones we should have for the occasion. We can *mimic*, copy their emotional display, which can then induce commensurate feelings in ourselves. We begin to feel what we have imitated.[42, 43] Other processes of emotion transfer are *empathy* and *identification*. We see empathy in Blair's attempts to capture the pain and sorrow of the nation and reflect them back to the audience. It is trying to feel the feelings of others by putting ourselves in their shoes. Identification happens if we *have* been in their shoes, such as experiencing similar loss or grief. Some of these processes are especially present among coaching leaders in organizations, who encourage both bonding and empowerment.

Charisma fade

Charisma is ephemeral; it rarely lasts. This is because it is more than just what the leader is or does. It is a relationship sustained by what followers perceive and need: whether their desires are met or betrayed, how their anxieties are soothed, whether the crisis has passed. As the social and organizational context shifts, so does the leader's credibility. We need leaders, but we also need to reject them to move on. Leaders are readily cast as yesterday's heroes – or villains or fools.[44]

After the Second World War, British prime minister, Winston Churchill, lost his political standing and was generally marginalized in public affairs. His charisma faded as his role as wartime leader, albeit a successful one, came to an end. He had contained the nation's fears. In peacetime, the role was redundant. On the industrial front, Jan Carlzon was unable further to mobilize his employees in Scandinavian Airlines once the main crisis had passed; he could not reinvent a rousing message.

Other former high-profile leaders trade on the vestiges of past charisma, attracting curious, sometimes nostalgic, audiences. Previous national leaders, as well as retired captains of industry, can sometimes make a sizeable income from the international lecture circuit, proffering advice, sharing wisdoms and recounting past glories. A rare few retain their original lustre and luminosity, and may even acquire more. They are socialized charismatics of an exalted order. Nelson Mandela, for example, rarely fails to draw a huge following wherever he travels. He has touched the hearts of many by enacting one of the most poignant 'grand narratives' of civilization – social justice for the oppressed.

FEAR AND ENVY IN LEADERSHIP

Some leaders have gained a formidable reputation for their use of fear. Al Dunlap, in the opening of this chapter, is a prime example. Sam Goldwin, the movie mogul said: 'I don't want any yes-men. I want everybody to tell me the truth, even it costs them their jobs'.[45] Lee Iacocca, reminiscing on his days with the Ford Motor Company:

> Each time Henry [Ford] walked into a meeting, the atmosphere changed abruptly. He held the power of life and death over all of us. He could suddenly say 'off with his head' – and he often did. Without fair hearing, one more promising career at Ford would bite the dust . . . This arbitrary use of power wasn't merely a character flaw. It was something Henry actually *believed* in.[46]

Management by fear is a power-and-control view of leadership. Fear tends to rob an organization of its energy. It creates a nervous, defensive, workforce and squeezes out creativity. Yet fear still flows in many organizations – such as when downsizing is in the air (see Chapter 12), when people are anxious about their jobs and security, when their trust in their boss is low, and when the scramble for status and position rests on secret deals and favouritism.[47, 48] A culture of fear undermines moral concern and mutual care, where surviving by 'keeping your nose clean' and 'doing what you are told', becomes the right thing to do. Robert Jackall's dark picture of politiking in corporations reveals just such pragmatism. In the words of a manager in his study:

> What is right in the corporation is not what is right in a man's home or in his church. What is right in the corporation is what the guy above wants from you. That's what morality is in the corporation.[49]

Fear has a close partner in envy – the resentment aroused by another's fortune, possessions or qualities. A modicum of envy oils the cogs of capitalism, sparking competition, spurring leadership and feeding ambition. But what if envy gets out of hand? Leaders who surround themselves with extravagant symbols of power, such as a disproportionately large salary, huge bonuses and stock options, generous pension rights and material luxuries, can produce a sharp sense of envy amongst less-favoured employees. Leaders themselves may envy the relative ease of their subordinates' work-life compared to their own. The better qualifications and skills of those jostling for leadership can feel threatening to the leader's position and security.[50] Nepotistic employment practices and perceived poor quality in the leader can fan the flames of envy: 'He doesn't deserve his position; even I could do better than that'.

The closer, and more dependent, we are on a leader, the more the likelihood of envy. Yet envy is like a grenade that explodes in the envier's hand. An envious attack will often damage the attacker, who worries about retaliation.[51] To raise the envy threshold requires a close examination of the leadership and cultural practices in an organization that contribute to perceptions of unfairness and inequity.

Soaking Up the Pain

By their blunt, fear-inducing, approach, some bosses generate *toxicity*, energy-sapping emotions that can spread, miasma-like, throughout the organization. The emotional fallout is aggravated in periods of turbulence, such as organizational change, downsizing or redeployment. At worst, the effect can be paralysing, creating a defensive and depressed workforce.[52]

Yet this does not always happen. Certain people can act as protective buffers or sponges, absorbing and defecting the worst of the organizational fear or pain for the good of others. As one manager put it:

> I feel very protective towards them because the are my team and I built that team and they are working for me. Some of the stupidity of the politics – it would be unfair to allow it to hit them.[53]

Frost and Robinson talk of such people as *toxic handlers*.[54] They are managers who 'take the heat', coming between the pain generator and the receiver. They translate, soothe and absorb. Toxic bosses can work, wittingly or unwittingly, in tandem with toxic handlers. The handler, or emotion minder, presents the boss's messages in a more acceptable manner, such as by filtering out the anger or aggression. So, 'I need the delivery from that damn lazy bunch in the assembly department by tomorrow afternoon at the latest!' is translated by the minder into, 'The boss is keen to help us get through the current crisis; what do you think we can do?'. Or, in the words of a team manager in a UK bank:

> The things I say to people are couched round in more positive terms rather than go in with a 'this is absolutely fucking crap and it's going to tear this department apart'.[55]

Frost and Robinson illustrate the life of one toxic handler, in the Intel Corporation:

> Dave Marsing . . . was assigned to turn round one of Intel's microprocessor fabrication plants near Alberquerque, New Mexico. The situation he inherited was dire: the plant's yield rates were bad and getting worse. The company's senior managers were pressing very hard for a quick solution to the problem. Employees were in pain, too, saying unrealistic pressure from above had them anxious and frustrated. 'I was trying to be a human bridge between all parts of the company and cope with all the emotions . . . On the outside, I was soothing everybody, and work was getting back on track. But on the inside I was in turmoil. I couldn't sleep, couldn't eat'. Two months after Marsing arrived on the job, he suffered a near-fatal heart attack. He was 36 years old.[56]

This example highlights a common observation: the handler of emotional toxins is both a hero (usually unsung) and casualty.[57] They are, to borrow Frost and Robinson's evocative words, 'amateurs, toiling unprotected in danger zones'.

VULNERABLE LEADERS: 'YOU NEVER SHOW YOU CAN'T COPE'

> Why should Johnny listen to you, you are only a woman, he doesn't like women.

Here speaks an angry mother to a female school principal. Her son was in the process of being suspended from school.[58] Women and men in leadership positions have to manage their emotions, and they are often sandwiched between different demands: parents and staff, customers and the organization, lower and top management, new staff and older ones, various trade unions. Once again, we enter the realm of emotional labour, the potential burden of showing only those feelings that are right for the role and circumstances (see Chapters 2 and 3). For many organizational leaders, leadership *is* emotional labour.

Gender politics and stereotypes cut across the picture. Angry outbursts from male managers are more likely to be tolerated (as 'masculine and assertive') than from female managers. However, women can show sadness (as 'feminine and passive').[59, 60] In the above school setting, women principals were expected to provide the nourishing emotions of care, warmth, patience and calm. Yet they had to deny their anger and rage because they were culturally unacceptable feelings for women in leadership positions, and for a school culture that privileged headwork over heartwork. The leader's pain, despair and uncertainty gave way to the rule: *You never show you can't cope . . .*

> You have to be careful about the people you ask advice from . . . I wouldn't ask advice from another principal, especially if it was a male because I would be afraid that they would be making judgements about my not coping.[61]

Organizational leaders are potentially both powerful and vulnerable. The vulnerability is especially complex for women who have to conform to male emotion-norms, which are dominant in most organizations. When women are the prime movers in creating a business there is the likelihood of more feminized emotion culture. For example, Anita Roddick, founder of The Body Shop, takes a decisively feminist stance. She has created a large, multinational, company, where the majority of middle and senior (but not top) managers are women. There is evidence that she has instilled a culture of emotion-openness, including respect for others' emotional limitations and a feeling of 'being oneself' at work. In her own words:

> The company talks about the body, having relaxed forms of interaction. [People are] risky, touch, hug, kiss. Women are so excited by their work. They have an emotional support system. They are valued. They have ways of communicating.[62]

Such feminization is exceptional, although we are now finding some key, male, corporate leaders openly celebrating more feminine styles of management. Percy Barnevik, chairman and of ABB Zurich, extols the benefits of compassion, and is dismissive about the 'macho managers who show up on the "toughest managers in the U.S." lists'.[63] Jack Welch, who was chairman and chief executive of General Electric for 20 years, talks of the 'hugs' as well as the 'kicks' that have brought the best out in him, and that he uses to bring out the best in others.[64] Ricardo Selmer is praised for his unusual organizational methods. He is president of Semco, the Brazilian marine and food-processing machinery manufacturer. Self-managed teams replace hierarchy and workers choose their own bosses. Extolling 'feminine, intuitive intelligence', Selmer asserts:

> Managers overrate where they are going, understanding what business they are in, defining their mission. [Such a rationalist approach is a] macho, militaristic, and self-misleading posture. Giving up control for freedom creativity and inspired adaptation is my preference.[65]

These words, as well as those of other top managers, are a refreshing contrast to the 'tough male' thinking that has, traditionally, dominated the leadership ethos of many organizations.

CONCLUSION

Leadership is a process that unites leaders and followers in a complex emotional web. Reducing leadership to just the leaders – their special attributes and emotional needs – is half the story, possibly the poorer half. The other half is about the followers, people seeking comfort, stability, direction, challenge and meaning. It is, perhaps, curious that companies, trainers, management consultants and business schools, place enormous emphasis on leadership and its skills, but none on the issues (skills, needs, challenges) of being a follower. And most of us, in one way or another, are followers.

The leadership tale is also one of mixed emotions. Each leader's success story can be matched with one about failure or redundancy. This is not because the leader suddenly becomes incompetent (although some are clearly more adaptable and have a wider range of skills, than others). But that the feelings and expectations of followers change over time, as personal social circumstances shift or develop – such as one's family, career, the economy, social values, personal wealth, downsizing. Leaders who cling to power, or cannot adapt, after their 'expiry date', are usually doomed to rejection.

Leaders perform on a stage where their emotional performance is under scrutiny. Dealing with balance sheets, strategic plans, and marketing information is one thing. Handling one's own, and others', fears, pains, anxieties and insecurities is a very different ballpark. Reflecting and expressing the joy, dejection or despair of followers, without appearing trite or condescending, requires a degree of empathy and emotional sensitivity not often credited to the technical specialists who achieve high office. The emotional labours of such leadership can be, as several of the accounts in this chapter attest, very real. They are sometime onerous, sometimes uplifting and exhilarating. What is often under-appreciated is that the leader's ability to 'get the job done' requires more just than good business knowledge. It also requires emotional knowledge and sensitivity.

FURTHER READING

Conger, J.A. and Kanungo, R.N. (eds) (1988) *Charismatic Leadership: The Elusive Factor In Organizational Effectiveness*. San Francisco: Jossey-Bass.
Frost, P.J. (2003) *Toxic Emotions at Work*. Harvard: Harvard Business School Press.
Kets de Vries, M.F.R. and Miller, D. (1984) *The Neurotic Organization*. San Francisco: Jossey-Bass Wiley.

REFERENCES

1 <http://www.pbs.org/bottomline/html/dunlap.html>.
2 Badcock, C. (2000) *Evolutionary Psychology*. Cambridge: Polity Press.
3 Freud, S. (1985) *Civilization, Society and Religion*. Harmondsworth: Penguin.
4 Anonymous (2001) 'The father figure', *Harvard Business Review*, 79 (11): 17.
5 Gardner, H. (1997) *Leading Minds: The Anatomy of Leadership*. London: Harper-Collins.
6 Gabriel, Y. (1997) 'Meeting God: When organizational members come face to face with the supreme leader', *Human Relations*, 50 (4): 315–42, especially p. 320.
7 Kapuscinski, R. (1983) *The Emperor*. London: Picador. p. 113.
8 Biggert, N. (1989) *Charismatic Capitalism*. Chicago: University of Chicago Press, p. 142.
9 Bryman, A. (1992) *Charisma and Leadership in Organizations*. London: Sage.
10 Zaleznick, A. (1977) 'Managers and Leaders: are they different?', *Harvard Business Review*, (May–June).
11 Burns, J.M. (1978) *Leadership*. New York: Harper and Row.
12 Spears, L.C. (ed.) (1995) *Reflections on Leadership*. New York: Wiley.
13 Aaltio-Marjosloa, I. and Takala, T. (2000) 'Charismatic leadership, manipulation and the complexity of organizational life', *Journal of Workplace Learning: Employee Counselling Today*, 12 (4): 146–58.
14 Heifetz, R.A. (1994) *Leadership Without Easy Answers*. Cambridge, MA: Belknap Press.
15 Weber, M. (1947) *The Theory of Social and Economic Organization*. New York: Free Press.

16 Heifetz, R.A. (1994) *Leadership Without Easy Answers.* Cambridge, MA: Belknap Press. p. 66.
17 Carlzon, J. (1987) *Moments of Truth.* New York: Harper and Row.
18 Iacocca, L. (1984) *Iacocca.* Toronto: Bantam.
19 Gardner, H. (1997) *Leading Minds: The Anatomy of Leadership.* London: Harper-Collins. p. 32.
20 Gardner, H. (1997) *Leading Minds: The Anatomy of Leadership.* London: Harper-Collins. p. 226.
21 Burns, J.M. (1978) *Leadership.* New York: Harper and Row.
22 Marcus, G.E. (2000) 'Emotions in politics', *Annual Review of Political Science*, 3: 221–50.
23 Gardner, H. (1997) *Leading Minds: The Anatomy of Leadership.* London: Harper-Collins. p. 33.
24 <http://www.iacenter.org/yugo_miloshague3.htm>.
25 Baumeister, R.F. (1997) *Evil: Inside Human Violence and Cruelty.* New York: Freeman.
26 Pelzer, P. (2002) 'The contemptuous manager: an introduction into an (almost) non-existing but ubiquitous topic'. The European Academy of Management, 2nd Annual Conference, May 9–11, Stockholm.
27 Rozin, P., Lowrey, L., Iamda, S. and Haidt, J. (1999) 'The CAD triad hypothesis: a mapping between three moral emotions (contempt, anger, disgust) and three moral codes (community, autonomy, divinity)', *Journal of Personality and Social Psychology*, 76 (4): 574–86.
28 Howell, J.M. (1988) 'Two faces of charisma: socialised and personalised leadership in organizations', in J.A. Conger and R.N. Kanungo (eds), *Charismatic Leadership: The Elusive Factor in Organizational Effectiveness.* San Francisco: Jossey-Bass.
29 Keithly, D.M. and Tritten, J.J. (1997) 'A charismatic dimension of military leadership?', *Journal of Political and Military Sociology*, 25 (Summer): 131–46, especially p. 131.
30 Conger, J.A. (1991) 'Inspiring others: the language of leadership', *Academy of Management Executive*, 5 (1): 31–45, especially p. 33.
31 Conger, J.A. (1991) 'Inspiring others: the language of leadership', *Academy of Management Executive*, 5 (1): 31–45, especially p. 35.
32 Fiol, C.M., Harris, D. and House, R. (1999) 'Charismatic leaders: strategies for effecting social change', *Leadership Quarterly*, 10 (3): 449–82.
33 Jackson, B. (2002) 'A fantasy theme analysis of three guru-led management fashions', in T. Clark and R. Fincham (eds), *Critical Consulting.* Oxford: Blackwell.
34 Lapierre, L. (1991) 'Exploring the dynamics of leadership', in M.F.R. Kets de Vries (ed.), *Organizations On The Couch: Clinical Perspectives On Organizational Behavior and Change.* San Francisco: Jossey Bass.
35 Hopfl, H. and Linstead, S. (1993) 'Passion and performance: suffering and the carrying of organizational roles', in S. Fineman (ed.), *Emotion in Organizations.* London: Sage. pp. 84–5.

36 Bensman, J. and Givant, M. (1975) 'Charisma and modernity: the use and abuse of a concept', *Social Research*, 42: 570–614.

37 Hamburger, Y.A. (2000) 'Mathematical leadership vision', *The Journal of Psychology*, 134 (6): 601–11.

38 Birchfield, R. (2000) 'Creating charismatic leaders', *Management*, (June): 30–1.

39 Fiol, C.M., Harris, D. and House, R. (1999) 'Charismatic leaders: strategies for effecting social change', *Leadership Quarterly*, 10 (3): 449–82, especially p. 477.

40 Little, G. (1999) *The Public Emotions*. Sydney: ABC Books. pp. 11–14.

41 Little, G. (1999) *The Public Emotions*. Sydney: ABC Books. p. 4.

42 Doherty, R.W. (1998) 'Emotion contagion and social judgement', *Motivation and Emotion*, 22 (3): 187–209.

43 Hatfield, E., Cacioppo, J.T. and Rapson, R.L. (1994) *Emotional Contagion*. Cambridge: Cambridge University Press.

44 Heifetz, R.A. (1994) *Leadership Without Easy Answers*. Cambridge, MA: Belknap Press.

45 Scarnati, J.T. (1998) 'Beyond technical competence: fear – banish the beast', *Leadership and Organization Development Journal*, 19 (7): 362–65, especially p. 362.

46 Iacocca, L. (1984) *Iacocca*. Toronto: Bantam. pp. 103–4.

47 Flam, H. (1993) 'Fear, loyalty and greedy organizations', in S. Fineman (ed.), *Emotion in Organizations*. London: Sage.

48 Jackall, R. (1988) *Moral Mazes: The World of Corporate Managers*. New York: Oxford University Press.

49 Jackall, R. (1988) *Moral Mazes: The World of Corporate Managers*. New York: Oxford University Press.

50 Stein, M. (1997) 'Envy and leadership', *European Journal of Work and Organizational Psychology*, 6 (4): 453–65.

51 Little, G. (1999) *The Public Emotions*. Sydney: ABC Books. p. 142.

52 Flam, H. (1993) 'Fear, loyalty and greedy organizations', in S. Fineman (ed.), *Emotion in Organizations*. London: Sage.

53 My thanks to Caroline Moore of Cranfield University for permission to quote from her PhD field interviews.

54 Frost, P. and Robinson, S. (1999) 'The toxic handler; organizational hero – and casualty', *Harvard Business Review*, 77 (4): 96–107.

55 Also from Caroline Moore's data.

56 Frost, P. and Robinson, S. (1999) 'The toxic handler; organizational hero – and casualty', *Harvard Business Review*, 77 (4): 96–107, especially p. 100.

57 Frost, P.J. (2003) *Toxic Emotions at Work*. Harvard: Harvard Business School Press.

58 Sachs, J. and Blackmore, J. (1998) 'You never show you can't cope: women in school leadership roles managing their emotions', *Gender and Education*, 10 (3): 265–79, especially p. 267.

59 Lewis, K.M. (2000) 'When leaders display emotion: how followers respond to negative emotional expression of male and female leaders', *Journal of Organizational Behavior*, 21: 221–34.

60 Baack, J., Carr-Ruffino, N. and Pelletier, M. (1994) 'Making it to the top: specific leadership skills. A comparison of male and female perceptions of skills needed by women and men managers', *Librarian Career Development*, 2 (1): 16–22.

61 Sachs, J. and Blackmore, J. (1998) 'You never show you can't cope: women in school leadership roles managing their emotions', *Gender and Education*, 10 (3): 265–79, especially p. 275.

62 Martin, J., Knopoff, K. and Beckman, C. (2000) 'Bounded emotionality at The Body Shop', in S. Fineman (ed.), *Emotion in Organizations, 2nd Edition*. London: Sage. p. 130.

63 Barnevik, P. (2001) 'Personal histories', *Harvard Business Review*, 79 (11): 28.

64 Welch, J. (2001) 'Personal histories', *Harvard Business Review*, 79 (11): 34.

65 Selmer, R. (2001) 'Personal histories', *Harvard Business Review*, 79 (11): 36.

7

Emotion and decisions

Emotions and decisions belong together, contrary to common wisdom. This chapter develops this theme:

- We rely on our feelings to make decisions.
- Organizational decisions rarely follow a rational, unemotional, path – we make them look rational.
- Moods infiltrate all decisions.
- Emotional performance can make or break a negotiation.
- Some decisions are shaped by strong feelings – such as of moral outrage, commitment, pride or pain.

The day was grey and gloomy as Eddie, chief executive of Merrywood Computers, guided his BMW into his usual parking place. He was deep in thought and looked grim. He'd had a restless night. 'Today's the day I said I'd do it', he reflected wearily. 'I'm dreading it. Maybe he's sick, or I could rush out on an emergency job. That would be a relief – for a bit. What will I feel tomorrow facing the rest of the staff, his friends here? Will we all live to regret it? Gee, and I can see his face now – he's going to be devastated. I guess I would be too. I'm beginning to hate this job. Maybe there's some other way round it. I might have missed something, something vital.'

Eddie was facing one of the most stressful decisions of his career. The company was being squeezed out of the market by the big, blue chip, manufacturers. It was bleeding. But the poor sales were not just due to the competition. George, the sales director, had failed several times to deliver on his own targets, and his plans for recovery were uninspiring. He was really an old school salesman, now overtaken by modern, fast moving, sales and marketing methods. For over a year now Eddie had felt uneasy about him, but had avoided the crunch, in the light of promises from George. But that's only half the story. George was an old, personal, friend and the staff loved him. He had that knack of connecting with people in the workplace and his cheerfulness was infectious.

But what else could Eddie do? George had to go . . . or did he? 'Maybe I can find him a different post here', thought Eddie, switching off the engine. 'But what? It would insult his pride, and it will be so embarrassing for us all. I can't afford to pay him a director's salary.' He slowly got out of the car and walked dejectedly towards his office.

UNFOLDING FEELINGS

Not all decisions in organizations are as angst-ridden as Eddie's, but his story encapsulates several salient features of decision making. First, it is often an unfolding, conflictual process, rather than a set of neat, programmed steps. Its apparent rationality in Eddie's eyes ('George has to go') is wobbly, emotionally infused. There are *background feelings* (Eddie's gloomy mood); there are *anticipated emotions* (Eddie's expectations of regret, embarrassment, devastation, insult); and there are *task-related feelings* (his discomfort and dread at delivering the news). All these are constituents of the decision process. They help make a decision a decision, shaping and shuffling ideas, hunches, dilemmas and actions.

Not that we always realize it. There is a strong Western predilection to rationalize our decisions – make them look unemotional. The rationalist tradition is strongly represented in conventional discourses on education, science and management. Rarely is emotion (feelings, hunches, moods, love, fear and so forth) regarded as a legitimate way of presenting ideas and conclusions or, more pointedly, how we reached those ideas and conclusions. Impulses need to be explained, rationalized, so we end up convincing others and ourselves that our decision making is, indeed, emotion-free – therefore proper and valid. The head is separated from the heart. Social values and gender stereotypes reinforce such impressions, such as legal or political decisions having to appear emotion-free and women deprecated for their 'emotional' approach towards decisions.

Revealing the messiness

We often tidy up our decisions, de-emotionalize them, for public presentation.[1] A classic example is the curriculum vitae (CV), or resumé. Our life's education and career achievements are normally listed in neat, chronological order, gaps smoothed over. The story we tell about them at job interviews is usually reassuringly logical and considered. It attests to our clear-headedness, wise planning and sound decision making.

The sanitized account reveals nothing of the emotional complexities that typically underpin life's 'real' CV – feeling lost after school, unsure about one's subject or destiny, studying at a foreign university to get away from home, taking a job because it was the only one available at the time, leaving

another job because of feeling harassed, unexpectedly being made unemployed, that chance meeting with an old friend who gave you a job, trouble
with a partner, and so forth. Being (or appearing to be) in control of one's
destiny is a valued managerial resource, not to be sullied by emotions. It
suggests order and predictability, a chimera on which all we all depend.
It also encourages a degree of self-delusion and myopia – a collective belief
that rationality is indeed the key to success.

Ironically, it is usually left to the successful and famous to break the
mould, to declare how it 'really is' or was. They are sufficiently secure to go
on record that their key decision making has been far from passionless. For
example, George Soros, the international financier, talks of his tortured time
at Quantum Hedge fund:

> As a fund manager, I depended a great deal on my emotions . . . The
> predominant feelings I operated with were doubt, uncertainty, and fear.
> I had moments of hope or even euphoria, but they made me feel insecure.
> By contrast worrying made me feel safe . . . By and large, I found managing
> a hedge fund extremely painful. I could never acknowledge my success,
> because that might stop me from worrying, but I had no trouble recognis-
> ing my mistakes. [But] . . . [w]hen I looked around, I found that most
> people go to great lengths to deny or cover up their mistakes.[2]

The 'gut feeling' that shifts or re-channels our preferences is celebrated by
some of the highest-profile executives, people who could be rapidly overwhelmed by all the alternatives before them. For example, Michael Eisner,
Chief Executive Officer of Walt Disney, describes it as an unusual feeling in
his stomach, other times his throat, and other times on his skin. The
sensation 'is like looking at a great piece of art for the first time'.[3] The bodily
feelings that Eisner (and many others) report are consistent with the neural
circuits of emotion to various part of the body (see Chapter 2).

Dealing with complexity and uncertainty requires an intricate mental
and emotional dance, taking shortcuts, rules of thumb or 'heuristics', to
make the impossible look possible. Daniel Isenberg's intensive study of
successful divisional heads in large corporations reveals how idiosyncratic
this can be. One manager explains:

> I have to sort through so many issues at once. There are ten times too
> many. I use a number of defence mechanisms to deal with this overload – I
> use delaying actions, I deny the existence of problems, or I put problems in
> a mental queue of sorts. This is an uncomfortable process for me. My office
> and responsibility say I need to deal with all these issues, so I create smoke
> or offer some grand theory as my only way to keep my sanity. One of the
> frustrations is that I don't want to tell my people that their number one
> problems have lower priorities than they think they should get.[4]

Isenberg concludes that decision making is often messy because:

- It is hard to pinpoint if or when managers, on their own, actually make
  decisions about major business or organizational issues.

- They rarely think in ways that might be viewed as 'rational' – that is, systematically formulating goals, assessing their worth, evaluating the probabilities of alternative ways of reaching them, and choosing a path that maximizes expected return.
- Difficult, novel or entangled problems are handled intuitively – 'unthinking', 'gut', responses.
- Retrospectively, effective executives often appear quite rational, and 'decisions' are justified using rationalistic rhetoric.

THE DEMISE OF RATIONALITY

Accounts, such as above, are not the experiences of 'weak' or 'flawed' individuals. Quite the contrary. They are the realities of people who hold responsible positions. The experience of decision making, of deciding, can be a fraught process, sometimes agonizing. It can range from tackling the everyday and mundane ('What on earth am I going to wear for work today?'; 'Which job shall I do first?'), to the highly complex, such as decisions concerning downsizing, formulating new organizational strategies and investment policies. At times, what feels good, right or comfortable ultimately solves the problem, unlocking the logjam of possibilities. But this sits uneasily with classical formulations about the cool-headed, rational, decision maker who carefully (and dispassionately) weighs up the pros of different alternatives before choosing the one that maximizes the payoff.

Some writers, especially those trying to explain economic behaviour and economic decisions, cling to the ideal of rationality. Emotions are regarded as interference to rationality. They are judgement mistakes, errors to be minimized, repaired or simply ignored. They are not regarded as intrinsic to decision making.[5] Others are more charitable towards emotion. They grant that it can be rational to set a *goal* that is emotional, such as seeking revenge, honour or love.[6] Indeed, people and nations will go to war to undo a previous shame, to restore pride, or exact revenge. Sociologist Thomas Scheff has described shame as a 'master' emotion (see Chapter 2). In the name of shame, humiliation and pride, historical decisions have been made implicating a tribe, an army or a kingdom, sometimes with catastrophic results.[7]

To a shamed Mafioso family, it is perfectly rational to seek retribution by the most lethal method available. In 2002, it made perfect sense to a humiliated, oppressed, Palestinian community, to conceal high explosives on a young person's body and send him or her to their death in a crowded Israeli metropolis. The rationality of this action was buttressed by the suicide victim's belief that he or she was not a victim, but a willing martyr to a greater cause. In the business context, the desire to dominate a competitor, or crush an opponent, serves greed, revenge and jealousy. It is a form of behaviour made respectable through the rational discourse of 'competition' and 'market forces'.

The idea of pure rationality, like many 'pure' models, stands up poorly against studies on what decision makers do in practice; that is, before the process is wrapped in the gloss of rationality. In the 1950s Herbert Simon offered an important qualification to rationality in the notion of *satisficing*.[8] Satisficing refers to the process of choosing some target criterion for one's decision that is the best available, or the most feasible, in the circumstances. When this criterion is met, the decision maker stops seeking further alternatives. It is time to halt and live with the decision. It is not possible to churn through all the possibilities to seek maximum gain. Rationality therefore is 'bounded', it can only go so far. Since Simon, all the assumptions of rational choice have been called into question, including the expectation that we can know, and dispassionately weigh, all alternative solutions. When uncertainty abounds, people rely on habit and stereotyping ('This is suitable for most women, so it should be OK for Jane'), and gut feeling ('Mm, it somehow feels right to me, but don't ask me why – it just does').[9]

Implicated emotions

Emotion is deeply implicated in these processes, yet curiously absent in major accounts of organizational decision making.[10–12] The costs and benefits of decision choices, in so far as they are assessed at all, can be dramatically influenced by strong emotions, such as of anger, shame or pride, as discussed above. When this is occurs, people will often expose themselves to considerable risks, whatever the consequences. Road rage (freeway violence) is a clear example. The infuriated road-rager does not sit back and carefully consider his or her options. There is only one option – swift, violent, revenge against the offending driver. Primal emotional urges are extraordinarily helpful in wiping out ambiguity and uncertainty. At the very moment it is self-evidently the best course, which is useful in conditions of physical threat. After the event, other feelings – such as relief, glee, pride – may reinforce the appropriateness of the rage. Alternatively, regret and guilt may kick in, a sign that a moral and legal line has been crossed.[13]

Once we begin to include feeling and emotion at the very core of decision making, its role becomes ever more fascinating. A landmark study by neuroscientist Antonio Damasio is especially revealing.[14–16] Damasio studied people who had suffered damage to a specific area of the prefrontal cortex of the brain. This is the site where, it is believed, we process some of our emotions. Patients responded normally to cognitive tasks: their use of language was fine, as was their coordination, their memory and intelligence. But, emotionally, they were impaired. They found it difficult or impossible to feel happy or sad. When they looked at an emotionally charged situation, such as photographs of gruesomely injured people, they felt nothing.

Damasio explored the link between this condition and decision making in a series of experiments. One seemingly innocent event illustrates this.[17] He asked one of his patients to choose between two dates for his next appointment. The patient consulted his diary and began a lengthy recitation of the pros and cons of the dates, including the possible weather at those times, his other commitments and their proximity. His logic was impeccable but, after thirty excruciating minutes, the man was still unable to make up his mind. Damasio made the decision for him. 'That's fine', responded the man, putting away his dairy and leaving immediately. According to Damasio, Descartes' famous credo, 'I think therefore I am', is flawed. Long before there was thought, there was feeling, and we are all primarily feeling beings. *I feel therefore I am.*

Our feelings are crucial for prioritizing, sorting and filtering possibilities; otherwise we become paralysed, or stuck in a perpetual loop. They guide us to what matters and what is relevant, not just to what makes sense.[18] Feelings are a source of information. They are our own, personal feedback on what is significant, irrelevant, dangerous or desirous in what we see, touch, smell or think about.[19] Artificial intelligence, which attempts to construct machines (robots and computers) that make 'intelligent' decisions, has struggled to produce more than the crudest representation of human preferences.[20, 21] Without emotion something crucial is missing. Machines cannot be 'intelligent' without emotions and, so far, no machines have emotions. Franks and Gecas recount the following tale to make the point:

> . . . when a computerized robot was put into a wagon with a bomb and told to figure out what to do before the bomb exploded at a prescribed time, it sat paralyzed from the preliminary stage of figuring out whether the distance between the wagon and China and the price of tea in New York was relevant to the problem.[22]

Damasio postulated the existence of *somatic markers*, bodily reactions that are aroused as we deliberate alternatives. They are emotional memory-keys, often subliminal, that machines have yet to simulate. They provide information on the desirability of different alternatives or choices. They are rapid reactions that interrupt and redirect cognitive processing, making choice possible and decisions decisive. Sometimes, when 'primary' emotions such as fear, dread or anxiety are involved, this process is literally thoughtless. The action is instantaneous, such as a mother's lunge as her child stumbles towards the kerb of a busy road. Imminent risk will short-circuit the head and pump action directly from the heart.[23]

FEELING FORWARDS AND LOOKING BACK

What would you feel like if your were working for a particular, new employer? How will you feel if you are living in a new, very different neighbourhood? If you accept the offer of promotion, what will it feel like to be in a different office, supervising the people who are now your colleagues? The short answer these questions might, understandably, be: 'I don't know. I'll only know when I get there'. In practice, however, our decisions are constantly shaped by *anticipated* feelings – imagining ourselves in new situations and how we might feel there – anxious, smug, guilty, joyful, scared, proud, and so forth. If we sense that we are taking a path we might regret, or feel disappointed about ('I think that job's beyond my abilities; I'll be so stressed'; 'That area of town is really far too posh; I'll feel uncomfortable there'), then we can shift to a safer, more comfortable, option.[24, 25] Anticipations serve a particular function: they reduce uncertainty. The less uncertain we feel, the easier it is to make a decision. Anticipated feelings reflect, in part, what we know, or have heard, about the new circumstances. They also represent our fantasies and wishes. If change is much desired, and if we are unhappy with our present circumstances, then some alternatives may appear especially warm and seductive.

We also reflect on the outcomes of important decisions we have made – with feeling. Has it turned out as pleasurable, exciting, or disappointing as we had imagined? There is evidence that we often get the emotional experience that we expect, at least in the first instance.[26] This may be because our predictions have been reasonably accurate. However, it is just as likely that, in order to justify our actions, we 'create' the feelings that we anticipated. We convince ourselves, and others, that it feels 'just as I had hoped -- even better!' The emotional investment in the decision is such that a degree of self-delusion relieves tension and 'dissonance'; it saves face. It also eases adaptation to the new circumstances. A classic example is a major holiday. Often much research, money and eager anticipation is devoted to what turns out to be a 'wonderful choice; a great holiday'. It is only after some months have passed that we feel confident enough to admit that 'It really wasn't that good; in fact I was pretty disappointed with the place.' The emotional costs of saving face and self-justification have faded over time and the admitted meaning of the event has shifted.

Regret, disappointment and the good times

But, of course, we also make decisions that we very soon regret. The decision seems obviously wrong, bad, ill judged. The anticipated pleasure, delight or excitement has not materialized. When fellow travellers, other decision makers, appear to have done better than us, envy or jealousy can add an extra edge to the disappointment. What we then do depends on the dominant feeling. Regret and disappointment are common reactions. Regret is felt when we feel responsible for the outcome – 'If only I'd taken that other offer'; or, 'I could have easily refused this move'. Regret comes from self-blame, mulling over what might have been. But regret also contains the seeds of hope: the opportunity to learn from our mistakes.

Disappointment has a different configuration. Disappointment is more likely to be attributed to factors beyond one's self: 'I'm disappointed with my new job, but no one knew there was about be a take-over from another company'. Disappointment, here, feels unavoidable. It leaves one sadder, but not much wiser. When the disappointment is seen as the responsibility of another person, it can convert to anger – and be less paralysing: 'I certainly *am* disappointed with my job! The manager who recruited me never revealed the true extent of the chaos in the department.'[27] Future decisions may be adjusted in the light of all these experiences, such as being prepared for possible regret or disappointment, or an increase in cynicism about the promises of change.

Looking back on how much we enjoyed, liked or loathed a particular experience provides important markers for future decisions. Generally (but not always) we are keener to repeat the good times and avoid re-creating the painful ones. However, when we look back at the good or bad times, what exactly do we recall? How, for example, do we use our memories of our feelings of a protracted downsizing, a long dispute with our employer, or the struggle to find a new job? We are unlikely to recall everything, like a literal action replay, so what are the feelings that linger to influence our decision making? This is a question that has intrigued psychologists, who talk of the *peak-and-end rule*.[28] The idea is that people can emotionally reconstruct a whole past episode from just two emotional nuggets, two key moments – the *most intense* emotional one and the emotion experienced at the *end* of the episode. These 'nodes' of experience are oozing with emotional meaning; they condense the whole event. So, if the worst aspect of job hunting was the despair you felt, but you were ecstatic in the end on getting an excellent new job, then going back to job hunting does not feel too bad. If, however, you remember the gloom of having to take a job you did not really want, then a new job hunt is not so welcome – the overall, peak/end, combination is a depressing one.

THE RIGHT MOOD

Scene 1: You arrive at work humming one of your favourite tunes. It's a sunny day and you're feeling great. It's been like that since you got up. The world's really rosy today.

Scene 2: You're late for work and you're fed up. The traffic's been appalling, like the weather. Nothing seems to have gone right this week. You're feeling pretty low.

We bring moods with us into work and they can linger. Some are more intense and enduring than others. Rarely are we not 'in' some sort of mood. There is always the background hum of a mood in decision-making contexts.

If we are with others, moods can be infectious, passed across the whole group. But do they affect our decision making? Do we handle information differently in, say, Scene 1 compared to Scene 2? It seems that we often assume that our moods, the daily ebb end flow of feeling, will affect how we *feel* about what we are doing, but that they will not materially affect important decisions. We will overcome them.

Recent evidence, however, indicates a more complex picture. The mood we bring to decision situations can have specific effects. Positive, even mildly positive, or negative moods influence our attitudes and values, the judgements we form about colleagues and tasks, the way we speak and respond to messages, and the way we plan and execute negotiations. They also influence the way we relate to well-known others. When we feel happy we are better at retrieving happy memories than when we are sad. Feeling joyful can shorten the search for alternatives. Positive moods can promote flexible and creative problem solving – new ways of looking at things and new sources of enjoyment. Anxiety fosters a more intensive search. Feeling sad can lead to more analytical thinking and longer response times.[29, 30] The more difficult and challenging the task, the more the influence of mood. For example, people who feel in a good mood will face danger or risk far more cautiously than people in a bad mood.[31]

In summary, different moods impel us unwittingly along particular paths that shape what we recall and what we take as important for the decision in hand. They influence *what* we think and *how* we think, acting as primers, or sensitizers, to the thoughts and memories we use in responding to decision demands.[32, 33] So, it is very likely that we will make different decisions in Scene 1 compared to Scene 2.

NEGOTIATING – PASSIONS ACROSS THE TABLE

> Frazier and Turner looked at each other in the eye. Somewhere a communication established itself without a word between them. The question in each other's eye was, 'If I move to 9 cents will you move to 9 cents?' Frazier said 'Well we are willing to give it some consideration . . .'. Turner nodded his acquiescence. The tension was gone.[34]

Eyeball-to-eyeball negotiation is the vehicle for all manner of significant decisions. In many countries it is how employer–employee agreements on working conditions, salaries, and organizational changes are made. Individual employees may negotiate their salary and workload when joining an organization. Trade unions negotiate. Politicians negotiate. Nations negotiate on world-shaping decisions, such as on how to prevent or halt a war; how to share disputed territory; trade and tariff agreements; protecting rainforests; reducing carbon dioxide emissions; oil prices; famine relief . . . and so forth. Negotiations are socially evolved mechanisms for managing differences and conflict, through which trust, a fragile commodity, is formed and deformed.

The negotiation setting is an intensive microcosm of the social-functions of emotions. It is where expressive performance – the show of emotions – really counts. Displayed emotions are not simple read-outs of private feelings, but are key devices for navigating the problems and vagaries of social interaction. They are, as Erving Goffman has shown, dramaturgically significant.[35, 36] They shape the staging, posturing, and strategic direction of the interaction. They are potent ways of conveying intention, power and meaning; of providing information and incentives; and of evoking complementary emotions.[37, 38] Flashes of anger, for example, can elicit fear, signalling the importance of the issue in hand and the desire for dominance. Embarrassment can trigger forgiveness, so restoring a disrupted relationship. Laughter and smiling can encourage the other party to follow a particular line, while frowning signals 'I don't like that'. Shame indicates ownership of a moral transgression, ceding power to the other party to decide one's fate.

All negotiations will feed on reciprocity of emotion, such as mutual displays of friendliness, interest and respect. But how such displays are enacted will be culturally dependent, confusing or complicating cross-cultural negotiations. While globalization has led to some smoothing of the differences, there are still significant cultural variations in the way feelings and emotions are valued and deployed in negotiations across countries.[39] For example:

- *North Americans* and *Northern Europeans* shake hands and make eye contact. Strength, 'logic' and argumentation are particularly important. Emotional sensitivity is not highly valued. Power is a key resource.
- *Japanese* bow and avert their eyes. They value feelings, but they must be hidden. Face saving and modesty is crucial, and decisions are often made on the basis of saving someone from embarrassment. They respect quietness when right and display patience with their opponent.
- *Latin countries* value emotional sensitivity and warmth. Negotiations can be passionate and lively. Trust and respect are important prerequisites for successful negotiations. Mexican negotiators, for example, often express strong objections to US negotiators' desire to 'get to the point'. Face saving is important to preserve honour and dignity, while it is worthy to be stronger, more 'macho', than one's opponent.

The negotiator is, in large part, an emotion manager in a highly dynamic process, tuning in, adapting to, and regulating, the emotions of self and others.[40] Practised negotiators are likely to be particularly sensitized to the emotion language of the encounter. The very start of a negotiation can carry an emotional history that, if not appreciated, can grind the process to a rapid halt. Memories of acrimonious exchanges, resentment about previous deals, hurt feelings, perceptions of unfairness, can colour the encounter. In some industries, union–management deals on pay and working conditions frequently have a stormy history. A past of hate and bitterness will foment mistrust from the outset, 'Can I really negotiate with this person? Can he be trusted?'. The faint smile, a nod, the raise of the eyebrows, or the shaking of hands, can break the ice and help the negotiation on its way.

A negotiation can end amicably or resentfully, so setting the mood for any future negotiations.[41] In hostile endings, the final act can be tense and confrontational: 'That's it! You have my offer. Take it or leave it!' There are instances where workers have knowingly sacrificed their jobs and have brought down the company they work for – in preference to accepting what they regard as an unsatisfactory offer from management. Students of emotion do not have to look far for an explanation. Negotiations, which are ostensibly about working conditions and pay, also have a hidden agenda – an emotional one. What is at stake is pride, feelings of dignity and status – on both sides of the negotiation table. An untimely 'insult' within a negotiation can harden attitudes. If a negotiator is made to look foolish, or is humiliated or embarrassed, then retaliation can follow, regardless of the consequences.[42] A final offer can be perceived as derisory, grossly unfair in relation to others' rewards. The offer is summarily rejected, in anger.

DIRE CHOICES . . . ON SPEAKING OUT

In August 2001, Sheeron Watkins, Vice President of ENRON, a large energy utility, made a momentous decision. She sent a memo to ENRON's chairman, warning him that the company might implode in a wave of accounting scandals because of the financial irregularities she had spotted. The warning was ignored, company officials pocketing millions of dollars in false stock market gains. The company collapsed in December 2001, just before it was able to eject Watkins. ENRON's 'core values' were 'RICE' – *Respect, Integrity, Community,* and *Excellence*. The slogan was reproduced on company T-shirts, on its intranet, pamphlets, paperweights and on a giant banner inside the lobby of its Houston headquarters. Watkins was, perhaps, one of the few ENRON executives who practised what the company preached.[43]

This is a prototypical story about a *whistleblower* – a person who feels impelled to speak out on some ethical malpractice in their organization. Whistleblowers are remarkable in what they reveal about the emotional sub-substructure of individual, morally impelled decisions, and about organizational responses to them.

But why speak out? Why expose yourself in this way? There are emotional explanations. Moral choice would be impossible without feelings for other people – sympathy, empathy, love, compassion, or care. Without these feelings – actual or anticipated – there would be no moral impulse, no wrong to put right, no harm to allay or atone for. Morality and emotion intertwine in ways that are obscured in rational portrayals of 'how to make ethical decisions in business', checklists of do's and don'ts.[44] For whistle-blowers, the passion of the cause is overwhelming. Any personal costs of speaking out are swamped by feelings of righteousness about their concern.[45–47]

Whistleblowers talk of the shame and repulsion of being in an organization that does not seem to care about the consequences of its actions.[48] For instance, a chemist in Fred Alford's study of whistleblowers worked for a state environmental protection agency. Several times his boss refused to allow him to testify before a state panel. They were investigating the agency's failure to test the purity of well water near sites where hazardous material had been dumped. Eventually he contacted a state senator and told him his story. Shortly afterwards he was fired. The state civil service commission made the agency take him back, but he was given no work to do and an office that was once a janitor's closet:

> I just felt so polluted by the whole experience. I felt ashamed to listen to their lies . . . Everyone has the right to know what's in their environment. I spoke up for the right. Now my colleagues won't come near me, they're afraid, like I'm contaminated or something.[49]

Another whistleblower expressed his incredulity and indignation about his employer:

> It was amazing. Here we were dumping poison into the [environment] and nobody wanted to talk about it, as if talking about it would make it real. Well, it was real all right, but we went around pretending it wasn't. I thought I was going crazy. Like it wasn't happening. You think I'm some kind of hero 'cause I blew the whistle. The only reason I spoke up was because I didn't want to go crazy. I had to say what we were doing.[50]

On such issues, whistleblowers find it very hard to perform the emotional hypocrisy that is key to maintaining organizational order (see Chapter 2). They say what they feel. They are unable to 'double', to live in emotionally different worlds.[51] For them, their actions are unquestionably rational – they are doing what is right. For those they expose, they are regarded as anything but rational. Consequently, they are at once ill fitted to organizational life and uniquely valuable in exposing ethical misconduct. They are somewhere between heaven and hell.

Knowing too much

Retaliation against the whistleblower is normally severe. Up to two-thirds lose their jobs.[52, 53] Most cannot get further employment because of an informal blacklist between employers. Many suffer depression, alcoholism and family strain, while their complaints can drag on for years.[54] Seniority or rank offers little protection. If anything, the organization feels most threatened by, and most unforgiving towards, senior members who speak out.[55] Rarely do whistleblowers' exposés get resolved, unless they are relatively unthreatening to key people in the organization. If the whistleblower speaks from a 'non-authorized' position, out of role, he or she has even more trouble being heard.[56]

As the organization progressively closes down on the whistleblower, the whistleblower's anger, passion and self-righteousness increase. Alford speaks eloquently of the whistleblower as the scapegoat who bears the sins of the tribe and is cast out into the wilderness. His or her sin is knowing too much, disturbing the impression of a coherent moral order in the organization. Loyalty keeps the order in place; disloyalty and insubordination is problematic, disruptive. But loyalty also seals in corruption and ethical malpractice.

An epic struggle

The struggle between the whistleblower and the organization has an epic quality: the brave, desperately honest individual pitched against the uncaring, fearful, but all-powerful organization. Rothschild and Miethe suggest that the experiences of the whistleblower teaches '. . . that while resistance in the workplace challenges the practices, the ideology and the authority of those in power, it also about the struggle for dignity and integrity in work organizations'.[57] The tension between the two parties is an excruciating one, revealing of both. As the whistleblower demonizes the organization, the organization responds in kind, labelling the whistleblower as 'sick' or 'disturbed', and ultimately as an 'insubordinate, problem worker'. The organization has now created grounds for the whistleblower's demotion and dismissal, carefully ducking the substance of the whistleblower's claims.

The whistleblower has a naïve faith in organizational justice and in the expectation that his or her cries will be heard. But the sober reality is that organizational norms, working procedures, profit goals and production deadlines, can anaesthetize consciences. Decisions are often focused on the immediate pragmatics of commercial survival. It becomes important to protect one's self-interest and the interest of ones immediate allies. To explore this point, a management researcher presented the following scenario to four groups: executives, blue-collar workers, students, and housewives:

CASE STUDY

A large auto manufacturer has developed a safety device that could reduce traffic injuries by as much as 50 per cent. However, the device would increase the cost of each car by more than $300, which would undoubtedly cause the company to lose sales to competitors. Therefore the company decided not to use the safety device unless all manufacturers are legally required to use it.

Fifty-one per cent of executives believed the company acted unethically – compared to 66 per cent of blue-collar workers, 73 per cent of students and 76 per cent of housewives. In another seven scenarios, executives were consistently less likely to see the decision as unethical.[58]

Is this a picture of evil executives plotting to produce dangerous vehicles, or deliberately cut back on safety requirements (or falsify accounts, or harass employees)? Unlikely. As private individuals, as caring parents, as loving partners, most of them would probably be disturbed by such events, among the first to condemn them. But within their organizations they can fast become submerged in working, 'commercial', rationalities. Caring for the commercial health of the organization (and their own jobs) becomes an 'obvious' priority, pushing into the background the consequential damage of what they do. It is rather like living in parallel moral universes. Trying too hard to bridge them is dangerous, as the whistleblower soon finds out.

THE COMMITMENT TRAP

> **Scene 1:** Your romantic relationship is falling apart, and you both know it. Weeks turn into months and neither of you can make the decision finally to part – it seems like a lingering death, but . . . who, knows, maybe things will improve?
>
> **Scene 2:** You're at the railway station waiting for your train. It's now 45 minutes delayed because of a signal failure, and the delay will continue for an unknown period. You resignedly decide to wait on, despite the fact that you could walk to your destination in 20 minutes.

Here are examples of *committed* decisions. Normally we praise commitment. It suggests loyalty, staying power, keeping an eye on the ball and not giving up. But, in these instances, we have *over* commitment to courses of action in the light of clear signs that they are failing. It would be better to stop, to do something else. However, the more one puts into a particular course of action, the harder it is to disengage. This is *escalation of commitment*.[59, 60]

Escalating commitment occurs when a decision maker has made an initial investment – of time, passion, money and self-identity – into a project that has bright prospects. However, after a period it becomes evident that all is not well: 'Shall I pull out now?' 'How much more would it need to turn the corner?' 'What should I do?' In taking the decision to continue, past efforts are regarded as investments, not sunk costs: 'Just a bit more will get me there'. Each time that the decision maker faces his or her lack of progress, optimism, or blind faith, wins the day. The expectation, the hope, is that the investment will finally pay off. The decision maker is in too deep to get out.

Escalating commitment can shadow many types of organizational decisions, such as investing more and more funds into a failing business, or
deciding not to leave a job, despite clear signs that you should. Each assumes
that things will come right in the end with a little more application,
commitment or time. The nature and strength of this expectation will depend
on what failure means to the decision maker; the intensity of commitment to
initial goals, how important they are; and the extent to which valued others
are implicated in the decisions.

Emotionalities are fundamental to this process. Psychodynamically,
one's self image, or ego, is bound up in the decision. Feelings of worth and
competence hang upon the project's success. When the vision becomes
tarnished, decision makers may suppress that reality (from themselves and
others), ignoring or downplaying negative information, seeking out information to support their own view of the world. It becomes crucial to demonstrate to the self and others that the original decision was correct, and
becoming ever more committed does just this. Pride and fear of failure
intermix to fuel persistence and commitment to the original vision. Being
seen to lose is embarrassing, even shameful. As matters deteriorate it
becomes ever more difficult to hide failure, but the decision maker marches
on to avoid humiliation, sometimes to commercial suicide.[61]

This was very much the pattern with London's Millennium Dome. The
Dome was to be a celebratory landmark on the south bank of the river
Thames, but was blighted with controversy from the outset. At the centre of
the difficulty was the dogged, escalating commitment of a few powerful
supporters. They propelled a dubious, and very costly project, to its realiza-
tion and ultimate demise. The reputation of the Prime Minister was at stake,
as well as 'British pride'. The main events are summarized below.

CASE STUDY

A Doomed Dome

The incoming Labour government in 1997 inherited the Millennium Dome
plans. It was to be a showpiece to mark the new millennium, built on
wasteland on the south bank of the Thames. It would be a vast, temporary,
structure, housing a number of unspecified 'attractions', financed by
business.

There was immediate public controversy, as well as resistance inside
government at cabinet level. Members of parliament were dismayed at the
huge shortfall in business contributions, now falling to government to meet
– some £150m. There followed a trail of scandals involving the salary of
the head of the company who managed the project and the safety of the
design. Labour MP Clare Short referred to the Dome as 'a silly, temporary,

building'. Cash-flow difficulties resulted in the Dome Company receiving £50m public subsidy.

High-profile ministers closed ranks to support their initial decision. The Prime Minister, Tony Blair, declared grandly that the Dome will be 'a triumph of confidence over blandness, excellence over mediocrity'. Peter Mandelson, one of the ministers with responsibility for the project, turned angrily on its critics: 'they lack a sense of greatness. It's pathetic and I hate it.'

The Dome's opening day was chaotic and by February 2001 only a tiny fraction of the expected visitors had arrived. In coming months, heads rolled in an attempt to improve matters and more public money was injected to cover the costs of disappointing visitor numbers. The new minister for the Dome claimed that the project had created jobs and had regenerated a decaying part of London: 'This will benefit the whole country.' 'It was a risk worth taking and an honourable risk.'

Forty-four Labour MPs signed a parliamentary motion condemning the use of public money to bail out the Dome. After ticket price-reductions and yet more public money, Tony Blair finally stopped defending the Dome and admitted that it had failed to meet public expectations. The Dome closed at the end of December 2000 – and proved very costly to keep closed.

Powerful, political, investment in a decision is often regarded as an important ingredient for organizational success. The Dome story illustrates that it does not always work out that way. Commitment can energize, but it also blinds. It offers hope, but also lays a trap for the unwary. It can dull the critical perspective of the committed, where winning at any cost becomes an obsession.

Frozen commitment

Commitment can freeze organizational decisions. Withdrawal becomes too troublesome, often inconceivable, an attack on one's pride. Belief that the project is right and good, and that those involved with it are right and good, provides a psychological protective bubble which filters out any bad news. This can happen to any organizational project, big or small, such as a major new building, an IT system, a theme park, a new high-street store, or a new road. Even a country's war plans can be afflicted, as was the case with the USA's 'Bay of Pigs' fiasco.

CASE STUDY

In April 1961 a brigade of about 1,400 Cuban exiles invaded Cuba in an area know as the Bay of Pigs. The CIA and the US Navy and Air Force supported them. Their objective was to topple Castro, communist leader of Cuba.

Nothing went as planned. Supply ships were sunk and the brigade was rapidly surrounded by 20,000 of Castro's troops. After three days 1,200 members of the brigade were captured and the rest were killed.

President John F. Kennedy and a core group of prestigious advisors shaped the disastrous plan. Kennedy was mortified by the outcome: 'How could I have been so stupid to let them go ahead?'.[62] How could he?

The event has been pored over by social scientists seeking explanations. Significant to our present discussion is the behaviour of the advisory group. Irving Janis points to the complacency and over-confidence of the group in the face of uncertainties and explicit warnings about the operations. Kennedy was regarded as charismatic and seductive, so sealing in feelings of invulnerability and euphoria. Some of his advisors feared that their personal status and political effectiveness would be damaged if they challenged the good mood and solidarity. The plan was never seriously questioned. Commitment blinded participants to fatal flaws in the plan. Arthur Schelsinger, one the advisors, reflects:

> In the months after Bay of Pigs I bitterly reproached myself for having kept so silent during those crucial discussions in the Cabinet Room, though my feelings of guilt were tempered by the knowledge that a course of objection would have accomplished little save the to gain a name as a nuisance.[63]

TOXIC AND INFLAMMATORY DECISIONS

Decision makers are often reluctant to take organizational decisions that will hurt others. Denial and avoidance is one way out. It gives the decision maker temporary protection from the anxiety associated with facing the issue; it holds a lid on the problem. But suppressed problems can grow in intensity. When unexpressed feelings in the organization are finally given voice, they can release an avalanche of organizational distress, which compounds the initial problem. Hakan Ozcelik and Sally Maitlis refer to these as *toxic decisions*, echoing the metaphor discussed in Chapter 6 on toxic leadership.[64] They discovered that toxicity in an organization can build up and diffuse in three main phases: *inertia*, *detonation* and *containment*. Each phase is influenced by a distinctive set of interactions among decision makers.

In the inertia phase, the issue is avoided. In their own study of symphony orchestras, there were several instances of musicians who persistently performed poorly. Managers were reluctant to take responsibility for confronting, and, possibly, dismissing them. When the offending musicians were finally informed of their fate, it released both expected and unexpected emotions. In one instance, a musician felt humiliated and shamed, while his immediate colleagues reacted with anger, fear, pity and embarrassment. The stored tension from the inertia phase exploded. Toxicity spread through the organization as members spontaneously engaged with the victim's 'tragic' story, empathizing with him. Some showed their discontent in a deputation to management, threatening not to play for a scheduled concert.

Finally, the containment phase. Managers tried to quell the fermenting emotion by getting tough – reasserting their control and proposing new structures that might help avoid the problem in the future. The orchestra's leaders responded, in part, to their own weariness, defensiveness and guilt. Such containment, however, merely intensified a volatile context. The musicians' anger and distrust were organizationally suppressed rather than acknowledged and addressed in their own terms.

Risky moves

Some organizational decisions, like the one above, are risky because they involve unpredictable or unforeseen consequences for others. They can hurt, offend, or infuriate people, in ways that the organization has failed to anticipate. And when the organization insists that it own decision is correct, faultless, the scene is set for an inflammatory, and costly, conflict.

For example, in 1995 Shell announced its decision to sink a massive, redundant, oil platform in the deep Atlantic waters off the west coast of Scotland. British Government scientists approved the action as an environmentally satisfactory, low-risk solution. Greenpeace thought differently. In one news release they claimed it was a 'heavily contaminated oil installation . . . loaded with toxic and radioactive sludge'.[65]

They boarded the Brent Spar, beginning a campaign of more than three weeks of direct, often dramatic, resistance against Shell's decision. They recruited the world's media and called for boycotts of Shell service stations. Shell responded by denying Greenpeace's claims and by deploying its own security forces, escalating the conflict into something resembling a naval battle.

Anger, frustration and recrimination were expressed on both sides, each defending its own position. Shell portrayed Greenpeace activists as 'emotionally disturbed' and themselves as the voice of reason and sound science. In turn, Greenpeace claimed the moral high ground: regardless of actual pollution-risk, Shell had no right to use the Atlantic as a dumping ground. They were outraged at Shell and its insensitive action. It was a mood that caught the public attention, and, in the face of public and political opposition in northern Europe, Shell abandoned its plans. But the company stood by its claim that deep sea disposal represented the best environmental option.

To supporters of Greenpeace, the victory was a thrilling one, only slightly tarnished by the discovery that Greenpeace had made a substantial over estimate of the oil remaining in Brent Spar's storage tanks. In 1998 Shell announced its decision to re-use much of the main steel structure in constructing of a new harbour facility in Norway. It would now include stakeholder consultation in is environmental policy, and aim to win the 'hearts and minds' of those whose decisions it effects.[66, 67]

A moral from this tale is that the decision maker's rational discourse can collide with the emotional discourse of those to be persuaded of the wisdom of the decision. Repeating the findings of 'science' and 'risk-statistics' simply serves to widen the gulf of understanding, credibility and sympathy. The onus is on the corporate decision maker to find ways of including the emotional considerations in all stages of the decision process – from inception to implementation.

Not in my backyard NIMBY ('not in my backyard') circumstances illustrate the issue of risk even more graphically. These are situations where a company, public utility, or other agency makes a strategic decision to site an environmentally sensitive process (such as an incinerator, a nuclear-waste processing plant, a new road, a chemical works, or a quarry) near a community, which is likely to object. The organization's task is to gain community consent. The typically favoured approach is to present the scientific facts which show, 'beyond doubt', that the installation will be safe and well managed, and that any fears are 'unreasonable fears'. It is a technical/engineering outlook on the decision. But what is reasonable to the organization can, as we have observed, be seen and *felt* as anything but reasonable by those affected by the decision.

A small US community, Clarion County, faced just such circumstances in the 1990s. A developer wanted to site a hazardous-waste processing facility in the neighbourhood. The company presented their plans coolly and rationally, stressing risk minimization. They compared the danger of the installation to the risks of driving a car, receiving chest X-rays or eating peanut butter. The community's immediate response was of mistrust, personal danger and emotion. The developer was characterized as frightening and repressive. The rational corporate rhetoric was met with moral outrage and passionate resistance.[68] The two parties were soon communicating past each other.

The Developer: I think the unfortunate thing is that people don't want to hear the facts . . . it's very easy for people to develop false impressions and misunderstanding about the risk of these facilities.

The Community: Risk assessment is not confusing, it's misinformation. [The developer's] tactic of comparing 70 years of exposure to hazardous waste with the consumption of diet soda is highly suspect. Get real, industry!

Emotion was a strategic resource in the decision process. Doubtless, many Clarion County citizens felt fear and anxiety, and the developer became frustrated and angry. But while the developer presented a bland, anti-emotional face to reinforce the sensibleness of their position, the community openly expressed their mistrust, fear and anger to demonstrate (a) the intensity of their objection, and (b) the meaninglessness, to them, of the developer's arguments and science. For them, the decision process had to be emotional because the subject matter *was* emotional. After three years, the developer withdrew its proposal, a decision described by a company spokesperson as 'strictly business'.

CONCLUSION

Sound decision making has been popularly defined as something in which emotion has no part. Why this myth is preserved (and promulgated in many management textbooks) is an interesting question. It is grounded in the assumption that emotions are interferences, and can only produce biased, contaminated or corrupt decisions.

But, as this chapter shows, the so-called bias and contamination of emotions are, essentially, what makes decision making possible, and decisions decisive. Our beliefs about de-emotionalized rationality are comforting illusions, cultural ideas that support the notion that we are in complete control of how we make decisions and what we decide. In many professional and managerial circles it is hard to admit that strong feelings, or ambivalence, shaped decisions that involved, say, a major organizational change, a merger or other peoples' careers or care. But feelings steer, shape and signal our thoughts and actions throughout the decision process. They propel our moral choices. The resolve tiebreaks – 'do I do this or that'? Without them we would be lost, often paralysed for direction: managers could not manage, decision makers could not decide.

This does not mean that we are random in our thought processes and respond impulsively to every emotional urge. There are too many feeling and emotional display-rules for that to happen, learned and internalized for appropriate occasions. It does mean, though, that what we think of as rational – the careful arranging of aims, choices and outcomes – evolves from a running interplay of thoughts and feelings until it feels right, or right enough, to 'decide'. In negotiations, some of these feelings are played out with subtlety and skill. On some occasions, a driving feeling, such as of fear, revenge, shame or pride, swamps the whole process. The decision is self-evident. When this adds up to very strong commitment, curious, or extreme, things can happen – like the Millennium Dome experience, the whistle-blower's plight and the polarizing of camps – for and against a decision.

Decision making is made all the more challenging when we realize that feelings and emotions are often our friends, not enemies. At the very least, they require our respect. They are not to be dismissed as an inevitable nuisance, or something to suppress. They are important signals about the shaping and outcomes of decisions. This is a challenge to organizations where 'getting to the point' and 'being quick and clear' permeates the decision-making ethos (an especially Western, male, predilection). Carefully voicing some feelings – uncertainty, anger, unease, excitement, ambivalence,

distress, delight – can provide helpful data, not distractions. Instant rational-
izations can be a dead hand, smothering the very emotionality that tests the
pathways to a decision and the quality of the outcome.

FURTHER READING

Alford, C.F. (2001) *Whistleblowers: Broken Lives and Organizational Power.*
Ithaca: Cornell University Press.
Barry, B. (1999) 'The tactical use of emotion in negotiation', in *Research
on Negotiation in Organizations.* Stamford, Connecticut: JAI Press, 7:
93–121.
Brockner, J. (1992) 'The escalation of commitment to a failing course of
action: Toward theoretical process', *Academy of Management Review,*
17 (1): 39–61.
Forgas, J.P. (ed.) (2000) *Feeling and Thinking: The Role of Affect in Social
Cognition.* Cambridge: Cambridge University Press.

REFERENCES

1   Toda, M. (1980) 'Emotion and decision making', *Acta Psychologica,* 45:
    133–55.
2   Soros, G. (1998) *The Crisis of Global Capitalism.* London: Little,
    Brown and Company. p. 24.
3   Hayashi, A.M. (2001) 'When to trust your gut', *Harvard Business
    Review,* 79 (2): 59–65, especially p. 62.
4   Isenberg, D.J. (1984) 'How senior managers think', *Harvard Business
    Review,* 62 (2): 81–90, especially p. 87.
5   Bazerman, M.H. (1986) *Judgment and Managerial Decisions.* New
    York: Wiley.
6   Harrison, E.F. (1999) *The Managerial Decision-Making Process, 5th
    Edition.* Boston: Houghton Mifflin. pp. 75–6.
7   Scheff, T.J. (1997) *Emotions, the Social Bond, and Human Reality.*
    Cambridge: Cambridge University Press.
8   Simon, H. (1957) *Administrative Behaviour.* New York: Macmillan.
9   Zey, M. (1992) 'Criticisms of rational choice models', in M. Zey (ed.),
    Decision Making: Alternatives to Rational Choice Models. Newbury
    Park: Sage.
10 Miller, S., Hickson, D. and Wilson, D. (1996) 'Decision-making in
    organizations', in S. Clegg, C. Hardy and W. Nord (eds), *Handbook of
    Organization Studies.* London: Sage.
11 Beach, L.R. (1997) *The Psychology of Decision Making: People in
    Organizations.* Thousands Oaks: Sage.

12 Salaman, G. (ed.) (2002) *Decision Making for Business*. London: Sage.

13 Fessler, D.M.T. (2001) 'Emotions and cost-benefit assessment: the role of shame and self-esteem in risk taking', in G. Gigerenzer and R. Selten (eds), *Bounded Rationality: The Adaptive Toolbox*. Cambridge, MA: The MIT Press.

14 Hayashi, A.M. (2001) 'When to trust your gut', *Harvard Business Review*, 79 (2): 59–65, especially p. 62.

15 Bechara, A., Damasio, H. and Damasio, A.R. (2000) 'Emotion, decision making and the orbitofrontal cortex', *Cerebral Cortex*, 10 (March): 295–307.

16 Damasio, A.R. (1994) *Descartes' Error*. New York: G.P. Putman's Sons.

17 Damasio, A.R. (1994) *Descartes' Error*. New York: G.P. Putman's Sons. pp. 195–6.

18 Lutz, C. (1988) *Unnatural Emotions: Everyday Sentiments on a Micronesian Atoll and their Challenge to Western Theory*. Chicago: University of Chicago Press.

19 Clore, G.L. and Isbell, L.M. (2001) 'Emotion as virtue and vice', in J.H. Kuklinski (ed.), *Citizens in Politics*. Cambridge: Cambridge University Press.

20 de Sousa, R. (1987) *The Rationality of Emotion*. Cambridge, MA: The MIT Press.

21 Dennett, D.C. (1978) *Brainstorms: Philosophical Essays on Mind and Psychology*. Cambridge, MA: The MIT Press.

22 Franks, D.D. and Gecas, V. (1992) *Social Perspectives on Emotion: A Research Annual*. Connecticut: JAI Press. p. 10.

23 Loewenstein, G.F., Weber, E.U., Hsee, C.K. and Welch, N. (2001) 'Risk as feelings', *Psychological Bulletin*, 127 (2): 267–86.

24 Loewenstein, G.F., Weber, E.U., Hsee, C.K. and Welch, N. (2001) 'Risk as feelings', *Psychological Bulletin*, 127 (2): 267–86.

25 Mellers, B.A. and McGraw, A.P. (2001) 'Anticipated emotions as guides to choice', *Current Directions in Psychological Science*, 6 (December): 210–15.

26 Olson, J.M., Roese, N.J. and Zanna, M.P. (1996) 'Expectancies', in E.T. Higgins and A.W. Kruglanski (eds), *Social Psychology: Handbook of Basic Principles*. New York: Guildford Press. pp. 211-38.

27 Zeelenberg, M., van Dijk, W.W., Manstead, A.S.R. and van der Pligt, J. (2000) 'On bad decisions and disconfirmed expectancies: the psychology of regret and disappointment', *Cognition and Emotion*, 14 (4): 521–41.

28 Fredericksen, B.L. (2000) 'Extracting meaning from past affective experiences: the importance of peaks, ends, and specific emotions.' *Cognition and Emotion*, 14 (4): 577–606.

29 Isen, A.M. and Baron, R.A. (1991) 'Positive affect as a factor in organizational behaviour', in L.L. Cummings and B.M. Staw (eds), *Research in Organizational Behaviour*. Greenwich, CT: JAI Press. Vol. 13, pp. 1–53.

30 Mellers, B.A., Erev, I., Fessler, D.M.T., Hemlrik, C.K., Hertwig, R., Laland, K.N., Scherer, K.R., Seeley, T.D., Selten, R. and Tetlock, P.E. (2001) 'Group report: effects of emotions and social processes on bounded rationality,' in G. Gigerenzer and R. Selten (eds), *Bounded Rationality: The Adaptive Toolbox*. Cambridge, MA: The MIT Press.

31 Isen, A.M. (2000) 'Positive affect and decision making', in M. Lewis and J.M. Haviland-Jones (eds), *Handbook of Emotions*. New York: The Guildford Press.

32 Forgas, J.P. and George, J.M. (2001) 'Affective influences on judgments and behavior in organizations: an information processing perspective', *Organizational Behavior and Human Decision Processes*, 86 (1): 3–34.

33 Forgas, J.P. (ed.) (2000) *Feeling and Thinking: The Role of Affect in Social Cognition*. Cambridge: Cambridge University Press.

34 Peters, E. (1952) *Conciliation in Action*. New London, CT: National Foremen's Institute. p. 18.

35 Goffman, E. (1959) *The Presentation of Self in Everyday Life*. New Jersey: Anchor Books.

36 Goffman, E. (1967) *Interaction Ritual*. New Jersey: Anchor Books.

37 Dachler, K. and Ekman, P. (2000) 'Facial expression of emotion', in M. Lewis and J.M. Haviland-Jones (eds), *Handbook of Emotions*. New York: The Guildford Press.

38 Morris, M.W. and Dachler, K. (2000) 'How emotions work: the social functions of emotional expression in negotiation', in B.M. Staw and R.I. Sutton (eds), *Research in Organizational Behavior*. Greenwich, CT: JAI Press. Vol. 22, pp. 1–50.

39 Hellriegel, D., Slocum, J.W. and Woodman, R.W. (1995) *Organizational Behavior*. Minneapolis/St Paul: West. pp. 450–2.

40 Thompson, L.L., Nadler, J. and Kim, P. (1999) 'Some like it hot: the case for the emotional negotiator', in L.L. Thompson, J.M. Levine and D.M. Messick (eds), *Shared Cognition in Organizations: The Management of Knowledge*. Mahwah, NJ: Lawrence Erlbaum.

41 Barry, B. and Oliver, R.L. (1996) 'Affect in dyadic negotiation: a model and propositions', *Organizational Behavior and Human Decision Processes*, 67 (2): 127–43.

42 Brown, B.R. (1968) 'The effects of need to maintain face on interpersonal bargaining', *Journal of Experimental Social Psychology*, 4: 107–22.

43 Anonymous (2002) 'The right way to blow the whistle', *Business Week*, Jan 29.

44 Hellriegel, D., Slocum, J.W. and Woodman, R.W. (1995) *Organizational Behavior*. Minneapolis/St Paul: West.

45 Solomon, R.C. (1991) 'Business ethics, literacy, and the education of emotions', in R.E. Freeman (ed.), *Business Ethics: The State of the Art*. New York: Oxford University Press.

46 Bos, R.T. and Willmott, H. (2001) 'Towards a post-dualist business ethics: interweaving reason and emotion in working life', *Journal of Management Studies*, 38 (6): 769–93.

47 Solomon, R.C. (1996) 'Emotions, ethics, and the "internal ought"', *Cognition and Emotion*, 10 (5): 529–50.

48 Alford, C.F. (2001) *Whistleblowers: Broken Lives and Organizational Power*. Ithaca: Cornell University Press.

49 Alford, C.F. (2001) *Whistleblowers: Broken Lives and Organizational Power*. Ithaca: Cornell University Press. p. 75.

50 Alford, C.F. (2001) *Whistleblowers: Broken Lives and Organizational Power*. Ithaca: Cornell University Press. p. 13.

51 Lifton, R.J. (1993) *The Protean Self: Human Resilience in an Age of Fragmentation*. New York: Basic Books.

52 Glazer, M. and Glazer, P. (1989) *The Whistleblowers: Exposing Corruption in Government and Industry*. New York: Basic Books.

53 Miethe, T.D. (1998) *Whistle-Blowing at Work: Tough Choices in Exposing Fraud, Waste and Abuse on the Job*. Boulder, CO: Westview Press.

54 Davis, M. (1989) 'Avoiding the tragedy of whistleblowing', *Business and Professional Ethics Journal*, 8 (4): 3–19.

55 Devine, T. (1997) 'What to expect: classic responses to whistle-blowing.' in *The Whistleblower's Survival Guide: Courage Without Martydom*. Washington, DC: Fund for Constitutional Government.

56 Miceli, M.P. and Near, J.P. (2002) 'What makes whistle-blowers effective?', *Human Relations*, 55 (4): 455–79.

57 Rothschild, J. and Miethe, T.D. (1994) 'Whistleblowing as resistance in modern work organizations: the politics of revealing organizational deception and abuse', in J. Jermier, W. Nord and D. Knights (eds), *Resistance and Power in Organizations*. London: Routledge. pp. 252–73, especially p. 267.

58 Sturdivant, F.D. and Cocanougher, A.B. (1973) 'Where are ethical marketing practices?' *Harvard Business Review*, 51 (November–December): 10–12, especially p. 12.

59 Brockner, J. (1992) 'The escalation of commitment to a failing course of action: Toward theoretical process', *Academy of Management Review*, 17 (1): 39–61.

60 Staw, B.M. and Ross, J. (1987) 'Understanding escalation situations: antecedents, prototypes and solutions', in B.M. Staw and L.L. Cummings (eds), *Research in Organizational Behaviour*. Greenwich, CT: JAI Press. Vol. 9.

61 Drummond, H. and Kingstone Hodgson, J.A. (1996) 'Between a rock and a hard place: a case study of escalation', *Management Decision*, 34 (2): 29–34.

62 Janis, I.L. (2002) 'A perfect failure: the Bay of Pigs', in G. Salaman (ed.), *Decision Making for Business: A Reader*. London: Sage. p. 11.

63 Janis, I.L. (2002) 'A perfect failure: the Bay of Pigs', in G. Salaman (ed.), *Decision Making for Business: A Reader*. London: Sage. p. 31.

64 Ozcelik, H. and Maitlis, S. (2001) 'Toxic decision making: the misman-agement of emotional issues in organizations'. Annual Meeting of the Academy of Management, Washington, DC.

65 <http://archive.greenpeace.org/~comms/brent/brent.html>.

66 Jordan, G. (2001) *Shell, Greenpeace and the Brent Spar*. London: Shell.

67 Shell (2001) *People, Planet and Profits*. London: Shell International, PXXL (Publications): London.

68 Welcomer, S.A., Gioia, D.A. and Kilduff, M. (2000) 'Resisting the dis-course of modernity: rationality versus emotion in hazardous waste siting', *Human Relations*, 53 (9): 1175–205.

8

Emotion and change

LEARNING OBJECTIVES

Change triggers many different feelings. This chapter explores the way change-feelings develop, and their organizational implications.

- Change is a process of unfolding feelings, before, during and after the event.
- Change can involve dealing with loss and anxiety.
- Resistance to change is rooted in disturbed social and political relationships, and threatened self-identity.
- Changing an organization's culture treads on sensitive emotional territory.

> Merely to alter the arrangement of the furniture in a room or to appoint just one new member of staff can be enough to set the cats of anxiety and selfishness amongst the pigeons of stability and cooperation.[1]

Changes in work settings occur in myriad different ways. Some are local and contained – a shift in offices, a new personal computer, a different colleague or immediate boss, or learning a new skill. Others stem from wider organizational moves and displacements (all of which contain many local changes) such as a merger or takeover, a corporate restructuring or downsizing, joining a new work team, a different accounting system, or a re-formed organizational culture (see also Chapter 12). Still others mark the beginning, middle and end of jobs or careers, such as first joining an organization, promotion, or retirement. Some of these events will be imposed, beyond the direct control of those affected; others can be negotiated or voluntary.

It is hard to envisage changes like these as emotion free. Emotions will shape the *anticipation*, the *experience*, and the *aftermath* of change. They are not just the consequences of a change 'event'. Consider, for example, the following scenario:

There is an announcement in your department that there will be a restructuring. Over the next two months your department will be split into two different sections to ease congestion in the workload. You will have to move your office and work with a different team and manager. You feel shocked – it's unexpected news; you weren't consulted. After a few days, and sleepless nights, your anxieties crystallize. You're nervous about who you will be working with, and for. You've heard rumours that a section manager from another team will take over, and she has a reputation as a 'difficult' woman. On the bright side, it looks like you will get a larger, less cramped, office, and that pleases you.

When the day of the move approaches, it's chaos. Nothing seems to be ready. Confusion reigns. The prospective new manager has refused the job and is resigning. A relief for you in a way, but now there's a vacuum in leadership. The office is indeed bigger, but it's still crowded. More staff have been allocated to it, several with no prior experience. You're fed up, stressed and wonder how you will cope. The best thing about the change is that all the computer equipment is brand new and very smart, and there's now more secretarial support. That feels good, a bit of a relief. Also, there's an added bonus: you're now just round the corner from the coffee room.

Three weeks after the move and there's still no manager in your section. The mood is gloomy. No one has time to give support to the newcomers. The effectiveness of the section has dropped rather than improved, as had been promised. In the coffee room, everyone complains, morale is low. You feel resentful, angry with top management for having mishandled the whole affair. You're seriously thinking of looking for a new job.

Change in this story is not simply a switch from one state to another. It is a process of unfolding and conflicting feelings – before, during and after the event. Emotionally speaking, change is occurring long before the material shift in circumstances, as well as during and after it. Expectations of change prompt a process of adaptation and learning, which can be long and excruciating, or short and sweet. It rather depends on how the change is construed – what it means to the person or people affected.[2, 3] Furthermore, as the above account illustrates, change is not just a matter of positive *or* negative feelings. Mixed feelings are common – simultaneously positive and uneasy about things.[4] Fear can coexist with exhilaration, liking with disliking, loving with frustration, suspicion with delight. Resolving, or learning to accept, these tensions, is part of the struggle of change. Let us examine this further.

THE CHANGING EXPERIENCES OF CHANGE

Going through a major change is often intensely personal. We get wrapped up in our fluctuating feelings: doubts, excitement, ambivalence, fear. Our feelings shape the meaning and sense we make of new circumstances. Sometimes the emotion work can be arduous as adjustment takes place, particularly when change dislocates comfortable routines and threatens our identity. This is especially likely for professional and managerial employees, whose self-images fuse with their jobs.[5, 6] Roger Stuart interviewed 63 such people, managers in two UK industrial organizations who had experienced an organizational-wide restructuring. The change fundamentally challenged their views about their jobs and themselves. Stuart was keen to examine the development of reactions during the change journey, noting how people sensed what was happening.[7] Two of his summary accounts of individual managers illustrate this:

'ON THE ROAD TO RUIN'

Journey	Reaction
Shock	*'It's happening! It wasn't an exercise'*
Minimizing	*'I couldn't believe it'*
Protest	*'I felt very angry. Exceptions were made. I felt guilty'*
Yearning	*'I was proud of what we were. It was like a family and someone dying. I'd been with them through good and bad times. It was almost like grief, living through that dying'*
Disorganization	*'I felt split. It was all too much. It wasn't real'*
Testing, protest testing and disorganization	*'Everyone was rushing around play acting and saying the buzz words'; 'How could they forget what's going on?'; 'we were working ridiculous hours. I was stressed'; 'people aren't honest about the reality – I don't see it happening; I'm confused, butterflying, not in control. I'm in a muddle and totally inefficient'*
Realization	*'Suddenly, I came to the conclusion – nothing will change. How much do people change when it comes down to it – neither people's attitudes nor the behaviour at the top'*
Despair	*'I'm yo-yoing up and down. I feel a sense of failure . . . I'm on the road and to ruin? Sad'; 'I hope this is temporary – I don't think I could live with it'*

'GOING THROUGH THE PAINS'

Journey	Reaction
Shock	*'Out of the blue . . . we were thrust into a completely different scene'*
Minimizing	*'I wanted to see it as still the same job – and thought that way'*

Yearning	'I enjoyed my work. I miss it, it was very interesting. I have great difficulty withdrawing from it – but it's still there, and when you want to get your fingernails dirty, you can'
Acceptance	'It's very painful to let go of what you're good at, enjoy and feel comfortable with. But there you are'
Testing	'Stepping into unknown waters is difficult'
Realization	'I've complete control over the process!'
Acceptance	'That's tremendous'
Testing	'Exciting and new . . . but going through the pain is very difficult'
Meaning, protest and yearning	'I can now see why . . . but it takes some getting used to. I'm seeing it evolve and starting to understand, but our days are numbered'; 'There is no reason why I should agree with what's being done but, in my job, you have to preach the gospel. I choose my words very carefully'; 'At heart, I'm an engineer. I miss it – most of us were not brought up in a step-back environment. I was right in the middle of it and now I delegate. Only three years ago, we were little families. I miss that'

These events show two things. First, that the effects of a major change *unfold* over time. There are struggles with one's self, one's beliefs about the organization and about professional and occupational identity. There is an image of lives in extraordinary flux as the managers grapple for meaning out of disruption, seeking a resolution, settlement or peace. Second, that feelings and emotions reverberate throughout: the shock of the news; nostalgia, pride and regret as they cling to images of the past job or situation; fear about an unknown future; denial of the change; excitement mixed with the pain of loss. Some of the managers in the study 'learned' to be helpless, resigned to their fate.[8] Indeed, there is a strong unifying theme throughout of people less able to manage their own work lives, as they once had.

Understanding change as 'loss'

Change often involves loss, as the above confessions reveal. In some circumstances the loss is welcomed, warmly or cautiously – a disliked boss (but will the new one be any better?) or an under-demanding job (but will the change give me what I want?). However, many losses are regretted, especially those that erode one's *self-identity*. For some people, their job is the centre of their universe, providing meaning, purpose and status. They have lost a major part of themselves, and grieving can occur.

Grieving is a psychological process of adjusting to loss, to recover meaningful patterns.[9] Its basis, according to Parkes, is in 'a reluctance to give up possessions, people, status and expectations'.[10] At its core is the emotion work that goes into accepting, making real, the fact of the loss. Grieving often moves through stages, beginning with *shock, numbness and denial*; then to *pining for what has been lost*; to *disorganization and despair*; and finally towards *acceptance and recovery.*[11, 12] The sequence is not always neat or precise, but interfering with, or trying to short-circuit, the grieving process can prolong adjustment.

'Managerial time' (short-term, eager for results) and 'grieving time' (less predictable, open-ended) are often out of sync. Managerial exhortations, or self-attempts to 'work normally', or 'snap out of it', miss the vital importance of allowing time and space for recovery. Hence the initial gains from radical organizational restructuring often do not materialize. The emotional currents are swirling as people try to come to terms with their loss (some never do). In death, grieving has long been a social, as well as a private, process. Different religions and cultures have developed sometimes elaborate rituals to support those who suffer loss, as well to legitimize the expression of distress. Work organizations that expect 'commitment as usual' after a major change have yet to make the connection between these events and the support that staff need to manage the loss of deeper meanings of their work.[13] The capability of senior managers to 'hold' others' uncertainty and pain is important in this respect. This means avoiding rushing into 'doing things' – creating new ventures, new plans, new schemes. These very actions may help leaders displace their own anxieties but, meanwhile, add to the burdens of others trying to adjust to change.[14, 15]

ANXIETY AND CHANGE

All learning is fundamentally coercive because you either have no choice, as is the case for children, or it is painful to replace something that is already there with new learning. (Edgar Schein)[16]

Some observers debunk the idea that change and new learning can be fun. It may be fun to realize the *outcomes* of a newly acquired skill. It can be enjoyable to find that there are fresh career opportunities after requalifying. But the process of getting there often involves anxiety and, at times, despondency, as familiar knowledge and routines are eroded or displaced. Indeed, anxiety, pain and struggle are often inevitable partners to successful learning and unlearning (letting go of habitual ways of operating). It is high distress and insecurity that are impediments to learning and change (see also Chapter 9).

Yet, what exactly is there to be anxious about? Consciously, our anxiety can stem from the shame of not being able to learn new skills or new ways, when others can. There is the embarrassment of failing to keep up with competitive colleagues or of being excluded from a peer group. There is the damage to one's pride and self-image in realizing that the change and new learning is beyond you: 'Am I stupid?' 'Am I too old to learn new things?' Or from the threat to one's material security: 'I might lose my job if I can't take this change'.[17] Some of our anxieties may be rooted in unconscious fears: the shadows of past failures, the guilt at letting down a leader or parent figure, the dread of being left out or rejected. These impulses lurk dimly in our emotional make-up, carried since childhood and reactivated when change beckons or threatens.

RESISTANCE AND CHANGE

As anxiety about change increases, so does resistance. Resistance is an expression of opposition by members of an organization to official or unofficial forms of control. Indeed tackling, or overcoming, resistance to change has become something of a managerial mission. From a managerial mindset, resistance to change can severely hamper an organization's plans and objectives. It can happen within or across levels of the organization, so it is not simply the stereotypical picture of workers resisting management initiatives. Middle managers may resist senior management, and supervisors can resist middle managers.

Employee resistance may be organized or disorganized, individual or collective, conscious or unconscious, continuous or one-off. It includes aggression towards management, frustration, arguing, undermining, rule breaking and ignoring.[18–20] Even small gestures, such as 'illegally' keeping a button undone on a uniform, or inscribing company property with graffiti, can be acts of resistance. Radical forms of resistance are strikes or sabotage. For instance, LaNuaz and Jermier report how some employees erased computer records and leaked confidential information on product development.[21] Resistance can be camouflaged through satire and humour, directed against the instigators of change.[22, 23]

From a top-down perspective, resistance is often an irritation for which employees are blamed: 'really awkward', 'bloody minded, 'irrational' or 'troublemakers'. Such judgements are themselves expressions of managerial frustration, but they do not go very far in appreciating the nature of resistance. Change, *per se*, is rarely resisted. People in organizations often hunger for constructive change. They will readily point to things in their organization that need addressing, improving, rethinking, or that are simply wrong. Kotter, for instance, found that, in over 100 companies, employees often understood the new corporate vision and wanted to make it happen.

Their objection came when they were forced to make choices that compromised their own self-interest.[24] Managerial prescriptions that feel uncomfortable, or 'not right', excite feelings of resistance.

Resistance's roots

When people resist, they are mobilizing their own power against some other source of power because they feel uneasy, put upon, insecure or fearful.[25] Organizational changes that bring about different work arrangements, increased impersonalization, more emphasis on measuring the quality and quantity of outcomes, altered promotion prospects and closer surveillance, may make good business sense in the executive boardroom. But to the receivers of change, they can mean and feel very different.

For a start, they may contravene the psychological contract, the unspoken agreements between employer and employee, particularly when those affected have had little control over the nature and pacing of the change programme.[26] The tacit give-and-take balance has been upset. Trust and identity are on the line. This feels worse for employees who strongly value their professional autonomy, and need to reaffirm it. Such as, for example, the following nursing manager's feelings about an imposed change:

> I resented greatly the dictation, the dictatorials from head office – you will do this, you will set this up – and I'm thinking, who the hell do they think they are? Individuals, we are.[27]

Second, resistance, that looks spiteful to management, may be perfectly reasonable to the resistor. For instance, the changes might require the employee to engage, or collude with, unethical practices – such as secretly monitoring staff's telephone calls, paying temporary workers below legal minimum wages, or trading with regimes that have a poor human rights record (see Chapter 10). Resistance, therefore, is rooted in (a) disturbance to the social relationships and moral/political order that binds a person to the organization, and (b) the anxiety and uncertainty that change can bring to person's sense of identity, security and self-worth.

Emotional balancing

Signs of resistance indicate important differences in the way a change is seen, presented, or negotiated.[28, 29] Resistance, if accurately 'read', provides important diagnostic information on the way change is being introduced, delivered and supported. It also indicates the feelings that have to be addressed if operational continuity, a semblance of normal organizational service, is to be sustained during the change. Failure to do so risks the organization sliding into paralysis or chaos. Huy calls this process *emotional balancing*. It falls upon managers, he argues, to work with their own and their subordinates' feelings, if both change *and* continuity are to be achieved.[30]

Huy illustrates the balancing principle in a study of contrasting responses to managing change in a large information technology company.[31] An aspect of the change involved closing ten call centres in small towns and consolidating them into one site. It meant a reduction of some 20 per cent of the workforce. The company's vice president was bullish about the project. He kept 'a state of insecurity and one must be an agent of change or be out. I [keep] the managers cranked up'. Following his lead, one middle manager expressed her intolerance of her subordinates' personal worries about the change:

> We had an open line for questions. Ninety percent of them were basically the same: how was it going to affect my work scheduling, my vacation. Not about the business structure or how customer segmentation works. In future should we take these calls? No!

She failed to restore psychological stability to those who had to continue delivering the service. But another middle manager's response was very different. He was sceptical about the change, but masked his feelings. He then reached out to his subordinates:

> I realized that one could not deal effectively with emotions when one was with a crowd. So I began to set up smaller meetings in groups of seven or eight, and I told them I would be available for private meetings after the group discussion . . . It was a winning formula. Every case was different: One service rep from a small town emotionally told me in a public meeting that she could not move to [Dallas] immediately. In private she explained to me that she was going through a divorce. Another one was worried that her handicapped child could not find a specialized school, so I looked for a job that would suit her needs. Others have sick parents. Relocation is a very emotional thing. We addressed that by offering them paid visits to the new location a few months in advance.

His sympathetic actions eased the anxieties and doubts that fuelled resistance, and helped carry people through the change.

CHANGING THE CULTURE

> I came back to the finance director and said, 'I've been on this course [on creativity] and I learnt that there's nothing wrong with sitting back and doing a bit of day dreaming now and again, so I've got to do an hour's day dreaming each day. I'll just sit there with my eyes closed – so don't think I'm wasting time will you!' Rubbish! I got a suitable response for winding him up, but no, I haven't been more creative![32]

There is long history of corporate attempts to change bits, or all, of an organization's culture. They aim to create loyalty, creativity and commitment among employees by instilling a particular set of values – what the company 'stands for'. For instance, Hewlett-Packard proclaims an informal corporate culture that is open and flexible, and where trust, respect and teamwork prevail. Many large companies make similar statements, marking out their cultural territory for the benefit of recruits, old and new. Some enshrine their manifesto in corporate brochures and on wall plaques, and there they can remain, largely forgotten in the daily mêlée of business. Others, however, are more determined to practise what they preach. The elements of corporate culture – shared values, language rituals and myths – are stripped out and reshaped by management, to engender commitment and enthusiasm. The company instigates training, in-house seminars, Outward Bound programmes, 'inspirational' talks from the chief executive, rousing sales conferences in smart hotels, aimed at inculcating the company 'way', and to get people to feel part of the corporate 'family'. (The popular use of the family metaphor is somewhat ironic given that many actual families are strife-ridden and broken). Such interventions, it is claimed, create the right emotional environment for commercial success – such as found in IBM, Proctor and Gamble, McDonalds, Plessey, Sainsburys and Schweppes.[33, 34]

The shaping of organizational–culture passions and feelings reaches back to the late 1930s (although not always under the 'culture' label). Early, influential management thinkers, such as Chester Barnard, saw the role of the executive as creating a cooperative social system, and in proclaiming appropriate values.[35] In the 1950s cultural change was openly indoctrinational; General Electric, for example, had *The GE Indoctrination Centre* to provide employees with the messages and sentiments that the company wanted to get across. IBM took the singing route, distributing the *IBM Songbook* to all employees.[36] By the 1970s and 1980s 'learning' and 'culture' came into fashion and, in particular, ways of creating 'strong', uniform, cultures with shared zeal. 'In culture there is strength' was the stark proclamation of business gurus, Deal and Kennedy.[37] Today, strong cultures are seen as something of handicap, reducing the flexibility of companies that have to change fast. Many of the strong culture companies of the 1980s have failed to sustain their advantage.[38] The quest for commitment has been further shaken in an era of downsizing, job insecurity and 'Me plc'.

There are heated debates over the nature and meaning of organizational culture, and significant doubts have been raised over whether culture can be managed, let alone changed.[39–44] Nevertheless, the belief persists in management circles that *some* cultural change is possible and desirable. What happens in these programmes? A recent study by Turnbull gives an indication of the typical range of responses. She studied a major organizational change in a large engineering organization. The aim was to instil a new set of values, which, ultimately, would, lead to increases in productivity. It was to be achieved through training and personal development that taught employees to behave in a less-macho manner, to reduce fear, and develop commitment and spontaneous passion for the organization's ideals.

She identified two types of respondents to the programme: *evangelists* and *actors*. The evangelists went willingly and uncritically with the flow of change. They were messianic about the programme. They relied on the company to provide meaning in their lives, and would work long hours, often to the detriment of family life. They bonded with their company and felt very good about it. One said 'I would die [for the company]. I live and breathe the company'. The actors, on the other hand, were sceptical, suspicious of the motives behind the change, but they acquiesced – they played along, acting out the part. As reluctant emotional labourers, however, their mask would sometimes slip (see Chapter 3). During the change programme they confided to Turnbull: 'Many are mimicking the change'; 'People have to say they are committed'. 'You keep your head down', 'You do what your manager wants you to do'.

Overall, there is a mixed, and complex, picture of cultural attempts to manage peoples' emotions.[45, 46] What might appear a well-intentioned executive effort to bring positive, warm, hopeful, feelings to an organization, is still an *executive* initiative. It can be seen, and felt, as gimmicky; learning imposed by the employer, rather than chosen by the employee. For these reasons, it can be resisted, or met with the kind of cynicism of the 'creative' manager speaking at the beginning of this section. It can create false camaraderie, a feeling of 'not being yourself', especially when people feel forced into uncomfortable 'learning events', such as the two below:

CASE STUDY

The Love Bath

As part of the company's transformation programme, participants were invited to take part in what was termed 'the Love Bath'. This was a group exercise in which participants were required to say 'nice things' about each group member in turn. This was supposed to improve self esteem. In practice, participants found the experience 'excruciating' . . . 'The Love Bath' was a humility-inducing experience because it robbed the participants of their dignity and made light of their discomfort.[47]

The Wave

In the first module of the Aerco programme, the managers were required by the consultants to hold hands and wave their arms in the style of a football crowd. The horror among these managers, 98 per cent of whom were male, was intense. Yet the same emotional display (even crying) would be considered normal behaviour by these same individuals if they were at a football match, for example. Interestingly, while a couple of the managers in the room did refuse to comply with the request, and were visible in opting out, over a hundred people in the room went through with the activity despite their intense dislike of it.[48]

Attempts to create 'positive bonds' that result in embarrassing or shaming people, is an ethically dubious practice. Companies seeking emotional changes tread in sensitive territory. As Edgar Schein soberly reflects, 'there are occasions when individuals do the organization a huge favor by refusing to learn'.[49] Commitment, especially, cannot be imposed. It may be voluntarily given and, if necessary, voluntarily withdrawn.

CONCLUSION

The ability to manage change in others is typically considered a key skill for effective management. Consequently, ideas and prescriptions for creating change abound. Most are top-down, focusing on change that is done to others.[50, 51] Advice is offered on ways that managers can overcome resistance to change to win the minds, and perhaps the hearts, of those they wish to influence. The leader's vision is regarded as important (see Chapter 6). Clear and regular information about the required change, quality circles, discussion groups and team-building exercises, can add to a sense involvement.

But, in practice, not all change in organizations is smoothly and sensitively executed. Change-management skills can be elusive or non-existent. Secrecy, hidden agendas and vested interests can mean that change is forced, without warning. Uncertainty and fear can dominate. A new chief executive might be the 'broom that sweeps clean', but with little appreciation of the value of the human 'debris' collected in the sweep. Sometimes sudden, unexpected events precipitate an organizational crisis – an oil shortage, a war, a terrorist act, a hostile takeover, the illness or death of a chief executive. In these circumstances, careful change management can give way to cruder approaches, such as immediate employee layoffs and closure of parts of the business (see Chapter 12).

It takes but little introspection to realize that when we, ourselves, face change we often confront conflicting feelings. It is working with these tensions that make change so challenging. Change is about feelings and emotion and chang*ing* is itself often emotional. When change is pressed upon us, or we force it on others, then the emotional cards are stacked against a smooth passage. Feelings pre, during, and post change, have trajectories which can easily be trampled on, or misread, especially by managers anxious to 'get on with the job'. In hierarchical and suspicious organizations, compliance rather than willing or eager embracement, is the most likely outcome. An organization of acolytes, evangelic employees ready to follow managements' desires, makes things much easier. However, it also makes for a rigid organization, where management initiatives are never seriously questioned.

When change is performed *with* people, rather than *on* them, then some of these anxieties dissipate. The managerial prerogative is not sacrificed, but it is flexible and open to negotiation. As organizational hierarchies begin to melt, we see autonomous teams in flatter organizations where managers facilitate change rather than command it. They work more closely with the needs, desires, fears and aspirations of employees and decision making becomes more emotionally transparent (see also Chapter 7). This is unlikely to make change any easier, but, with emotionally sensitive managers, it can be more effective – for everyone.

FURTHER READING

Coutu, D.L. (2002) 'The anxiety of learning', *Harvard Business Review*, 80 (3): 100–6.

Huy, Q.N. (2002) 'Emotional balancing of organizational continuity and radical change: the contribution of middle managers', *Administrative Science Quarterly*, 47 (1): 31–70.

Kunda, G. (1992) *Engineering Culture: Control and Commitment in a High-tech Corporation*. Philadelphia: Temple University Press.

Schein, E.H. (1992) *Organizational Culture and Leadership, 2nd Edition*. San Francisco: Jossey-Bass.

REFERENCES

1   French, R. (2001) '"Negative capability": managing the confusing uncertainties of change', *Journal of Organizational Change Management*, 14 (5): 480–92, especially p. 480.

2   George, J.M. and Jones, G.R. (2001) 'Towards a process model of individual change in organizations', *Human Relations*, 54 (4): 419–44.

3   Kiefer, T. (2002) 'Understanding the emotional experience of organizational change: evidence from a merger', *Advances in Developing Human Resources*, 4 (1): 39–61.

4   Pratt, M.G. and Doucet, L. (2000) 'Ambivalent feelings in organizational relationships', in S. Fineman (ed.), *Emotion in Organizations, 2nd Edition*. London: Sage. pp. 204–26.

5   Fineman, S. (1983) *White Collar Unemployment*. Chichester: Wiley.

6   Fineman, S. (1987) *Unemployment: Personal and Social Consequences*. London: Tavistock.

7   Stuart, R. (1995) 'Experiencing organizational change: triggers, processes and outcomes of change journey', *Personnel Review*, 24 (2): 3–88, especially pp. 41–2.

8   Seligman, M.E.P. (1975) *Helplessness: On Depression, Development and Death*. San Francisco: Freeman. p. 39.

9   Marris, P. (1986) *Loss and Change*. London: Routledge and Kegan Paul.

10 Parkes, C.M. (1986) *Bereavement: Studies of Grief in Adult Life*. London: Penguin. p. 39.

11 Parkes, C.M. (1986) *Bereavement: Studies of Grief in Adult Life*. London: Penguin. p. 39.

12 Kubler-Ross, E. (1973) *On Death and Dying*. London: Penguin.

13 Carr, A. (2001) 'Understanding emotion and emotionality in a process of change', *Journal of Organizational Change Management*, 14 (5): 421–32.

14 French, R. (2001) '"Negative capability": managing the confusing uncertainties of change', *Journal of Organizational Change Management*, 14 (5): 480–92, especially p. 480.

15 Frost, P.J. (2003) *Toxic Emotions at Work*. Harvard: Harvard Business School Press.

16 Coutu, D.L. (2002) 'The anxiety of learning', *Harvard Business Review*, 80 (3): 100–6, especially p. 103.

17 Antonacopoulou, E.P. and Gabriel, Y. (2001) 'Emotion, learning and organizational change', *Journal of Organizational Change Management*, 14 (5): 435–51.

18 Bovey, W.H. (2001) 'Resistance to organizational change: the role of cognitive and affective processes', *Leadership and Organization Development Journal*, 22 (8): 372–82.

19 Coch, L. and French, J.R.P. (1948) 'Overcoming resistance to change', *Human Relations*, 1: 512–32.

20 Argyris, C. and Schon, D.A. (1974) *Theory in Practice: Increasing Professional Effectiveness*. San Francisco: Jossey Bass.

21 LaNuez, D. and Jermier, J. (1994) 'Sabotage by managers and technocrats: neglected patterns of resistance at work', in J. Jermier, D. Knights and W. Nord (eds), *Resistance and Power in Organizations*. London: Routledge. pp. 219–51.

22 Piderit, S.K. (2000) 'Rethinking resistance and recognizing ambivalence: a multidimensional view of attitudes toward an organizational change', *Academy of Management Review*, 25 (4): 783–94.

23 Collinson, D. (2002) 'Managing humour', *Human Relations*, 39 (3): 269–88.

24 Kotter, J.P. (1995) 'Leading change: why transformation efforts fail', *Harvard Business Review*, 73 (2): 59–67.

25 Young, A.P. (2000) '"I'm just me." A study of managerial resistance', *Journal of Organizational Change Management*, 13 (4): 375–88.

26 Rousseau, D. (1995) *Psychological Contracts in Organizations*. Thousand Oaks: Sage.

27 Young, A.P. (2000) '"I'm just me." A study of managerial resistance', *Journal of Organizational Change Management*, 13 (4): 375–88, especially p. 382.

28 Nord, W. and Jermier, J. (1994) 'Overcoming resistance to resistance: insights from a study in the shadows', *Public Administration Quarterly*, 17 (4): 396–409.

29 Smith, K.K. (1993) 'On banning smoking in the workplace: a case of organization gridlock', *Administration in Social Work*, 17 (3): 81–97.

30 Huy, Q.N. (2002) 'Emotional balancing of organizational continuity and radical change: the contribution of middle managers', *Administrative Science Quarterly*, 47 (1): 31–70.

31 Huy, Q.N. (2002) 'Emotional balancing of organizational continuity and radical change: the contribution of middle managers', *Administrative Science Quarterly*, 47 (1): 31–70, especially pp. 50–1.

32 Turnbull, S. (2002) 'The planned and unintended emotions generated by a corporate change programme', *Advances in Developing Human Resources*, 4 (1): 22–38, especially p. 31.

33 Walton, R.E. (1991) 'From control to commitment in the workplace', in R.M. Steers and L.W. Porter (eds), *Motivation and Work Behavior*. New York: McGraw-Hill.

34 Martin, P. and Nicholls, J. (1987) *Creating a Committed Workforce*. London: Institute of Personnel Management.

35 Barnard, C.I. (1938) *The Functions of the Executive*. Cambridge: Harvard University Press.

36 Coutu, D.L. (2002) 'The anxiety of learning', *Harvard Business Review*, 80 (3): 100–6, especially p. 103.

37 Deal, T. and Kennedy, A. (1988) *Corporate Cultures: The Rites and Rituals of Corporate Life*. Harmondsworth: Penguin. p. 19.

38 Thompson, P. and McHugh, D. (2002) *Work Organizations: A Critical Introduction, Third Edition*. Houndmills, Basingstoke: Palgrave.

39 Bate, P. (1990) 'Using the culture concept in an organization development setting', *Journal of Applied Behavioural Science*, 26 (1): 83–106.

40 Deal, T. and Kennedy, A. (1999) *The New Corporate Cultures*. London: Textere.

41 Deal, T. and Kennedy, A. (1982) *Corporate Cultures*. Harmondsworth: Penguin.

42 Frost, P.J., Moore, L.F., Lundberg, C.C. and Martin, J. (1991) *Reframing Organizational Culture*. London: Sage.

43 Smircich, L. (1983) 'Concepts of culture and organizational analysis', *Administrative Science Quarterly*, 28 (3): 339–58.

44 Smith, P.B. and Peterson, M.E. (1988) *Leadership, Organizations and Culture*. London: Sage.

45 Kunda, G. (1992) *Engineering Culture: Control and Commitment in a High-tech Corporation*. Philadelphia: Temple University Press.

46 Van Maanen, J. and Kunda, G. (1989) '"Real feelings": emotional expression and organizational culture', in L.L. Cummings and B.M. Staw (eds), *Research in Organizational Behaviour*. Greenwich, CT: JAI Press. Vol. 11, pp. 43–104.

47 Hopfl, H. (1994) 'The paradoxical gravity of planned organizational change', *Journal of Organizational Change Management*, 7 (5): 20–31, especially p. 26.
48 Turnbull, S. (1999) 'Emotional labour in corporate change programmes', *Human Resource Development International*, 2 (2): 125–46, especially p. 136.
49 Coutu, D.L. (2002) 'The anxiety of learning', *Harvard Business Review*, 80 (3): 100–6, especially p. 106.
50 Schermerhorn, J., Hunt, J. and Osborn, R. (1988) *Managing Organizational Behavior*. New York: John Wiley and Sons.
51 Kreitner, R. (1995) *Management, 5th Edition*. Boston: Houghton Mifflin.

PART TWO
Emotional injuries

This part of the book examines circumstances in the workplace that leave emotional scars. They are revealed in different ways, such as the level of stress in an organization (Chapter 9), incidents of bullying and violence (Chapter 10), and sexual harassment (Chapter 11). They are also exposed in the traumas of 'downsizing' a workforce, where those who survive the shakeout become emotionally unfit for the very recovery that the organization desires (Chapter 12). Injurious work underscores organizations where power is abused, ethics ditched and feelings marginalized. It also reveals how human concerns can be overlooked or ignored in periods of economic myopia – when panic grips key decision makers. Why do these circumstances occur? Where does the responsibility lie – the worker, the management, the organization, or all three? What are the implications for reducing harm?

9

Stress as emotion and fashion

LEARNING OBJECTIVES

Stress has become a focus of how we fare, or survive, emotionally in the workplace. Stress has also become fashionable. This chapter explores how stress is used, abused and managed, discussing:

- Responsibility for stress – does it lie with the individual or the organization?
- Stress-sensitive and stress-mute organizations
- The nature of threat and organizational stressors
- Burnout, and blaming the victim
- Stress alleviation – myths and possibilities.

Stress is the second biggest cause of work-related illness. There are early warning signs you can look for and there are things that managers can do to reduce its effects. Next year sees the first management standards on stress in the workplace. You can be ready for them by phoning for your free Stress Action Pack today. Stress. Don't ignore it.[1]

Stress is a subject that is hard to avoid. Wherever you turn there are a multiplicity of guides on the nature of stress from psychologists, epidemiologists, therapists, consultants, journalists and so on. In academic texts or in popular media articles, we learn how stress is a fact of our busy modern lives, and how we should watch for the 'danger signs' of stress.[2]

Stress is everywhere, not least in the workplace. It has been called the disease of the twentieth and twenty-first century. We are in the Stress Age. Stress has now become an acceptable reason for being absent from work and, following in the footsteps of the USA, work stress in the UK has become a cause for litigation.[3] For example, in 1995 John Walker, a social worker, successfully sued his employer, Northumberland District Council, for their failure to prevent stress that led ultimately to his nervous breakdown. In 2000, a record compensation amount of over £200,000 was paid to a council worker for job-related stress.

The widespread use, and some say abuse, of stress, has also led to a backlash, some denying its existence. The criticism is that the stress label is now freely attached to just about any personal complaint and, despite volumes of research, it remains an elusive and problematic concept.[4, 5] There is force in this argument; stress is indeed becoming an overworked idea, yet its long 'popularity' suggests it is here to stay. Moreover, many of the indicators, or symptoms, of stress are decidedly emotional, such as doubt, despair, panic, worry, tension, frustration, confusion, depression, anxiety, fear and insecurity. Stress, as a concept, is unique in capturing such a cluster of feelings.[6–8]

THE CONTEXTS OF STRESS

Feelings of stress at work tell us that something is 'not right'. Stress-induced illnesses add to the picture: ailments such as heart and skin complaints, high blood pressure, back problems and migraines. Where does the responsibility for this lie? Is it with the stressed individual, who should be more resilient, or with the organization? What pressure does the organization put on the individual, such that stress is inevitable? This could be from long hours, conflicting expectations, job insecurity, or tasks that are clearly beyond the employee's qualifications or competence.

Finally, how does stress feature in the cultural ethos of an organization? In some organizations, for example, talking stress is regarded as a badge of honour. To appear stressed signals that you are a hard, committed worker. It also means that your weariness deserves respect, reward or remission. In contrast, there are organizations where *stress-muteness* is the dominant value. To admit to stress is to confess to a personal weakness, incompatible with being a strong manager, a tough police officer, an 'in control' doctor, fire-fighter or soldier.[9, 10] In these settings, stress is often denied by individuals and evaded by their organizations. In the event of a stress crisis, the stress-injured person is taken off their job for treatment or recuperation, or permanently removed from their post.

It is a particular irony that those who deal professionally with other people's stresses, such as psychiatrists, physicians and social workers, often find it difficult to voice their own stresses. I am reminded of a social worker I interviewed some years ago:

> In one of our meetings a social worker spoke with poignancy about her difficulties in coping with the demands of a particular client, when added to her home pressures. I asked her if she had shared her concerns with any of

her colleagues. 'Oh no!' she retorted, 'I wouldn't want to be social worked by them.' She then recoiled with a look of horror on her face. 'God, what am I saying? I can use my social work skills on clients but I can't accept them for myself?'[11]

Such confessions underline the stress trap of professionalism, where professional mystique is to be preserved, regardless of personal cost. Feelings of vulnerability, stress or incompetence are shielded, certainly from clients, but also from friends and colleagues, and often from oneself. The trap is reinforced by social expectations: certain professionals are to *appear* invulnerable, founts of wisdom, and rarely beset with the same problems experienced by ordinary mortals, such as their clients, patients, or consultees.

WHAT MAKES STRESS STRESSFUL?

Stress, in biological–evolutionary terms, is no accident and is more a blessing than a curse. In the face of physical threat and fear, the understanding goes, our cave-dwelling ancestors would be primed for action – for flight or fight. Arousal-inducing chemicals, such as adrenaline, would automatically flood the body. The person would be 'stressed' for action: dilated pupils, tensed muscles, sharpened hearing, raised blood pressure, and heart pumping. The elegance of this process for human survival is that it just happens, a genetically 'hardwired' programme that Charles Darwin would have much appreciated (see Chapter 2).

For evolutionary psychologists, who study the ancient pre-programming of human behaviour, fight-or-flight stress is a primitive and forceful emotional response, indelibly embedded in our nature. It is there to help our survival, especially in 'natural' organizational hierarchies where male dominance and competition prevail. Organizations that work against this evolutionary grain, who experiment with different organizational structures, will find stress more destructive than constructive.[12]

This is a controversial perspective. Are we really so tied to our Stone Age past that dysfunctional stress is inevitable in modern organizations? How do we know that Stone Age communities did not face their own social complexities, which could have been different, but no less burdensome than our own?[13–15] Can we assume, for instance, that men and women are programmed for similar flight-or-fight stress responses? Indeed, recent research suggests that, in the face of danger, women are more likely to 'tend-and-befriend' than fight-or-flight. They will run, but to their children to care and protect them, and to gather with other women for support and bonding.[16] We have to look closer at the biological, psychological and social context of stress to unpack its different elements.

THREAT, STRESS AND PERFORMANCE

Hans Seyle was a pioneer in exploring the physiological basis of stress. He identified a 'general adaptation syndrome' to threat as *perceived* by the individual.[17] The body generates an *alarm response,* which prepares it for *resisting* the threat. Significantly, however, prolonged exposure to the threat eventually depletes our capacity to resist and *exhaustion* sets in. That is when emotional-distress symptoms and stress-related diseases can begin to appear. But the twist in the stress tale is that it is cumulative. Different sources of threat, small and large, will add together to produce a larger effect. Prolonged low levels of stress accumulate and take a greater toll of the body, and thus increase symptoms of stress. We have, for example, the well-publicized relationship between stress and heart disease, due to long-term increases in blood pressure and heart rate. Prolonged stress suppresses the body's immune response, and increases susceptibility to viral and bacterial infection. Thompson and McHugh further add:

> . . . this model can be used to explain a multitude of phenomena from 'cold spots' in haunted houses (reduced bloodflow to the skin when something scares us) to 'butterflies in the stomach' when apprehensive or in love (reduced bloodflow to, and contraction of, the intestines).[18]

Selye offers an additional insight, often overlooked. Whereas most writers reserve the term stress for negative feelings, Selye postulated 'positive stress', the feelings and bodily activity that occur when we are psyched-up to face an important task. There is that peak feeling, or excitement, just before we race, compete, or get ready for a major challenge. Motivation and energy are high as the task ahead sparks many of the alarm reactions associated with negative stress, but they stimulate, rather than detract from, performance. It is when we become over-stressed that problems occur. This process is frequently represented as an inverted 'U' curve (see Figure 9.1) where, as the

FIGURE 9.1
The stress curve

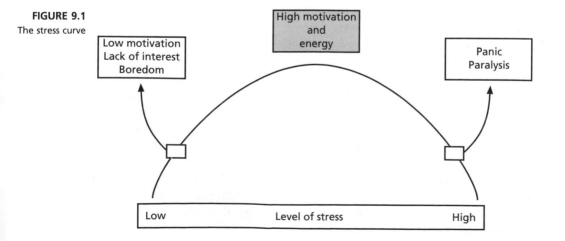

level of stress increases, performance shifts from initial listlessness, boredom and under-performance, to peak arousal and optimum performance (the top of the curve), to high anxiety, panic and desperation, where performance drops. Those fazed by examinations will readily recognize the pattern.

What's the threat?

What is, or is not, threatening will vary between individuals; people interpret danger differently. The gradient of the stress curve will depend on the issue and the person. Take, for example, promotion. For some people, promotion in their organization is a golden goal. Not only does it signal that they are valued by the organization, it promises extra status and financial reward. Consequently the annual appraisal and promotion round is met with antici-pation and trepidation. The psychological and material costs of failure are considerable: 'What if they think I'm no good? Maybe I *am* no good?' They are rapidly ascending the stress curve. After several sleepless nights, they are well over-stressed when the big day arrives. They cannot think clearly and become defensive and erratic in their responses to their appraiser's queries about their work-record.

By way of contrast, consider employees who have, for some time, regarded the prospect of promotion as more of a burden than a reward (unwanted extra responsibility, less free time). Moreover, their identity is far from submerged in their work. They like to do a competent job, but if they are seen under-performing in some areas, it is not something to 'take home' with them; little sleep will be lost. For them, appraisal is no big deal. When the day arrives they are relaxed about the event – a little too relaxed thinks their appraiser. They are barely in sight of the peak of the stress curve.

PERSONALITY OR SOCIAL CONTEXT?

The examples above show that the *personal meaning* of an event or situation is crucial. So, one person's threat can be another's opportunity or incon-sequence. Unless there is some perceived danger, stress reactions are unlikely to be triggered.

Personality

Personal meanings are partly biographical and partly social/cultural. The biographical element includes conscious and unconscious fears, long-held anxieties and vulnerabilities, and unmet aspirations. Psychoanalysts point to unresolved childhood and family tensions that are re-expressed in the workplace, rekindled when, for instance, we are judged, measured or evaluated.[19] The threats we feel are echoes from the past that have been suppressed or repressed because of the anxiety or pain they generate. They are now part of our personality and colour how we see the world and the way we react.

Our personality may be regarded as more or less 'neurotic', which has a bearing on stress.[20, 21] Neurotics are described as anxious, obsessive people, who are easily upset when things go wrong. Such predispositions have been incorporated into a profile of the 'stress-prone', or *Type A*, personality.[22–24] The person with a Type A personality is said to be quick to anger, has a sharp sense of time urgency and is excessively preoccupied with achievement. Type As work fast, do as much as they can in the day, keeping many 'balls in the air'. They will readily dominate others and will fly into a rage about issues that other people find quite trivial (such as in 'road rage'). One American self-assessment test for Type A personality includes the following items to agree, or disagree, with:[25]

> I have no patience for lateness.
> I hate to wait in most lines [queues].
> I feel guilty for taking time off from work.
> People tell me I have a bad temper when it comes to competitive situations.
> Even when I go on vacation, I usually take some work along.

Measuring and categorizing personality like this can be revealing. It has a long history, and chimes with our everyday tendency to pigeonhole people. Its weakness is that it freezes people in form and time. Once *labelled* in a particular, authoritative-sounding way ('Type A', 'neurotic', 'stressed') we can begin to *see* ourselves (and be seen) in that way and *behave* accordingly. Such is the nature of a self-fulfilling prophecy. Pencil-and-paper measures of personality have the added problem that the items can easily date, and rarely allow for the shades of meaning that we would wish to express.

Social contexts

Personality may go some way to explaining what becomes stressful, but it is only a part, and certainly partial, perspective on stress. An alternative, or complementary, position is that the social and organizational context is also very significant in explaining stress. By insisting that it is 'all to do with personality' we risk blaming the victim, rather than looking at the organization and its wider context.

The social context of stress is dramatically illustrated by *karoushi*, the Japanese term for 'sudden death from overwork'. The Japanese have been much admired for their diligence and extraordinary efforts at reconstructing their economy since the devastation of the Second World War. But in recent years some of the personal costs of this have come to light:

> Nakamura, an employee of a construction company, had recorded 135 hours of overtime around the time of his collapse. He was barely able to

squeeze in five hours of sleep a night. Assigned a job in Tokyo, he had to commute daily from Osaka for more than two months. Some days he worked so late that he spent the night in his office rather than trying to go home.[26]

The Nara Labor Standards Inspection Office ruled that the death of Taro Kimura, a worker in a ball-bearing factory, was caused by overwork. On his job, workers were not allowed to take any days off in order to keep the company's machines in operation for 24 hours a day.[27]

These tragic events are best understood as a consequence of oppressive, overbearing conditions of work. The most capable of individuals are likely to bend and break in such circumstances. The issue is reinforced by Japan's cultural tradition of hard work and mutual loyalty between employer and employee. These customs have recently proved doubly injurious as Japan enters recession. The historical one-employer-for-life concept has collapsed as all grades of workers have been displaced by unemployment. The threat to deeply ingrained pride, and intolerable shame, has forced some redundant managers and professionals onto the street, living rough. A number have committed suicide.[28]

Uncertainty and insecurity about work has also infected European workers. The pressure on those in employment, especially in the UK (where working hours are the highest in Europe) has led to a phenomenon of *presenteeism* (see Chapter 12). The fear of unemployment creates feelings of obligation to work all hours, regardless of personal stress and family strain. Once again, it is the wider social conditions that create the circumstances for such stress. Obviously, there will still be individual differences in how people interpret these circumstances, and some will be better equipped than others at coping with the threat of anticipated job loss. But the weight of pressure, and the levers to reduce that pressure, reside in the employment and organizational circumstances, beyond the normal reach of the individual employee. Responsibility for change here rests with managers, employers, trade unions and government.

Other organizational stressors

The organizational context of stress has been the subject of social research for many years. Checklists of potential organizational stressors regularly lengthen, to now include almost all features of an organization's culture, structure, decision-making processes, communications, and physical environment.[29, 30] There is an impression that just about anything can trigger stress. This may be true, but it is not particularly helpful to the overwhelmed practitioner. Targeting the major contributory factors is crucial, and the following are often revealed to be particularly significant:

- *Structures* Extreme organizational structures – either very rigid or very fluid and flexible (as is currently the vogue) – can particularly affect feelings and emotions. Rigid structures over-enclose some people; they feel stifled and denied room for self-expression. Conversely, loose and liberal structures offer some people too much psychological space, too few markers. They feel anxious and lost.

- *Superiors* Stress-provoking bosses tend to give inconsistent or inadequate instructions; fail to provide emotional support; over-emphasize productivity; and give feedback on poor, but not good, performance.[31, 32] 'Neurotic' leaders often create neurotic, stressed organizations.[33, 34]

- *Quantitative role overload* Too much work is, as our discussion of *karoushi* suggests, an obvious source of stress. Quantitative role overload comes about when the number, or frequency, of demands exceeds the jobholder's expectations of what is reasonable and manageable. While most of us manage periodic peaks in load, it is the persistence of quantitative overload that can be stressful.[35]

- *Qualitative role overload* This occurs when the job is beyond the worker's capacities – it is the *type* of work rather the amount. This may be a temporary blip as a new recruit learns the ropes, or when someone is transferred to a new position. Training as well as experience in the job can soften the stresses of qualitative overload. But when there is little organizational tolerance for inexperience, or the person is persistently working beyond his or her skills and abilities (such as being promoted to their 'level of incompetence'), then stress is more likely.

- *Role ambiguity* This is a further potential source of stress. Role ambiguity refers to how uncertain workers are about what their job entails because of mixed or vague demands from significant people who comprise their 'role set', such as superiors, colleagues and team members.[36]

- *Role conflict* Stress is more likely to occur when a person has conflicting expectations *within* their work role, or between separate, *competing* roles. For example, in my role as manager I am to do all I can to encourage my staff to develop and feel secure in their jobs. But this year I am also required to cut my training expenditure by half and not recommend any salary rises or promotions. How can I achieve all these requirements? This is within-role conflict. Competing-role conflict occurs when my position as chairman of the firm's environmental protection committee conflicts with my other position – company production manager. In the former role I know it is essential to redesign and update our pollution-control system, otherwise we will get prosecuted. But as production manager, I cannot afford any disruption to the production flow because, as it is, I am barely able to keep up with demand. Which way shall I turn?

The above organizational stressors are derived from studies that seek broad trends. As such, they cut across individual variations, differences in stress vulnerability or coping styles, and the nuances of particular organizational contexts. They are best read as starting points for 'stress housekeeping'. They are things to avoid, if possible, when designing, remodelling or managing an organization.

BURNOUT – THE FINAL INJURY?

What happens when failure to cope with threat is persistent; when stress keeps increasing and performance spirals downwards? We move to the bottom right-hand corner of the stress curve in Figure 9.1. In such chronic situations our on-the-run, ancestral caveman would probably have been dispatched by his mortal enemy, perhaps consumed – literally. The equivalent condition in today's workplace is being psychologically consumed. It is a state of *burnout*.

Burnout represents a condition of physical and emotional exhaustion combined with feelings of hopelessness and futility about work. Unrelenting job pressures transform the once hopeful and optimistic worker in to a cynic, who withdraws from colleagues and clients.[37–39] In principle, anyone who suffers prolonged stress at work can burn out, especially managers. But particularly vulnerable are those who work in helping, face-to-face professions, such as teachers, police, nurses and social workers. These occupations tend to attract people with high ideals about what they can achieve; and there lie the seeds of possible burnout.[40, 41]

Often, the expected achievements are not met. A combination of role overload, role conflict and resource scarcity gradually erodes enthusiasm.[42, 43] Clients (pupils, patients, offenders) frequently fail to improve as much as hoped, despite considerable personal effort from the worker. In the intensity of disillusionment, stress sets in. The worker's attitude gradually slides from caring to apathy. Emotional labour breaks down. Clients, once a source of challenge and excitement, are now no more than objects. Some are treated callously. It is a dramatic, self-protective, disengagement from the painful realties of the job. It is burnout.

Some of these patterns can be seen in accounts from practising social workers. Social work is often a highly rewarding profession, but is also especially emotionally demanding. The workers' high expectations and desire to help can sometimes flounder in the bureaucracy and intractability of the problems they face. Two social workers illustrate this.[44] The first is Jim, a young social worker, beset with disillusionment:

> When I first qualified, I was keen, eager and excited. I wasn't here for two weeks when my supervisor said, 'You're wearing the ticket – everyone's the same when they come out of college. Nothing's different. Calm down and you'll soon learn'. That smashed me – like a whack across the face. I always thought social workers were nice people – keen to help you. Actually, if I was a client I would think there are only five social workers here that I could trust and do their job well. This really frightens me. I'm tired generally. I want the job but the responsibility at times is too much, with all

the other things going on. My body is giving me warning signs. It's like having a clogged artery. I feel like chopping it off and a new one will grow. There's nothing holding me here.

The second is Ann, contemplating her emotional fitness for the job:

For the last six to eight months, I've been asking myself whether I should continue in social work – whether I've got enough to give – and I've run out. The job can be so depressing. Most of the people we deal with are inadequate. They're not going to change. You can't make up for years of deprivation. It makes me wonder – *why* do we bother? Why do we put up with the hassle? I really don't know. It's ridiculous when you look at the time and energy you put into someone when you know there will probably be no returns. And a lot of pain you get sometimes. Like a kid of mine just come up to court again. I could kill him – stupid idiot. It means that everything I've done for two years is wasted.

For some workers, however, burnout is no surprise – it is a normal part of being in a tough, stressful, occupation; an intrinsic part of the culture. It is something to accept and move through. Debra Meyerson reports the experiences of medical social workers in these terms.[45] One says:

It [burnout] means what we do here is stressful, that we are asked to always give and sometimes there isn't anything left to give, so we take a break and then we're OK.

Another reflects:

Burnout is the need to detach and I think that there is something healthy about letting yourself occasionally detach . . . And just like stress, it's not a bad thing when you start to feel the signs and symptom of stress. It's a warning to take care of yourself and it can be a very positive thing.

MAKING IT BETTER?

Can burnout and work-stress and be relieved or removed? Can the worst ravages be avoided or managed?

Burnout raises particular challenges because of its intensity, and the difficulty in communicating with people who have already withdrawn in despair. They are unlikely, for example, to be receptive to advice on how to relax or find purpose or joy in their workplace, which to them appears uniformly bleak. Against this gloomy backcloth there are, however, self-help groups who share their burnout experiences. Some are virtual. One website, for instance, calls itself FriedSocialWorker.com and offers resources, advice, as well as humour, to fellow sufferers.

The dominant wisdom, however, is that burnout is not a matter of poor attitude or individual weakness. The problem lies in organizational cultural expectations that (as we have seen) make burnout appear normal. The focus for change, therefore, is on the organizational procedures, expectations and conflicts that lead to unfettered emotional demands, frustrated aspirations and disillusionment. Maslach and Leiter, notable writers on burnout,[46] recommend that managers should ensure that:

- Staff have sufficient time and resources to accomplish their work.
- The needs of clients should be put above reducing costs.
- A sense community is fostered among workers, not eroded by demands for ever more production.
- Trust is cultivated by fairly applying staff evaluations, promotions and benefits.
- Personal worth is not undermined through tasks that staff regard as unethical, contrary to their personal values.

Such well-meaning prescriptions have major implications for the culture of the whole enterprise, and can easily fall on deaf ears in an overwrought organization. The key is to engineer change from the very top of the organization, where the organization's approach towards burnout is formed, and where strategic decisions are made.

Where stress is more generally addressed, it has been predominately victim-centred. Spurred by the cost to industry from stress-related absence, illness and litigation, company 'wellness' programmes have been developed to help individuals cope better with stress. Typically, they are reactive more than proactive, aimed at people who are already stressed. For example, Pepsico has 'fitness' centres; the US Control Data Corporation has a 'Stay-well' programme; Digital Equipment and the Trustee Savings Bank developed stress-management programmes.[47–49] Many companies use external stress consultants to run their programmes. These services are often inaccessible to smaller (but no less stressed) firms, because of their high costs.[50]

The rationale of such interventions is to reduce stress by making the employee more resilient, a better coper. Approaches include physical exercise, biofeedback (taking one's own pulse and breathing rate), assertiveness training (learning how to understand stressful situations and identify their causes), and behavioural self-control (learning more effective time-management and ways to cope with stress). Stress counselling is a favoured tool in helping people re-frame problems and reduce their threat. The efficacy of these techniques is mixed.[51–53] Participants often feel good in the short-term, but the sensation quickly fades, especially when returning to the same stressful conditions from which they have temporally escaped.[54] This is reminiscent of the UK's First World War approach to 'shell shocked' (traumatically stressed) officers. They were removed from their front-line posts to a safe, therapeutic, country house. When they showed some signs of improvement they were sent straight back into the heat of battle.

By saying 'what's wrong with him/her?' and 'treating' the individual, the organization avoids the more uncomfortable question of 'what's wrong with us?' It places the major responsibility for doing something onto the shoulders of the victim, who can be stigmatized as sick, weak or inadequate. Stress is individualized and privatized; the victim is blamed for their condition. This is a controversial, ideologically loaded, perspective. The UK's Labour Research Department makes the point:

> Where they exist, management 'stress control' programmes peddle individual victim-blaming approaches to stress problems that can only be solved by changing workplace organization and relations.[55]

Other observers, such as Thompson and McHugh, also raise concerns:

> At its worst, employee counselling often consists of a short interview with a hired-in consultant in response to episodic or acute problems, which cannot be solved in this fashion. What is taking place is, in effect, the location of the problem in the context of 'organizational reality' as in 'you need to pull your socks up or you'll be in trouble' . . . The role of the organization in producing unhealthy systems and condition of work is in danger of being ignored.[56]

An additional difficulty for stress programmes, be they victim or organization focused, is the interaction of work and non-work experiences. There is no, neat, psychological boundary between the two. Dealing with threatening life events will take its toll, irrespective of source.[57–59] There are the ups and downs of family life, failing personal relationships, divorce, deaths, pregnancy, personal injury or illness, a sick child, moving house or financial pressures. At work, we can try to cope, but the emotion work in maintaining an 'OK' face can be costly. The consequent stress will reflect in our moods, our performance, our level of tolerance and our health. A stress-tolerant organization is likely to pick up on these signs and respond sensitively and supportively – at an individual and organizational level.

CONCLUSION

Stress has become part of everyday talk about feelings at work, a powerful discourse with significant consequences. That is a social fact, regardless of squabbles about what stress 'really is', or whether it 'really exists'. When stress is not the thing to admit to in public, it is hidden in private corners or medicalized – taken to a physician or counsellor. Stress is then caught in a system that, in effect, makes stress more stressful. It loads the issue onto the backs of sufferers, rather than into the organization where the conditions and culture of stress can often exist.

Despite the increased openness about stress, it is still met uneasily by many organizations, and by individuals who are ashamed to admit that they cannot cope. Token responses, such as wellness programmes, tend to sideline stress, deflecting it from the everyday organizational practices that can produce stress in the first place. Stress, also, has now become a political tool, regardless of its personal symptoms. It is something for trade unions to negotiate about and for managers to be defensive about – because it can lead to litigation.

It would be naïve to believe that work stress is something that should, or indeed could, be entirely eliminated. The fluctuating threats – to our self-esteem, our competence, our relationships and our livelihoods – are a permanent feature of working and living. This does not, however, let organizations off the hook. Organizations can produce and sustain an emotional culture where damaging levels of stress are driven underground ('it doesn't really exist here'); grudgingly tolerated ('yeah, we all have live with high stress here, that's how it is'); deflected ('we send them to see our medics'), or even celebrated ('stress is what makes a manager a manager here; those who can't hack it have to leave'). Stress, in this sense, is a crude litmus test on how an organization is prepared to confront and talk about emotion, especially its difficult emotions. It gives us an 'instant' readout on the way emotionality is received, politicized and legitimized.

To cut through the cultural strands that buttress stress requires several initiatives. Societal pressure is one, such as from high-profile governmental initiatives, media exposés, trade union action, legal mechanisms and management education. Within organizations, stress-sensitive managerial approaches can permeate all levels of decision making. In practice, that means designing systems that (a) acknowledge that stress happens, (b) minimize the worst of conflicts, tensions and inconsistencies, (c) provide a climate that supports, rather than marginalizes the stressed, and (d) use these experiences to constantly review their cultural practices.

FURTHER READING

Cartwright, S. and Cooper, C.L. (1997) *Managing Workplace Stress*. London: Sage.

Kinchin, D. (2001) *Post Traumatic Stress Disorder: The Invisible Injury*. Didcot, Oxfordshire: Success Unlimited.

Maslach, C. and Leiter, M.P. (1997) *The Truth About Burnout*. San Francisco: Jossey Bass.

Newton, T., Handy, J. and Fineman, S. (1995) *'Managing' Stress: Emotion and Power at Work*. London: Sage.

REFERENCES

1 UK Government Health and Safety Executive, September 2002.

2 Newton, T., Handy, J. and Fineman, S. (1995) *'Managing' Stress: Emotion and Power at Work*. London: Sage. p. 5.

3   Cooper, C. and Payne, R. (1978) *Stress at Work*. New York: Wiley.

4   Preston, A. (2000) 'An elusive but expensive concept: stress', *Financial Times* (2 June), London.

5   Briner, R. and Reynolds, S. (1993) 'Bad theory and bad practice in occupational stress', *The Occupational Psychologist*, 19: 8–13.

6   Lazarus, R.S. and Cohen-Charash, Y. (2001) 'Discrete emotions in organizational life', in R.L. Payne and C. Cooper (eds), *Emotions at Work*. Chichester: Wiley.

7   Fineman, S. (1995) 'Stress, emotion and intervention', in T. Newton (ed.), *'Managing' Stress: Emotion and Power at Work*. London: Sage.

8   Ivancevich, J.M., Matteson, M.T., Freedman, S.M. and Phillips, J.S. (1990) 'Worksite stress management interventions', *American Psychologist*, 45: 252–61.

9   Fineman, S. (1996) 'Emotion and organizing', in S. Clegg, C. Hardy and W. Nord (eds), *Handbook of Organization Studies*. London: Sage.

10   Hearn, J. (1993) 'Emotive subjects: organizational men, organizational masculinities and the (de)construction of "emotions"', in S. Fineman (ed.), *Emotion in Organizations*. London: Sage.

11   Fineman, S. (1985) *Social Work Stress and Intervention*. Aldershot: Gower. p. 100.

12   Nicholson, N. (1997) 'Evolutionary psychology: towards a new view of human nature and organisational society', *Human Relations*, 50 (9): 1053–78.

13   Newton, T., Handy, J. and Fineman, S. (1995) *'Managing' Stress: Emotion and Power at Work*. London: Sage. p. 5.

14   Pollock, K. (1988) 'On the nature of social stress: production of modern mythology', *Social Science and Medicine*, 26: 381–92.

15   Sahlins, M.D. (1972) *Stone Age Economics*. Chicago: Aldine-Atherton.

16   Taylor, S.E., Kleine, L.C., Lewis, B.P., Gruenwald, T.L., Regan, A.R.G. and Updegraff, J.A. (2000) 'Biobehavioral responses to stress in females: tend-and-befriend, not fight-or-flight', *Psychological Review*, 107 (3): 411–29.

17   Selye, H. (1956) *The Stress of Life*. New York: McGraw-Hill.

18   Thompson, P. and McHugh, D. (2002) *Work Organizations: A Critical Introduction, Third Edition*. Houndmills, Basingstoke: Palgrave. p. 202.

19   Gabriel, Y. (1999) *Organizations in Depth: The Psychoanalysis of Organizations*. London: Sage.

20   Czander, W.M. (1993) *The Psychodynamics of Work Organizations: Theory and Applications*. London: Guilford Press.

21   Eysenck, H. (1965) *Fact and Fiction in Psychology*. Harmondsworth: Penguin.

22   Friedman, H.S. and Booth-Kewley, S. (1987) 'Validity of the Type A construct: a reprise', *Psychological Bulletin*, 104 (3): 381–84.

23 Friedman, M. and Rosenman, R. (eds) (1974) *Type A Behavior and Your Heart*. New York: Alfred A. Knopf.

24 Mathews, K.A. (1982) 'Psychological perspectives on the Type A behavior pattern', *Psychological Bulletin*, 91: 293–323.

25 Hellriegel, D., Slocum, J.W. and Woodman, R.W. (1995) *Organizational Behavior*. Minneapolis/St Paul: West. p. 254.

26 Hellriegel, D., Slocum, J.W. and Woodman, R.W. (1995) *Organizational Behavior*. Minneapolis/St Paul: West. p. 247.

27 Hellriegel, D., Slocum, J.W. and Woodman, R.W. (1995) *Organizational Behavior*. Minneapolis/St Paul: West. p. 247.

28 Hoffman, J.W. (1998) 'The dark side of dedication' <http://www.outsider.gol.com/magazine/june/article.html>.

29 Rollinson, D. and Broadfield, A. (2002) *Organisational Behaviour and Analysis*. Harlow: Pearson Education.

30 Champoux, J.E. (1996) *Organizational Behavior*. Minneapolis: West.

31 Fox, M.L.D., Dwyer, D.J. and Ganster, D.C. (1993) 'Effects of stressful job demands and control on physiological and attitudinal outcomes in a hospital setting.' *Academy of Management Journal*, 31 (2): 289–318.

32 Fieldman, G. (2002) 'Your boss could be damaging your health', *New Scientist*, 173 (2324, 5 January): 11.

33 Kets de Vries, M.F.R. and Miller, D. (1984) *The Neurotic Organization*. San Francisco: Jossey Bass.

34 Kets de Vries, M.F.R. (1999) 'What's playing in the organizational theater? Collusive relationships in management', *Human Relations*, 52 (6): 745–62.

35 Styhre, A., Ingelgard, A., Beausang, P., Castenfors, M., Mulec, K. and Roeht, J. (2002) 'Emotional management and stress: managing ambiguities', *Organization Studies*, 23 (1): 83–103.

36 Kahn, R.L., Wolfe, D.M., Quinn, R.P., Snoek, J.D. and Rosenthal, R.A. (1964) *Organizational Stress: Studies in Role Conflict and Ambiguity*. New York: Wiley.

37 Maslach, C. (1982) *Burnout: The Cost of Caring*. Englewood Cliffs, NJ: Prentice-Hall.

38 Paine, W.S. (1982) *Job Stress and Burnout*. California: Sage.

39 Pines, A. and Aronson, E. (1989) *Career Burnout*. New York: Free Press.

40 Evans, B.K. and Fischer, D.G. (1993) 'The nature of burnout: a study of the three-factor model of burnout in human service and non-human service samples,' *Journal of Occupational and Organizational Psychology*, 66 (1): 29–38.

41 Firth, H. and Britton, P. (1989) 'Burnout, absence and turnover amongst British nursing staff', *Journal of Occupational Psychology*, 62 (1): 61–77.

42 Edelwich, J. and Brodsky, A. (1980) *Burn Out*. New York: Human Sciences Press.

43 Cordes, C.L. and Dougherty, T.W. (1993) 'A review and integration of research on job burnout', *Academy of Management Review*, 18 (3): 621–56.

44 Fineman, S. (1985) *Social Work Stress and Intervention*. Aldershot: Gower. p. 41.

45 Meyerson, D.E. (2000) 'If emotions were honoured: A cultural analysis', in S. Fineman (ed.), *Emotion in Organizations, 2nd Edition*. London: Sage. pp. 167–83, especially p. 171.

46 Maslach, C. and Leiter, M.P. (1997) *The Truth About Burnout*. San Francisco: Jossey Bass.

47 Cooper, C.L. (1984) 'What's new in . . . stress', *Personnel Management*, (June): 40–44.

48 McKenna, E. (2000) *Business Psychology and Organisational Behavior*. Hove: Psychology Press.

49 Lucas, M. (1986) *How to Survive the 9–5*. Thames: Methuen.

50 Merrick, N. (1998) 'Getting to grips', *People Management*, (December): 39–41.

51 Cooper, C. and Sadri, G. (1991) 'The impact of stress counselling at work', in R.L. Perrewe (ed.), *Handbook of Job Stress*. Corte Madera, CA: Select Press.

52 Elkin, A.J. and Rosch, P.J. (1990) 'Promoting mental health in the workplace: the prevention side of stress management', *Occupational Medicine: State of the Art Review*, 5 (4): 739–54.

53 Reynolds, S., Taylor, E. and Shapiro, D.A. (1993) 'Session impact in stress management training', *Journal of Occupational and Organisational Psychology*, 66 (2): 99–113.

54 Briner, R. (1999) 'Against the grain', *People Management*, 30 (September): 32–41.

55 LRD (1988) 'Stress at work: the trade union response'. Labour Research Department, London. p. 2.

56 Thompson, P. and McHugh, D. (2002) *Work Organizations: A Critical Introduction, Third Edition*. Houndmills, Basingstoke: Palgrave. p. 283.

57 Dohrenwend, B.S. and Dohrenwend, B.P. (eds) (1974) *Stressful Life Events*. New York: Wiley.

58 Holmes, T.H. and Rahe, R.H. (1967) 'The social readjustment rating scale', *Journal of Psychosomatic Research*, 28 (3): 222–41.

59 Perkins, D.V. (1982) 'The assessment of stress using life events', in P.S. Goldberger and S. Breznitz (eds), *The Handbook of Stress*. New York: Free Press.

Bullying and violence at work

LEARNING OBJECTIVES

Bullying and violence are the dark side of work life. They are often hidden but invariably devastating for victims.

- Who bullies? Who are the victims? What are the emotional explanations?
- Bullying and violence involve a victim, a perpetrator and the organizational culture.
- Violence can be intrusive, consumer-related or organizational.
- Directions for action.

The tears ran down my face, hidden by my surgical mask. My consultant continued relentlessly, 'Why can't you do this? It really isn't hard. Are you stupid? Can't you see how to help me?'

I hated myself for crying. I avoided her eyes so she couldn't see my tears and the deep hurt in my eyes, but I couldn't speak without betraying myself. I managed a few one-word answers. The criticism continued, if not with words, then with sighs and angry tutting. The atmosphere in the operating theatre was tense. The staff had all seen this happen many times before – hard working, pleasant trainees reduced to non-functioning wrecks in the space of an operation. I looked helplessly at the scrub nurse, another trainee. She saw my distress immediately and gave me a supporting glance. But she too was suffering. 'No, not that one. Why do we have to have trainees in my operations? Not like that,' she lashed out at the scrub nurse. Another hard working, competent trainee, now shaking and anxious, her self-confidence fast diminishing.

I didn't know what to do. I felt uncomfortable continuing in such distress . . . Three hours of hostility and criticism. At the end I ripped off my mask and gloves and turned, only to find her standing behind me. She registered my swollen eyes and tear stained face in complete silence. I have never seen such a cold, emotionless stare, and I hope never to again.

I continued in this post for the complete six months, becoming increasingly anxious and depressed. I left my post feeling suicidal. I am now taking a year away from medicine . . . Despite being told that she treated everyone this way, I believed it was all my fault.[1]

My victimisation started in early 1998 straight after the redundancies. It was only by a fluke of luck that I was not made redundant. First of all my pay was affected. Then I was singled out. I was made a 'floating' labourer, the only one out of 8 other labourers to do so. I was to report to a supervisor every morning to find out where I was working. I was never allowed to settle or gain a routine, and an even more degrading job would be waiting for me every time I complained. I was the only one of 600 men to have to do this. I had served 8 years at the factory without having to do these things before. It was only after the introduction of the new management that things turned downhill.

It was like a cloud of evil had descended on the factory. Everyone was afraid of this evil. I complained to the recently 'elected' shop convenor. It was obvious that this man was a union man in name only, you could actually smell his apathy. This only made things worse.

I knew that I was being harassed and bullied, I felt like I was being forced into resigning. Every reasonable step I took to resolve my situation was refused or worse I was totally ignored. All the time my treatment seemed to get harsher. I was given totally menial tasks, which when complained about would result in me being given physically impossible tasks. It was like I was being mentally tortured by an experienced torturer.

To cut a long story short I eventually suffered a breakdown in October 1998. This not only devastated me but all my family too . . . I was re-diagnosed in June 2001 as suffering from 'stress reaction' to a real situation.[2]

These are people who have felt bullied at work. Someone more powerful has, in their view, deliberately intimated and persecuted them. The effects have been disastrous; the feelings and emotions are raw. Bullying is psychologically violent, and violating, elevating work-stress to extreme levels. The violence can also be more openly physical – either as part of a bullying work culture, or as a hazard of the type of work undertaken. This chapter will explore these issues, and the questions they raise for organizations.

UNDERSTANDING BULLYING

It is a sombre fact that bullying occurs in work settings, as the above confessions attest. Bullying can be found in blue- and white-collar jobs, among highly experienced professionals and with new trainees. A 2000 report by the European Foundation for the Improvement of Living and Working Conditions, estimates that there are some 12 million people subjected to psychological violence at work through bullying.[3] A British study, published in the same year, surveyed 5,300 employees. Forty-seven per cent of them had witnessed bullying in the previous five years, and one in ten said that they had been bullied in the previous six months.[4]

Bullying can inflict potent emotional injuries, more devastating than any other form of social stress in workplace. Victims of workplace bullying report insomnia, melancholy, nervousness, apathy, lack of concentration, fear of social groups, depression and psychosomatic complaints.[5, 6] Some will commit suicide.[7] These reactions have been associated with 'post-traumatic stress disorder', a cluster of severe emotional reactions – sometimes delayed – following a deeply shocking experience. If untreated, they can stay with a person for a lifetime.[8]

Bullying rarely 'just happens'. The target of bullying is usually entangled in escalating conflict at work that culminates in actual bullying.[9] The bully's aim is to humiliate, frighten, intimidate or punish the victim through teasing, badgering and insults. The victim eventually feels helpless, unable to retaliate. Indeed, bullies rely on their victims feeling so demoralized, their confidence so undermined, that they cannot be bothered to resist – and in so doing, they play into the bully's hands.[10]

Common bully-tactics include ridiculing others, attacking their competence, public humiliation and verbal and physical threats. Less direct, but no less injurious, is to socially isolate the victim and change their work task so that it is difficult, or demeaning, to perform (such as in the second story above). When such events are part of the culture of an organization, we can speak meaningfully of *organizational bullying*. Bullies, therefore, can be collectives as well as individuals.[11, 12] Group bullying, or 'mobbing' (the European terminology), can be especially brutal. It is often treated as an enjoyable, predatory, game by its perpetrators. Guilt is diffused amongst the group, so lessening any individual feelings of misdeed. Such behaviour can be found in authoritarian settings such as the military, on the factory floor, and in some schools.

In Japan, schoolteachers have sometimes become accomplices in the mobbing of school children. Jacqueline Treml describes the suicide note of a tormented 8th grade, Japanese boy, telling of his long-term physical and psychological torment. He once arrived at school to a particular humiliation. His desk was used as an altar and a card was left for him, signed by all who attended his 'funeral'. Four teacher's 'joined in the fun', signing the card *'May he rest in peace'*. The victim was useful to both students and teacher – in fusing together the class. One teacher hesitantly confessed: 'when someone in my class is being bullied, the rest of the class becomes animated and class work becomes much easier'.[13] Treml points to the Japanese proverb, *The nail that sticks up gets hammered down*, as indicative of the societal value placed on conformity. It contrasts to the Western emphasis on individuality, such as: *Just because everyone else is doing it doesn't mean you have to.* The boy took his own life. His teachers said he was a weak person.

Defining bullying

Such incidents raise the question of what constitutes bullying? Some definitions are broadly encompassing and complex, of the sort: *repeated practices that are directed to one or more workers, unwanted by the victim, which may deliberately or unconsciously cause humiliation and offence, and may also interfere with job performance.*[14] Others, with an eye on legal niceties, emphasize specific times and frequencies, such as at least once a week for a period of six months. Different practitioners have their different slants. There are personnel officers, for instance, who look upon physical contact, isolation, non-cooperation, victimization, and setting impossible deadlines, as bullying. But they regard gossip, slander, offensive posters, graffiti, offensive language and obscene gestures, as harassment – a lesser sin. In contrast, trade union officials consider all of these behaviours as bullying.[15]

Bullying, while often devastating to the victim, is enmeshed in the social constituency in which it occurs. Its meanings, causes and consequences are, almost invariably, contested. Like feeling 'stressed', it has now become prevalent to use the language of 'bullying' to describe a wide range of felt injustices in the workplace. This does not dilute its psychological validity, however it makes bullying harder to pin down in specific terms. For the victim, this can be like opening a Pandora's box of troubles that exacerbate, rather than relieve, their distress. In the UK, should the victim go to law, he or she will find no direct protection against bullying. The case has to be based on the nearest suitable law, which can range from stalking and sex discrimination, to health and safety.

The examples at the beginning of this chapter, as well as the tragic tale of the Japanese schoolchild, underline, how institutionally unsupported a victim can feel, especially when they are seen as 'the problem':

> 'It's really his own fault'
> 'She's far too touchy',
> 'He exaggerates; wants to make trouble',
> 'A neurotic person'

Like the accounts of whistleblowers in Chapter 7, the victim's complaints can ruffle the established order of the organization, so they are treated lightly or rejected outright. As they are 'difficult' people, their bullying claims 'must be' exaggerations, or pure fantasy.[16–18]

Who bullies and why?

Bullying is associated with differences in power and status. Superiors are the main culprits. Their victims appear to suffer more than the victims of co-worker bullying.[19, 20] Nearly 20 per cent of 761 UK public-sector workers claimed to have been repeatedly bullied, mostly by their managers. The experience left them feeling undermined and powerless and angry.[21]

The aim of bullying, in many victims' eyes, is to expel them from the company or community; to get rid of them. Mobbing is regarded as conspiratorial, where a person with a grudge mobilizes others against the victim.[22] Any apparent difference or personal characteristic can attract a bully's attention, such as extremes in work performance, religion, ethnicity, gender, sexual preference, handicap or status. In some occupations, such as fast food, its low status marks out the worker for bullying – from customers. These may be physical assaults (see later section of this chapter) or public humiliation. A New York fast-food cashier explains:

> When the customer come in, if they have to wait on their food they be nasty to you and then they say. 'You better be glad you have this job because I think it is the only job you can get'.[23]

However, not everyone bullies and not everyone is bullied, so we have to take a closer look at the bully–bullied relationship to appreciate its dynamics.

The bully   A dominant perspective is that the root of the problem lies with the tormenter. It is the individual bully's own emotional problems, or psychopathology, that creates what he or she is. The typical bully, it is suggested, has a fragile self-esteem derived from troublesome life experiences, possibly being bullied themselves as a child. At work, these feelings are acted out by diminishing others. Some bullies are said to show symptoms of a *narcissistic personality disorder*.[24, 25] Narcissists are deeply obsessed with themselves and their own accomplishments, to the exclusion of others. They are interpersonally exploitative, taking advantage of others to achieve their own ends. They want attention, are emotionally cold, and are unable to appreciate the feelings and needs of others. We have remarkably little information on the explanations that bullies give for their own behaviour, other than the target 'deserved it', or that the conventional rules on how to treat others only apply to 'losers'.

The victim   Could victims be complicit in their own fate? In some manner 'inviting' the bullying? This view deeply divides people. Many find the very suggestion repugnant.[26, 27] Why should anyone set up situations in which they will be attacked and diminished? Because, claim some psycho-analytic writers, of their own sense of guilt and worthlessness. Unconsciously they will feel they deserve the punishment meted out to them, while consciously they may not feel they have contributed in any way to the bullying.[28] Victims with a 'general anxiety disorder' that existed before the bullying will, it is argued, contribute both to triggering and intensifying the bullying.[29]

There is a danger in taking any one of these positions as *the* explanation for bullying. Both explanations neglect the organizational context that makes bullying more or less possible, and victims deserve protection, not blaming, whatever their emotional background.

The bullying culture

A cultural perspective highlights the apathy, acquiescence, or antagonism towards bullying that is embedded within the organization's culture.[30] Bullies will bully only if they have the explicit or implicit support of their colleagues and superiors. Turning a blind eye, perhaps fearful of confrontation, is tantamount to accepting bullying. Without that, bullies are aware that they are vulnerable to censure or punishment.

Workgroup climates will vary. Bullying, or bullying-like, behaviour can be proscribed, quietly tolerated or, in some cases, even celebrated. The Fire Service, where bullying is often endemic, is a powerful illustration. I here draw on David Archer's revealing description of a UK Fire Brigade.[31]

CASE STUDY

The UK Fire Service is a culture based on power. It is structured by rank and has a highly prescriptive discipline code. It has all the trappings of a paramilitary organization where obedience to orders is paramount. Its long-standing traditions favour the employment of white males, for whom exclusion from their buddy group is a powerful reason to not to fall foul of local conventions and practices.

Archer interviewed two groups, 21 people in all. The first group included those who had experienced bullying directly as a victim or a witness. The second comprized those who had dealt with the outcomes of incidents of bullying, such as senior officers, equal opportunities managers, welfare officers, occupational health doctors and union officials. More than 20 per cent of respondents reported experiences of bullying. They spoke of isolation and exclusion, offensive sexual innuendo, being targeted as a 'volunteer', and unnecessary physical contact. Some were set unachievable work objectives, faced intimidatory discipline, or were denied access to training.

Managers behaved in ways that they believed were expected of them by the organization. Being a 'strong', results-driven, manager was part of this, a style that condoned behaviour that could be unacceptable in other organizations. The Brigade Equal Opportunities Officer made the point: 'When we referred to the person as an officer bully, the reply was, "He gets things done"'.

People adopted bullying behaviours if they saw them as influential and valued, especially for promotion. A fire fighter, and victim of bullying, described this as a 'tradition' in the Service, while another asserted that it was a tradition that 'hurts a lot of guys'. Management regarded the physical abuse of new recruits as 'horseplay', which contributed to 'team building', 'character formation' and 'bonding'. It was a matter of pride to the Equal Opportunities Officer that he had been harassed on joining the Service; it had 'made him a man'. Everyone was at risk of being bullied, but some more than others:

'Anyone can be a victim of bullying – but if you are in a minority by either gender or race – the likelihood is dramatically increased.' (Fire fighter)

'There's no room for diversity on watches, they are looking for a type. If the person doesn't conform then the culture is we have got to change the person to meet the type.' (Union official)

'Differences' that raised a person's risk of being a victim, included: not liking football, not wishing to go to the pub each day, possessing a university degree, being female, being young, being black or simply being keen to pass examinations.

This case demonstrates the way bullying behaviour can penetrate the cultural warp and weft of an organization. It is not simply an issue of victim and perpetrator. Bullying is broadly accepted, or tolerated, intrinsic to what the organization is and always has been. For management, it is so taken for granted that it has become regarded as an essential ingredient in the socialization of workers. The institutionalization of bullying in this manner (like the institutionalization of racism) leaves victims feeling especially powerless and alone. Their emotional costs are not counted because they are not seen, or looked for, as 'costs'. They are invisible, filtered through the sieve of 'tradition', with its machismo pride and prejudice.

Helping the odd victim, or expelling the obvious bully, does not achieve change in these circumstances. It requires a root-and-branch examination of the way the organization perpetuates bullying through its power structure. And then, how the old-order can be reformed through, what change literature calls 'second order change' – the radical questioning of the very organizational assumptions that keep bullying alive.[32, 33]

Bullying without a bully

A cultural perspective on bullying raises the possibility of the bully *being* the organization, rather than a single individual, or a definite group of people. In other words, victims see features of the organization's style, expectations, or procedures as oppressive, and, in their eyes, bullying. A study by Andreas Liefooghe and Kate Mackenzie Davey[34] nicely illustrates this. They encouraged UK telecommunications employees to talk, in any way they liked, about bullying. They all worked in call centres dealing with telesales or customer complaints.

No one felt bullied in the traditional, person-to-person sense, but many regarded organizational practices as bullying – such as the way statistics were used against them, call-handling time, sickness policy, and threats of dismissal and discipline. In their own words:

> It's quite an oppressive environment that we work in. Umm. We have to work within strict confines. It damages your self-esteem, it makes you feel worthless . . . I think we kind of, it's a bit of a robotic process, we all become numbers . . . I feel bullied by the statistics.

> I mean, getting back to the call-handling time, that could be construed as bullying or manipulating. I mean the number of times some us need to seek advice or help from other areas . . . No sooner do you get through then you get cut off you know and I'm sure that's only because that person has had a bad day and is worrying about their call handling time . . . Everyone, is like, scared stiff . . .

There were oblique references to the culprits 'up there', but the blame was more often attributed to the organization as a whole. Even the managers themselves felt trapped by the culture:

> I always hate to think that any of my people are bullied, and I would hope they, um. There are things that I do as a manager that I don't want to do . . . But there are some things that you have to do . . .

An organizational culture that bullies, like a culture that supports bullying, is far more difficult to deal with than isolating an individual bully and his or her victim. Call-centres, for example, epitomize new work arrangements where skills are routinized, running costs pared down to the bare minimum, and the surveillance of workers often close and unforgiving. Workers can feel especially powerless in such circumstances, unable to influence the conditions of work they regard as bullying – scary, demeaning, stressful. An organization that profits from such conditions exploits a mobile, floating, population of relatively unskilled workers. In the absence of more enlightened senior management, change needs to come from external pressure – government, legal measures and unionization.

WORKING DIRECTLY WITH VIOLENCE

> The reality for many workers in this new millennium can involve being sworn at, spat upon, insulted on racial grounds or being physically attacked in the course of their work.[35]

Much of what we have discussed so far entails psychological violence in the workplace. Violence begets violent emotions, such as rage, anger, revenge and betrayal. It inevitably trades on fear, although reactions can vary over time and are intimately connected with the subjective meaning of the event to the victim.[36, 37] Of the many faces of workplace violence, some are more direct, physical and brutal. There are at least three different forms: *intrusive*, *consumer-related* and *organizational*.[38]

Intrusive violence

Intrusive violence is the 'smash and grab' sort: criminal threat or assault in vulnerable work settings such as banks, post offices, or places where drugs are stored (pharmacies, doctors' surgeries). Doctors out on-call have been assaulted for the drugs they may be carrying.[39] Violence in these situations is aimed at removing, or 'neutralizing', the worker, who stands on the path of a much-desired object. Recent forms of intrusive violence have been terrorist attacks on aircraft, where flight staff and passengers are taken as hostages to the terrorists' cause.

Intrusive violence has its fashions. As I write, UK farmers of genetically modified produce, and organizations that specialize in the use of animals for experimentation, are vulnerable to violent protest. More widely, activists in the 'anti-capitalist' movement have targeted businesses such as McDonald's and international banks as symbols of their grievances, sometimes with tragic results for the staff. Such events confront workers with violence that can injure, maim, or even cost them their lives. In response, many organizations have enhanced their security procedures, a move that can reassure staff, but also create oppressive feelings of working in a fortress. Victims of intrusive violence can be plagued with stress symptoms well after the event.

Consumer-related violence

There is consumer violence towards employees. 'Flight rage', for example, puts flight attendants at risk, when passengers, sometimes inebriated, often rowdy, assault them. Journalists and international peacekeepers are exposed to violence when they work in highly charged, tense, situations. Fast food and pub workers can be subject to physical ill treatment from customers. However, it is care-and-control professionals that are most vulnerable: social workers, nurses, police officers, security staff, traffic wardens, psychiatrists, lawyers, and judges.

The first recorded fatality of such a worker is thought is to be a nurse in the mid-nineteenth century. Social workers were regarded a high-risk group from the mid-1970s.[40] The control exerted by these professionals is always precarious, liable to be resented and resisted, so it is no accident that skills of defusing violence are often part of their training. But we need also to look beyond the immediate worker for explanations. Government policies, such as cutbacks, can adversely affect public services by increasing waiting times. They can try the patience of customers and increase the risk of violence to employees. For instance, waiting many hours to be treated in a hospital Accident and Emergency Unit can foment frustration and trigger aggression in some patients. Sometimes it is wiser to seek ways of reducing waiting times and queues, rather than focus exclusively on ways of policing and restraining violent patients.[41]

Psychologists and psychiatrists dealing with 'difficult' clients can be subject to sudden, and seemingly unprovoked, violence. One such instance is described by Breakwell,[42] which reveals some of the reasons behind the attack.

CASE STUDY

A 21 year old woman hit her psychiatrist across the head and repeatedly punched him about the torso when he suggested that she might consider having an abortion. As she did so, she shouted 'You should know I'm a Catholic'.

No simple explanation of this young woman's violence in terms of religious sentiment will work when one considers the case a little further.

[She] had been picked up by police walking in the middle of a busy road against the traffic. This was the second occasion on which this had happened . . . [She] had been in psychiatric wards where she had witnessed assaults on staff . . . [Her] psychiatrist knew she had three children, all of whom had been taken into care. Each of her children had been fathered by a different man, and what the psychiatrist did not know was that one of these men (whom the woman now hated) had just gained a residence order for his child, claiming the woman was an incapable mother. The woman explained . . . that she was facing eviction from her council house . . . [and the] night before she had been picked up by the police, she had also been deserted by the man with whose child she was pregnant.

None of these circumstances help soothe the psychiatrist's bumps and bruises, nor his probable shock. The attack is out of proportion to the apparent provocation, and is clearly socially unacceptable, whatever the cause. What they do, however, is reveal that the explanations for the outburst are more complex than initially appears, and that violence also needs tackling at its social and psychological roots. The assailant was clearly a troubled person. Her violent reaction to the offence against her Catholicism can be seen alongside her huge personal stresses and the 'loss' of one of her existing children. The psychiatrist was, unwittingly, both a trigger and convenient target for her overwhelming distress and anger.

Vulnerable teachers School teaching staff have, traditionally, been managers of classroom discipline, including aggression between students. But now they face the possibility of violence, sometimes appalling, to themselves:

> The teacher let us go out and see what was happening and when we left the classroom, 3–4 metres in front of there was a masked person in black holding his gun from his shoulder . . . [He] stretched out his gun and shot. We saw a teacher fall to the ground.[43]

The date of this incident was 26 April 2002. The place was Erfurt in Germany. The gunman was a 19-year-old former pupil of the school who had been expelled the previous autumn. He had secured a permit to buy guns soon afterwards and had planned the attack for months. He succeeded in killing 13 teachers, two girl students, a police officer and, finally, himself.[44]

Such shootings have become very worrisome. In the USA, the Secret Service's National Threat Assessment Centre (normally charged with assessing threats to US presidents) produced a report on 37 school shootings, including interviews with attackers.[45] Rarely, it concluded, did students act impulsively, suddenly 'snap'. The events were all carefully planned, even advertised: '"I told everyone what I was going to do", said Evan Ramsey, 16, who killed his principal and a student in remote Bethel, Alaska, in 1997. He told so many students about his hit list that his friends crowded in the library to watch.'[46]

Like the case of the psychiatrist's client, the perpetrators' emotional background in the schools' shootings is an important consideration. Often there was a grievance, bad feelings about the school or particular individuals, and a desire for revenge. Most felt persecuted, and had been long-time bullied, threatened, attacked or injured by others prior to the incident. More than half the attackers had a history of feeling very depressed, desperate or suicidal, and many had to cope with a change to a significant relationship in their life.

Protective measures in schools, such as metal detectors and police officers, can be reassuring, but fail to touch the social and emotional difficulties. Attention, then, turns to the student's social circumstances, his family and friends, and the way his various stresses are addressed – if at all. Where is the student able to go with his or her emotional problems? Who will listen? Home and school pressures will interact such that personal slights at school can be hugely magnified. The school, at best, can try to cultivate an ethos where the telltale signs of a built-up grievance are spotted and reported, and where anger and persecution cannot be fomented.

The battered client   It is not always the worker who is the victim of care-and-control violence. There is also violence by staff to clients – neglect, verbal abuse, sexual assault, and even homicide. Abuse by a carer is a gross abrogation of professional trust and power, often causing lifetime emotional trauma to the victim.

Violence can take place in children's hostels, care homes, police stations, hospitals, and doctors' surgeries. A notorious example is Dr Harold Shipman, a British physician who, in January 2001, was convicted of causing the deaths of 15 of his patients. Estimates of the actual number he killed range from 76 to 1000. Another example is the 'Angel of Death', a Swiss male nurse. In September 2001 he confessed to killing 27 elderly patients. In a similar manner, a British nurse, Beverley Allitt, was sentenced to 13 life sentences after killing four young children in her care in the early 1990s, and severely injuring a further nine. These kind of events have lead one commentator to reflect, caustically: '. . . medicine has arguably thrown up more killers than all the other professions put together, with nursing a close second'.[47]

Notwithstanding the personal motives behind these incidents, they spotlight the kind of institutions in which they take place. Mechanisms to screen possibly violent professionals are invariably inadequate or non-existent. More of such procedures are very important and often called for in the immediate aftermath of the tragedies. But attention is also required to the way an emotional culture of violence and secrecy can be produced in some organizational settings. Of special concern are 'closed' institutions, such as hostels, care homes, and 'special' schools, where fear and shame among the victims mixes with the perpetrators' power and anxieties about being discovered. This is an emotional recipe for a strong code of silence, a code reinforced in conditions where staff burnout is high and there is a vacuum in effective leadership. There is a strong potential for abuse of power when carers no longer care and there is no one caring to whom they are responsible.

Organizational violence

Like organizational bullying, we can speak of organizational violence when violence, intended or otherwise, is embedded in the values of the organization. It translates into practices that systematically cause danger, risk or exploitation to employees. Emotionally, the employer can feel indifferent, even derisory, about its workers and their psychological or physical well-being: 'there are always more out there'. The worker may feel equally indifferent, but trapped in the job.

Organizational violence is most virulent when applied to poorly protected, low skilled, workers (such as recent immigrants anxious for work) or in regions where unemployment is very high. Such circumstances provide opportunities for less-scrupulous employers to flout safety regulations and ignore basic human rights. Workers can toil unprotected with dangerous machinery, be exposed to poisonous fumes in a manufacturing process, and work gruelling hours – with little power to resist. It is where misery and vulnerability flourishes.[48, 49] In May 1998 Simon Jones, a Sussex University student, died after starting work unloading stone from a cargo ship. His head was crushed in the jaws of a mechanical excavation claw, which had been adapted to lift bags of concrete from the ship. The machine had not been tested for safety.[50] In the USA, Daniel Rothenburg has eloquently described the plight of present-day migrant farm workers who, in fear and desperation, are threatened and cheated out of their wages, housed and transported in dangerous conditions, and sometimes held in peonage – tied to the employer until all debts are paid.[51]

Some major brand-names, global manufacturers, have been accused of exploitation and violence towards their employees in third-world countries, where a combination of low wages, very long hours and minimal comfort facilities, can create oppressive working conditions. To meet the stringent and relentless deadlines of the employer, and to drive down costs, local management can be authoritarian and unforgiving.[52] These are organizations that enjoy the commercial benefits of a docile, fearful, workforce, and where the employees have little organized power. The fear of losing one's job suppresses dissent. Nike, for instance, has been subject to criticism for the conditions and treatment of its sub-contracted employees in Vietnam. The account below, by Richard Senser, appeared on the web-based *Human Rights for Workers Bulletin* in 1996.[53]

CASE STUDY

Warning to Nike Workers: Do It – Or Else
'Did you know about the workers who were made to kneel on the ground – 45 of them for 25 minutes – with their hands in the air?'

A reporter from CBS' '48 Hours', Roberta Baskin, put that question to a Nike public relations man, and she quickly asked another one. *'Does that bother you?'*

'Roberta,' he replied on camera, *'it bothers me very much when things happen to workers – it bothers me very much.'*

'Were you aware of that incident?' Baskin continued.

'I was not aware of that incident,' he said, obviously embarrassed.

That exchange closed a '48 Hours' broadcast on October 17 titled 'Just Do it – Or Else.' The incident the two discussed occurred at one of five factories in Vietnam, where 25,000 Vietnamese, mostly young women, work six days a week making Nike shoes at 20 cents an hour. Low wages are not the worst of the problems faced by these workers.

One of the worst is physical abuse. Beatings and other violence against workers are not unusual in the Asian plants rushing to make shoes, garments, toys, and other products for the global market, but the reports about such acts are seldom documented first-hand. The CBS broadcast provided evidence directly from 15 workers who were punished for making mistakes in stitching Nike shoes. The 15 young women demonstrated how a Korean supervisor had struck them, two or three times each, on the back of the head and the side of the neck, with a Nike shoe. Two of the workers went to the hospital for treatment.

The supervisor in the case is said to have been dismissive, saying: 'It's not a big deal. It's just a method for managing workers'. Events such as these are often reported in partisan fashion, yet still alert us to the way some international corporations win their profit on the backs of ill-protected, sub-contracted, workers, far away from the glitz of corporate headquarters. Few of the positive emotions of 'good' human resource management are apparent. Given their vested interest, organizations accused of violence to their employees are typically defensive, proffering explanations of the sort:

We try, but we cannot enforce our usual high standards in another country.
Local labour is still better off in our factories than out of them.
The local culture is more violent; that's not our fault.

Labour, it appears, can be differently valued, depending on where it is sited and what is taken from it. The reactions also sidestep the often considerable political influence of a major corporation in its host country and how, and where, it chooses to direct its profits.

CONCLUSION

The phenomenon of victim and victimization is ancient, long evidenced in social organizations of all types. It is especially prevalent when people are embroiled in politics of gain and envy – winning at somebody else's cost. Hence work organizations are more likely to become sites of bullying and violence when they ferment such conditions, though an exaggerated emphasis on winning, greed, privilege, power and management-by-fear.

When bullying, violence and the infliction of pain becomes an accepted part of organizational processes, they raise crucial questions:

* Who profits, materially or psychologically from such conduct? How can that profit be challenged and reduced?
* How does it become normalized in an organization, silencing and frightening its victims and their witnesses?
* Who polices professionals who abuse their clients? How might such professionals be better screened?
* What are the cultural elements in an organization that turn a 'decent' citizen into an oppressor?
* What organizational structure and surveillance systems become domineering, creating fear and loathing, rather than constructive engagement in the work?

If societal violence and prejudice spills over into the workplace, the organization is then itself a victim of wider issues. Yet the organization is not entirely helpless. Much depends on the willingness and skills of management to treat all forms of organizational violence as issues to be tackled at both individual and organizational-cultural levels.

FURTHER READING

Bassman, E. (1992) *Abuse in the Workplace*. Westport, CT: Quorum.
Gill, M., Fisher, B. and Bowie, V. (eds) (2001) *Violence at Work*. Cullompton: Willan.
Randall, P. (1996) *Adult Bullying: Perpetrators and Victims*. London: Routledge.

REFERENCES

1 Anonymous (2001) 'Bullying in medicine', *British Medical Journal*, 323 (7324): 1314.
2 <http://www.success.unlimited.co.uk/bullylcase12.htm>.
3 EFILWC (2000) 'Violence at work', Second European survey on working conditions. European Foundation for the Improvement of Living and Working Conditions, Dublin.
4 Hoel, H. and Cooper, C. (2000) 'Workplace bullying in Britain', *Employee Health Bulletin*, 14: 6–9.
5 Einarsen, S. (1999) 'The nature and cause of bullying at work', *International Journal of Manpower*, 20 (1/2): 16–27.
6 Zapf, D. and Einarsen, S. (2001) 'Bullying in the workplace: recent trends in research and practice – an introduction', *European Journal of Work and Organizational Psychology*, 10 (4): 369–73.
7 Leymann, H. (1990) 'Mobbing and psychological terror at workplaces', *Violence and Victims*, 5: 119–26.
8 Kinchin, D. (2001) *Post Traumatic Stress Disorder: The Invisible Injury*. Didcot, Oxfordshire: Success Unlimited.
9 Leymann, H. (1996) 'The content and development of mobbing at work', *European Journal of Work and Organizational Psychology*, 5 (2): 165–84.
10 Crawford, N. (1999) 'Conundrums and confusion in organisations; the etymology of the word "bully"', *International Journal of Manpower*, 20 (1/2): 86–93.
11 Einarsen, S. (1999) 'The nature and cause of bullying at work', *International Journal of Manpower*, 20 (1/2): 16–27.
12 Zapf, D. and Einarsen, S. (2001) 'Bullying in the workplace: recent trends in research and practice – an introduction', *European Journal of Work and Organizational Psychology*, 10 (4): 369–73.
13 Treml, J.N. (2001) 'Bullying as a social malady in Japan', *International Journal of Social Work*, 44 (1): 107–17, especially p. 111.
14 Hadjifotiou, H. (1983) *Women and Harassment at Work*. London: Pluto Press.
15 Lewis, D. (1999) 'Workplace bullying – interim findings of a study in further and higher education in Wales', *International Journal of Manpower*, 20 (1/2): 106–18.
16 Leymann, H. (1990) 'Mobbing and psychological terror at workplaces', *Violence and Victims*, 5: 119–26.
17 Leymann, H. (1996) 'The content and development of mobbing at work', *European Journal of Work and Organizational Psychology*, 5 (2): 165–84.
18 Einarsen, S., Raknes, B.I. and Matthiesen, S.M. (1994) 'Bullying and harassment at work and their relationship to work environment quality

– an exploratory study', *European Work and Organizational Psychologist*, 4: 381–401.

19   Einarsen, S. (1999) 'The nature and cause of bullying at work', *International Journal of Manpower*, 20 (1/2): 16–27.

20   Brodsky, C.M. (1976) *The Harassed Worker*. Toronto: Lexington Books.

21   UNISON (1997) 'Bullying Report'. UNISON, London.

22   Zapf, D. (1999) 'Organisational, work group related and personal causes of mobbing/bullying at work', *International Journal of Manpower*, 12 (1/2): 70–85.

23   Talwar, J.T. (2002) *Fast Food, Fast Track*. Boulder, Colorado: Westview Press. p. 66.

24   Holmes, D. (2001) *Narcissm*. London: Faber.

25   Beaumeister, R., Boden, J. and Smart, L. (1996) 'Relation between threatened egotism to violence and aggression: the dark side of high self-esteem', *Psychological Review*, 103 (1): 5–33.

26   Adams, A. and Crawford, N. (1992) *Bullying at Work: How to Confront and Overcome It*. London: Virago.

27   Bassman, E. (1992) *Abuse in the Workplace*. Westport, CT: Quorum.

28   Crawford, N. (1999) 'Conundrums and confusion in organisations; the etymology of the word "bully"', *International Journal of Manpower*, 20 (1/2): 86–93.

29   Zapf, D. (1999) 'Organisational, work group related and personal causes of mobbing/bullying at work', *International Journal of Manpower*, 12 (1/2): 70–85.

30   Brodsky, C.M. (1976) *The Harassed Worker*. Toronto: Lexington Books.

31   Archer, D. (1999) 'Exploring "bullying" culture in the para-military organization', *International Journal of Manpower*, 20 (1/2): 94–105.

32   Bartunek, J.M. and Moch, M.K. (1987) 'First-order, second-order and third-order change and organizational development: a cognitive approach', *Journal of Applied Behavioral Science*, 23 (4): 483–500.

33   Bate, P. (1994) *Strategies for Cultural Change*. Oxford: Butterworth Heinemann.

34   Liefooghe, A.P.D. and Mackenzie Davey, K. (2001) 'Accounts of workplace bullying: the role of the organization', *European Journal of Work and Organizational Psychology*, 10 (4): 375–92, especially pp. 381–383.

35   Paterson, B. and Leadbetter, D. (2002) 'Standards for violence management training', in M. Gill, B. Fisher and V. Bowie (eds), *Violence at Work*. Cullompton: Willan. p. 132.

36   Budd, T. (1999) *Violence at Work: Findings from the British Crime Survey*. London: Health and Safety Executive.

37   Diamond, M.A. (1997) 'Administrative assault: A contemporary psychoanalytic view of violence and aggression in the workplace', *American Review of Public Administration*, 27 (3): 228–47.

38 Bowie, V. (2002) 'Defining violence at work: a new typology', in M. Gill, B. Fisher and V. Bowie (eds), *Violence at Work*. Cullompton: Willan.
39 Fineman, S. (1990) *Supporting the Jobless*. London: Routledge.
40 Leadbetter, D. and Trewartha, R. (1996) *Handling Aggression and Violence at Work*. Lyme Regis: Russell House.
41 Paterson, B. and Leadbetter, D. (2002) 'Standards for violence management training', in M. Gill, B. Fisher and V. Bowie (eds), *Violence at Work*. Cullompton: Willan. p. 132.
42 Breakwell, G. (1997) *Coping with Aggressive Behaviour*. Leicester: BPS Books. pp. 18–19.
43 Hooper, J. (2002) 'Teachers massacred', *The Guardian* (27 April), London: 1.
44 Anonymous (2002) 'Gunman's plot', *The Guardian* (1 May), London.
45 U.S. Secret Service National Threat Centre (2000) 'Safe school initiative. An interim report on the prevention of targeted violence in schools', (October), Washington, DC.
46 Dedman, B. (2000) 'Deadly lessons: shooters tell why', *Chicago Sun-Times* (16 October), Chicago.
47 Kinnell, H. (2000) 'Serial homicide by doctors. Shipman in perspective', *British Medical Journal*, 23 (321): 1594.
48 Southerland, M., Collins, P. and Scarborough, K. (1997) *Workplace Violence: A Continuum from Threat to Death*. Cincinnati, OH: Anderson Publishing.
49 Walraff, G. (1985) *Lowest of the Low*. London: Methuen.
50 Anonymous (2001) 'Company fined over student's death'. BBC News (29 November), London. <http://news.bbc.co.uk/1/hi/uk/england/1683080.stm>.
51 Rothenberg, D. (1998) *With These Hands: The Hidden World of Migrant Farmworkers Today*. New York: Harcourt Brace.
52 Klein, N. (2000) *No Logo: Taking Aim at the Brand Bullies*. Toronto: Knopff.
53 Senser, R. (1996) 'Warning to Nike workers: do it–or else', *Human Rights for Workers Bulletin*, 1 (10 November): 1. <http://www.senser.com/bu10.htm>.

11
Sexual harassment

LEARNING OBJECTIVES

Sexual harassment at work contains elements of bullying and violence and stirs similarly powerful feelings. This chapter investigates its contexts, causes and consequences, examining:

- The dominance of male power at work
- The emotions of sexual harassment
- Work settings and structures that encourage sexual harassment
- Helplessness and vulnerability
- Challenging sexual harassment.

Our sexuality is at once intensely private and very public. It involves fluctuating physical desires and passions. Sex and sexuality are experiences to feel cautious and uncomfortable about, or to be easy and open about. It depends on our culture, religious beliefs, family upbringing and personality.

In recent years there has been growing confusion over what constitutes acceptable sexual behaviour and sexual feelings at work, and appropriate boundaries between public and private. We may carefully camouflage our sexuality at work, or flaunt it. It may be corporately used (with our consent) or exploited. It is rarely 'not there', as evidenced by the ebb and flow of sexual gossip, innuendo, teasing and flirtation.[1] Sexuality and romance in the workplace are an inevitable part of the life force of an organization. But when is sexual attention coercive, rather than fun? When is the line crossed from OK, to not OK and harassment? What is the emotional substructure of sexual harassment as it crosses paths with other injuries – stress, bullying and violence?

POWER AND THE MALE IMPERATIVE

Like bullying and violence, sexual harassment is inextricably linked to power, especially the power of men over women. The main, but not only, victims are women in junior positions, sexually harassed by male superiors or colleagues.[2, 3] Women in traditionally male working environments can be perceived as threatening to men, 'taking their jobs', and are more likely to face sexual harassment. Indeed, as the number of women in traditional male jobs and roles has increased, so have complaints of sexual harassment. This has lead to an opening-up of the issues and a little less stigmatization, but victims still remain exposed to subtle forms of blame[4] (see the cases described below).

Sexual harassment operates through different channels of power. Steven Lukes' 'three-dimensional' framework is helpful in unravelling some of them.[5, 6] There is *one-dimensional power*. This is sheer coercion, such as a sexual proposition backed up by the force of higher rank. *Two-dimensional power* is subtler; it is built into the organization's culture, such the acceptability for, or indulgence of, harassment. It is an invisible, often macho, agenda that 'invites' victims to keep silent for fear of embarrassment or reprisal. The agenda favours a male view of 'appropriate' sexual conduct. For example, women are far more likely than men to see offence in sexual jokes, suggestive comments by a supervisor or colleague, pin-up calendars, leering at the body or intimate questions about one's sex life.[7]

Finally, there is *three-dimensional power*. This form of power is rooted in the ideas and ideals that make up the social, political and economic system in which the organization operates. The assumption, for instance, that men will prevail over women in economic affairs and leadership. Also, sexual stereotypes and gender scripts, such as women as warm, nurturant and fickle, and men as emotionally controlled and assertive. These ideas spill over into work settings, and are used or abused in interpersonal relationships. For example, a female personal assistant can be treated as a women first ('feminine', 'soft', 'available', 'temperamental'), and a worker second. As one young, female, employee recalls:

> I came to work in a smart trouser suit and Paul greeted me with 'Did you forget to take your pyjamas off Suzie?' (He knows I hate being called Suzie). A little later I was trying to print some documents and said 'This printer is so temperamental!' and Paul quipped 'It's obviously female . . . that's what happens when you let women near machines'.[8]

Sexual harassment of men by women is less common, yet it occurs, and it appears to be on the increase.[9] In a major survey of 20,000 active duty military personnel, 17% of males reported that they had been sexually harassed (compared to 64% of females).[10] Women are more likely to harass men in work settings that are predominately female, and where women define the main rules of sexual conduct. Men, however, are inclined to construe such events as embarrassing rather than humiliating or offensive, possibly as a way of protecting their male pride. It is regarded a 'tame' form of harassment.[11]

OFFENSIVENESS AND FEELINGS

Being sexually harassed can be distressing and stressful. Prolonged harassment can lead to anxiety, tension, irritability depression, headaches, sleeplessness and fatigue. Personal relationships suffer. Work morale, time keeping and performance can deteriorate.[12]

As sexual harassment has come out of the shadows, there have been attempts to formalize its manifestations. The European Commission, for instance, outlines five categories of sexually offensive acts: *non-verbal* (pin-ups, leering, suggestive gestures); *physical* (unwanted touching); *verbal* (unwanted sexual proposition and innuendo); and *intimidation* (offensive comments on dress or performance, and sexual blackmail). They are described as pollutants to the work of millions of women and many men.[13, 14]

Essentially, it is their *unwantedness* and *offensiveness* that marks them out as harassment, which allows for variations in work and national contexts. For example, in occupations such as theatre and film, there has long been accepted a degree of open physical contact and intimacy among workers. Their hugs, kisses and embraces are part of the social norms of the profession, unlike, say, steelworkers or police officers, where handshaking and backslapping would be more common. Likewise, nations from the Mediterranean region are more tactile than Nordic ones. These differences do not obviate sexual harassment, but they set different social expectations about what is, or is not, acceptable.

CONTEXTS: THE HOTEL, THE REFINERY AND THE UNIVERSITY

Particular organizational settings reveal more detail about the way harassment and its emotions operate. Three contrasting ones are described below. The first is the hotel industry, where the customer is 'sovereign'. The second examines the plight of a female employee in a male-dominated oil refinery. The final example describes what happens when a female student confronts her harassing mentor at university.

The hotel

> Our friendly, helpful staff go out of their way to make guest feel welcome. If there's anything we can do to make your stay more pleasurable, we will. (Holiday Inn)[15]

Promises like this are common in the highly competitive hotel industry. They reinforce the strong rhetoric of the sovereignty of the consumer, or the customer is king, something of a mantra in twenty-first century commerce.[16, 17]

But the pledge has a darker side. It is made in an industry where employees are mainly women, young people and disadvantaged ethnic groups. Hotel receptionists, waiters and chambermaids are of lower status than guests and clients, therefore more vulnerable to sexual harassment – suggestive remarks and looks, unwelcome physical contact and verbal abuse.[18] The division of labour in the hotel industry is gendered. Women, such as chambermaids and breakfast waitresses, often feel that they are viewed as maternal homemakers. Others, such as receptionists, sales and marketing staff, are groomed as sex objects: glamorous and seductive for the benefit of male customers.[19]

Hotels have an unusual emotional form, criss-crossing public and private domains. The hotel is a temporary home for guests, yet free from the normal constraint domesticity. Hotel bedrooms, restaurants and bars all hold promise of sexual activity, such as the business fling, 'adult' movies and prostitution.[20] Sex is in the air, so to speak, as hotel staff enter the private space of a guest's bedroom, a vulnerable position for chambermaids who usually work alone. One of the interviewees in a study by Guerrier and Adib, recounts the experiences of a chambermaid confronted by a naked man while she was cleaning his room. He 'really came on strong'. She had to phone the hotel manager who 'discretely spoke to the customer'. Another slapped the face of a man who was harassing her. She was dismissed from her job. In both of these instances, preserving the customer relationship took priority over the victim's feelings.

The atmosphere is tipped further towards possible harassment in the way the hotel encourages its staff to present an 'attractive' image, consonant with the advertised 'warmth' and 'friendliness'. Emotional labour, therefore, becomes a major part of the job, aimed at sustaining an image of front-desk glamour and friendliness in meeting the guest's 'pleasure' (see Chapter 3). One young, male receptionist recalls the sexual traps that can ensue:

> One guest, oh my God, he comes down and says, 'Do you have any entertainment?' And we said 'What?' 'Can you send one of your colleagues up to our room?' and I said 'Hm – no I don't think she'll go up to your room' and he goes 'Well, you'll do anyway' and I said 'No, we don't provide that service' and walked off.[21]

Hotels also run restaurants and table service. The traditional image of the de-sexed, invisible, waiter and waitress has now given way to the waiter who is your friend, even confidant(e), someone who builds a relationship with you – or so it seems. Impression management is key, especially displaying warm feelings towards the customer.[22] Expressing sexuality through flirtatiousness and flesh-revealing clothes can be part of the script, perfected by restaurants such as *TGI Friday*.[23] Commercial and sexual/emotional logic blend in these circumstances; it is seen as a successful recipe for repeat business.[24] However, the opportunity for sexual harassment and abuse, by customer or employer, is markedly increased.

'Below stairs' the opportunities for harassment shift from customers to co-workers. Students on work placement in a hotel are at the bottom of the power–status pecking order, so are especially vulnerable to exploitation. A survey of 274 of such students revealed over half who declared that they were sexually harassed by their work colleagues or managers, including chefs. The majority of victims were female, although 12 per cent were males.[25] Dominant feelings were of disgust, cheapness, anger and embarrassment. A proportion reported continuing emotional and physical damage from the experience. Nevertheless, a few were flattered by the event, underlining the idiosyncratic way that some sexual approaches can be interpreted. One person's harassment is, sometimes, another's pleasure or fun.

The oil refinery: Kate's story

Traditionally, oil refineries are bastions of maleness and masculinity. Social interactions tend to be shaped around male feeling, and emotional display-rules. Kate's story, related by Kiely and Henbest, is from a study of a refinery where there were 10 males to every female.[26] Kate was a 28-year old, single, process operator.

CASE STUDY

Kate . . . is employed on a totally male shift, working a four-day/four-night rota. Reluctantly, she recently brought a complaint to the human resources department about her male shift manager. He initially started harassing her by making suggestive remarks in front of the other males, which Kate ignored but found unnecessary and humiliating. Her other work colleagues noticed the comments, but did not give Kate any support, as she believed they found it highly amusing. The comments continued for a period of about one month, and Kate began to feel very uncomfortable in his presence. More importantly to Kate, he threatened that she would receive poor appraisals and that she would not pass her final process-leader tests if she did not comply with his wishes. Kate ignored all the comments and declined all invitations.

However, she started receiving telephone calls late at night at her home, and letters further harassing her. She confided in one of her male work colleagues, who admitted that he did not realise the extent of the harassment, or how it was affecting her. The shift manager became very hostile during this period as Kate continued to decline his offers.

After three months of being subjected to such behaviour, Kate rang the HR department for some guidance on her rights and where she stood in terms of the complaint procedure. She was advised that she ought to visit the department and discuss in depth the harassment complaint. At this stage, she was unsure if she wanted to follow the company reporting procedure and did not visit the HR department until about one month later. Kate stated that she intended to report the incidents in the belief that she would have support from several of her male work colleagues, two of whom had agreed to substantiate her claims. The HR department interviewed both Kate and the shift manager on several occasions separately, with two senior members of management present, and a work companion of Kate's choice.

The Outcome

The shift manager was transferred to another shift, causing the transfer of several other shift managers to accommodate this move. This created a degree of bad feeling within the entire process staff, and Kate was made a scapegoat by her fellow work colleagues, and held responsible for the upheaval and 'rocking of the boat'. The process staff did not welcome the general uncertainty surrounding the shift changes, and as a result Kate was blamed for setting the ball in motion. She said that since making the complaint she has been isolated by several of her former work colleagues and she has heard a number of jokes being made at her expense.

Kate's experiences are salutary and emotionally complex. The strong, male, culture isolated and diminished her, giving tacit support to her harasser. Her distress was her colleagues' mirth. Her rejection of her tormentor fuelled his further harassment. Feeling spurned, possibly from hurt pride, he redoubled his efforts, coupled with direct threats. By 'coming out', exposing her harasser, Kate unwittingly threatened the tacit emotion subculture of the workgroup – where they were all 'comrades' and where 'banter' (male defined) was acceptable. Preserving the status quo and the male bonding was more important to most of her colleagues than responding sympathetically to her complaint which, to them, appeared unreasonable – the 'typical' outpouring of a woman who 'could not cope'.

The procedures followed by the Human Resources Department were textbook in every way, so that should have been the end of the matter. But the emotional ripples of harassment are not so easily contained. Removing the harasser sowed the seeds of resentment among the workgroup. Kate was lampooned, made a scapegoat, a target for their resentment. The effects of this were sufficient to make Kate feel unsure of herself, doubtful about the wisdom of her action.

Kate took on more than a distressing harasser. It was a whole way of male-attuned life in the department. A long-standing manager described his male colleagues as 'working class', with traditional views about women. They had wives who lead 'the housewife style' life and the managers believed claims of sexual harassment to be exaggerated. There was little cultural space for Kate's feelings, and much tacit tolerance for resentment and revenge directed at her.

The university

At first glance, universities would seem the last place to encounter sexual harassment. The stereotypical picture of the academic environment is one of tolerance, sympathy and understanding. A liberal educational atmosphere is the right kind of antidote to the narrow thinking of the oil refinery, or the exploitative status differences in the hotel industry.

The reality, however, is different. Sexual harassment occurs, and is of sufficient concern for most universities to have an anti-harassment policy, a formal mechanism of complaint, as well as in-house counselling services. Following the wider pattern, sexual harassers are chiefly men who target female students, especially ones under stress. The students are likely to be anxious and unsure about their academic work and relatively non-assertive in their style.[27] Male students are less prone to report being harassed, mainly because they do not regard 'sexual harassment' as an appropriate description of their experiences of sexually-suggestive remarks.[28, 29]

American studies indicate that some 30 per cent of women students are sexually harassed by at least one superior, while, in the UK, the incidence appears to be higher.[30-32] These statistics reflect the typical imbalance of power between harasser and harassed. The student is subordinate to the instructor in the university's pecking order and the instructor's judgment can often make or break a student's academic career. The academic hierarchy normally stretches from full professors and lecturers down to post-doctoral students, doctoral students and undergraduate students. Harassment can occur anywhere along this line.

The following account is taken from Fiona Wilson's records of students' harassment.[33] It is the story of the experiences of a female doctoral student, badgered and distressed by a male post-doctoral student, who could influence her academic progress.

CASE STUDY

This student . . . felt she had been 'polite and civil' to her alleged harasser though she did not like him. He had gained his doctorate with the same supervisor and offered to help her by proofreading her thesis and offering constructive criticism before she submitted her thesis. Although he was married with children, he seemed obsessively interested in her. She said he hung around in corridors to see her, followed her, asked questions after each weekend where she had been, then checked her car mileage to see if this was true. He talked to the departmental secretary about how much he liked her and how unhappy he was with his marriage. He waited for an opportunity to find the student alone at work in the evening. In an attempt to protect herself, she persuaded colleagues to stay on in the laboratory with her if she was working late.

Her colleagues did not share her view that she was being harassed and had advised her to be friendlier as he 'had considerable influence over her work' (he worked with her supervisor, thoroughly understood her research area and would be proofreading her thesis, which was almost ready for submission). In an attempt to appear friendlier, she accepted an invitation to go to the cinema; he said that others from her research group were going but none of them appeared. She went to 'keep him happy' but was ill at ease which became clear to him. 'He made a big deal out of it and called me into his office the next day.' She felt obliged to account for her behaviour. She realized that he had been going through her belongings in her desk as he had found out that she had recently moved house.

She asked him to leave her alone but he ignored this request. He sent her a large bunch of flowers, had them delivered to work, then followed this with a long letter saying he wanted to leave his wife and how strongly he felt about her. He then asked the secretary what the student had thought of the flowers while his wife was present. The student said 'He is not quite rational. He has no shame. It is all a fantasy built up in his head.' The final harassing incident had happened the day before when she could not face going into work and had stayed at home. He went to her house; she was on her own there. When she did not answer the door, he lifted the garage door to see if her car was there. She had felt frightened and vulnerable. She had submitted the thesis, but she feared he could negatively influence the result of her doctorate.

At one level this story could be read as the action of an obsessive, infatuated, man consumed with desire, and with unhappiness about his own relationship. But the account demands deeper examination. As Wilson points out, the very notion of 'being harassed' becomes confusing as women are socialized to accept many non-consensual sexual interactions as a fact of life.[34] Men and women can read emotional signals differently in sexual encounters. The victim, therefore, seeks the affirmation of others about her harassment. Is she really being harassed as she feels she is? She fails to receive support and, confusingly for her, is persuaded to appear more welcoming and warm. In her anxiety, her surface acting is unconvincing, and the consequences prove to be disastrous. His anger, guilt and obsession propels him into ever-more reckless behaviour.

CONCLUSIONS

Work life is also sex life – openly, in secret corners, or lightly disguised in innuendo and banter. But sexual politics, emotions and organizational politics are all closely intertwined. Sexual feelings for others can become part-and-parcel of one's identity at work, a way power and excitement can be mobilized, a reason to enjoy more time and collaboration with some people more than others, a comfortable route to desired influence and favours, and a way of meeting unmet sexual needs. Sexual harassment, however, stretches and distorts these processes. It breaks the tacit consensuality of workplace sexuality. It transgresses the unspoken sexual boundaries and the emotion-rules that hold them in place. It violates the victim's private emotional space. For her (and sometimes him), fear and loathing replace the normal fun, flattery and attraction.

Breaking down sexual harassment means breaking down the emotion assumptions that are used to justify it, and the institutional processes that sustain them. For instance, what men do or say 'naturally', women can find offensive and intrusive. What men regard as banter, a 'bit of fun', women can construe as harassment. Less innocently, men can knowingly use innocuous-sounding terms as camouflage for behavior they know to be sexually intimidating and unwelcome. Sexual stereotypes shape the justificatory process, such as women as 'pets', 'whores', 'mother figures' or 'virgins'. They are fuel for the sexual harasser who wants to treat women as objects. In a male environment, where men shape the expectations of organizational conduct and the 'correct' emotions, their (hetero-) sexuality tends to win out. The woman can struggle to be heard, and it can be a painful struggle.

Written organization policies on sexual harassment scratch the surface of these issues. They can sometimes backfire on the victim – as we have seen in the oil refinery story. At best they help suppress the worst excesses; at worst they are tokenistic, more for public relations purposes than a genuine expression of concern and action. But this picture has blurred edges. Several decades of feminism have eroded some of the worst excesses, the 'male' agenda and traditional emotional folklore, such that the voice of women in organizations is now not as muted and suppressed as it once was. Women's feelings are more likely to be heard. The law and human resources departments have responded positively, if not entirely effectively, to curb the excesses of sexual harassment. In society, especially Western, the shifting and shuffling of roles between the sexes has helped. They have added ambiguity to what is right or wrong sexually speaking; but that is no bad thing. Uncertainty is a sign that old assumptions no longer prevail and a more open and balanced sexual agenda is possible.

FURTHER READING

Brant, C. and Too, L. (1994) *Rethinking Sexual Harassment*. London: Pluto Press.

Hearn, J. and Parkin, W. (2001) *Gender, Sexuality and Violence in Organizations*. London: Sage.

Stephens, T. (1999) *Bullying and Sexual Harassment*. London: CIPD.

Thomas, A.M. and Kitzinger, C. (1997) *Sexual Harassment*. Buckingham: Open University Press.

REFERENCES

1 Burrell, G. and Hearn, J. (1989) 'The sexuality of organizations', in J. Hearn, D.L. Sheppard, P. Tancred-Sheriff and G. Burrell (eds), *The Sexuality of Organization*. London: Sage.

2 Worsfold, P. and McCann, C. (2000) 'Supervised work experience and sexual harassment', *International Journal of Contemporary Hospitality Management*, 12 (4): 249–55.

3 Wilson, F. (2000) 'The subjective experience of sexual harassment. Cases of students', *Human Relations*, 53 (8): 1081–97.

4 Kiely, J. and Henbest, A. (2000) 'Sexual harassment at work: experiences from an oil refinery', *Women in Management Review*, 15 (2): 65–80.

5 Wilson, F. and Thompson, P. (2001) 'Sexual harassment as an exercise of power', *Gender, Work and Organization*, 8 (1): 61–83.

6 Lukes, S. (1975) *Power: A Radical View*. London: MacMillan.

7 Kiely, J. and Henbest, A. (2000) 'Sexual harassment at work: experiences from an oil refinery', *Women in Management Review*, 15 (2): 65–80.

8 Gabriel, Y., Fineman, S. and Sims, D. (2000) *Organizing and Organizations: An Introduction, 2nd Edition*. London: Sage. p. 178.

9 Baugh, S.G. (1997) 'On the persistence of sexual harassment in the workplace', *Journal of Business Ethics*, 16 (9): 899–909.

10 Webb, S.L. (1991) *Step Forward: Sexual Harassment in the Workplace: What You Need to Know!* New York: MasterMedia Ltd.

11 Pringle, R. (1989) 'Bureaucracy, rationality and sexuality: the case of secretaries', in J. Hearn, D.L. Sheppard, P. Tancred-Sheriff and G. Burrell (eds), *The Sexuality of Organization*. London: Sage.

12 Stanford, J. and Gardiner, J. (1993) *No Offence? Sexual Harassment. How it Happens and How to Beat it*. London: The Industrial Society.

13 Commission of European Communities (1991) Commission Recommendation of 12th November on the Protection of the Dignity of Women and Men at Work. Brussels.

14 Labour Research (1992) 'Standing up to sexual harassment', *Bargaining Report*, 17–18.

15 Holiday Inn <http://www.holiday-inn.co.uk/whyhi.shtml>.

16 Du Gay, P. and Salaman, G. (1992) 'The cult(ure) of the customer', *Journal of Management Studies*, 29 (5): 615–33.

17 Sturdy, A. (1998) 'Customer care in a consumer society: Smiling and sometimes meaning it?' *Organization*, 5 (1): 27–53.

18 Worsfold, P. and McCann, C. (2000) 'Supervised work experience and sexual harassment', *International Journal of Contemporary Hospitality Management*, 12 (4): 249–55.

19 Biswas, R. and Cassell, C. (1996) 'Strategic HRM and gendered division of labour in the hotel industry: a case study', *Personnel Review*, 25 (2): 19–34.

20 Guerrier, Y. and Adib, A.S. (2000) '"No, we don't provide that service": the harassment of hotel employees by customers', *Work, Employment and Society*, 14 (4): 689–705.

21 Guerrier, Y. and Adib, A.S. (2000) '"No, we don't provide that service": the harassment of hotel employees by customers', *Work, Employment and Society*, 14 (4): 689–705, especially p. 689.

22 Guerrier, Y. and Adib, A.S. (2000) '"No, we don't provide that service": The harassment of hotel employees by customers', *Work, Employment and Society*, 14 (4): 689–705.

23 Hall, E.J. (1993) 'Smiling, deferring and flirting: doing gender by giving "good service"', *Work and Occupations*, 20 (4): 452–71.

24 Glibert, D., Guerrier, Y. and Guy, J. (1998) 'Sexual harassment issues in the hospitality industry', *International Journal of Contemporary Hospitality Management*, 10 (2): 179–202.

25 Worsfold, P. and McCann, C. (2000) 'Supervised work experience and sexual harassment', *International Journal of Contemporary Hospitality Management*, 12 (4): 249–55.

26 Kiely, J. and Henbest, A. (2000) 'Sexual harassment at work: experiences from an oil refinery', *Women in Management Review*, 15 (2): 65–80.

27 Dziech, B.W. and Weiner, L. (1984) *The Lecherous Professor: Sexual Harassment on Campus*. Boston: Beacon Press.

28 Kitzinger, C. and Thomas, A. (1995) 'Sexual harassment: a discursive approach', in S. Wilkinson and C. Kitzinger (eds), *Feminism and Discourse*. London: Sage.

29 Metha, A. and Nigg, J. (1983) 'Sexual harassment on campus: an institutional response', *Journal of National Association of Women Deans, Administrators and Counsellors*, 46: 9–15.

30 Wilson, F. (2000) 'The subjective experience of sexual harassment. Cases of students', *Human Relations*, 53 (8): 1081–97.

31 Dziech, B.W. and Weiner, L. (1984) *The Lecherous Professor: Sexual Harassment on Campus*. Boston: Beacon Press.

32 Paludi, M.A. (1990) *Ivory Power: Sexual Harassment on Campus*. Albany, NY: State University of New York Press.

33 Wilson, F. (2000) 'The subjective experience of sexual harassment. Cases of students', *Human Relations*, 53 (8): 1081–97, especially pp. 1088–9.

34 Wilson, F. (2000) 'The subjective experience of sexual harassment. Cases of students', *Human Relations*, 53 (8): 1081–97, especially p. 1090.

12
Downsized

LEARNING OBJECTIVES

When organizations downsize it can diminish and distress all those associated with the process. This chapter discusses:

- Why organizations downsize
- The emotional effects on stayers, leavers and the executioners
- Dealing with guilt and anger
- The destruction of networks.

I never considered I'd be out of work. I was really shocked when I learned I'd have to go. The more people sympathised with me the worse it got. I felt very resentful at first and wanted to get my own back. I was there 14 years and most of this period I enjoyed my job. The company shrank from 120 people to around 40. I've been trying virtually everything to recover my self-respect and status. I'm feeling bitterly disappointed. (Chief Engineer)[1]

I used to go to work enthusiastically, now I just go in to do what I have to do. I feel overloaded to the point of burnout. Most of my colleagues are actively looking for other jobs or are just resigned to do the minimum. At the same time the CEO is paid millions and his salary is going up much higher than anyone else's. It makes me angry and resentful. (Middle Manager, Engineer)[2]

These are engineers speaking. The first was in the 1980s when white-collar unemployment was beginning to take hold. The second was in the late 1990s when vast swathes of job losses cut through many of the biggest and best organizations.

The distress of these two people is palpable. They have been injured – they are hurt, angry, resentful, disaffected. Yet, in other respects, their situations are very different. The first is jobless. The second remains in his 'downsized' company, retaining his job, but neither it, nor the organization, feels the same any more. Another difference is that the 1980s engineer was shocked at the very prospect of redundancy – it was not the expectation of his generation, where employment meant security. In over a decade, however, things had shifted dramatically. Job insecurity and temporary employment became the norm, a picture that shows little sign of changing.[3] Yet being still *in* work after a downsizing, a survivor, can be emotionally conflicting and complex, and some say that it is even more difficult to cope with than being one of the 'economic' casualties – the unemployed. This is because downsizing breaks up established social networks at work and leaves the survivor unsure about 'what next'? Their fate feels uncertain. Some feel guilty for having survived while their friends and colleagues have not.

THE DOWNSIZING PHENOMENON

Downsizing, as the term suggests, is a matter of reduction: reduction in costs by reducing the size of the workforce. The reasoning is dominated by transaction-cost economics. Costs are measured at each stage of the different transactions in the organization's work processes, and then evaluated to find ways of lightening expenditure and increasing profitability.[4] Outsourcing, subcontracting and part-time work, all play a role, as does a slimmed-down workforce. Overall, downsizing attempts to achieve more with less. Its potential, immediate savings are alluring, as employment costs normally range from 30 per cent to 80 per cent of the total costs of running a business.

Downsizing is typically portrayed as a last-resort initiative for the business in trouble. In an unpredictable, and increasingly competitive, global economy, the drive to reduce costs and improve performance has to be relentless, goes the reasoning. Downsizing removes the 'excess fat', the 'deadwood' (that is, people). Each slimming or pruning sets the baseline for the next, so some organizations go through successive downsizings in their attempts to survive. But downsizing is also used as a proactive tool for thriving companies, to give an even sharper edge to their competitiveness.

Between 1991 and 1994 some remarkable downsizings took place, such as 85,000 people from IBM, 83,500 from AT&T, 73,400 from General Motors and 50,000 from Sears. These leviathans of the corporate world, some famous for their paternalism, looking after their workers, downsized aggressively. Some employees were offered remuneration 'packages' to retire early. Three million US jobs were eliminated in the first half of the twentieth century, a pattern mirrored in Europe.[5, 6] Traditional notions of loyalty were badly shaken.

Alternatives to layoffs, such as pay cuts, shortening the working week, unpaid vacations, or job shares, are possibilities, but rarely occur. Downsizing remains a favoured approach. A twenty-first century snapshot is presented below. It is a sample drawn from news reports in February 2002. A close examination reveals some familiar names, such as General Motors, Black and Decker, Marconi, Dow Corning, Mitsubishi, Electric, Fujitsu and 7–Eleven. It also exposes the wide range of different businesses affected.

GM cutting 932 jobs in Canada
Homestore.com cuts 300 jobs
BA to slash 16,000 jobs
Dow Corning to cut work force by 700
Staples cuts 326 jobs, to close 30 stores
Marconi to cut 4,000 jobs as core sales fall
Mitsubishi Electric cuts 2,000 jobs

Amtrak to lay off 700
Air Services Group to cut 900 jobs
7–Eleven to close up to 120 stores
Auto Parts cuts 900 more jobs
Amtrak to cut 700 to trim shortfall
Xcel to cut 500 jobs in Denver

Liz Claiborne closing 12 stores
Steelcase to lay off 235 workers
Black & Decker to cut 2,400 jobs
Toys 'R' Us to close 64 Stores
Fujitsu cuts 1,000 jobs
PC maker Gateway cuts 2,250 jobs
Last day for 3,000 Boeing Workers

Does Downsizing Work?

For some senior employees, there are immediate gains. The stock market can take downsizing as a sign of prudence and the firm's stock value rises. This can give instant financial rewards to executives. For example, General Dynamics laid off 12,000 workers in 1992, which put double-salary bonuses into the pay packets of executives.[7] For deregulated monopolies, open to competition for the first time, a dramatically reshaped business can be the only way of effectively operating. But often, the expected performance-benefit of downsizing does not occur. After announcements of downsizing, performance frequently continues to decline, to become even worse after two years.[8] An American Management Association Survey shows that only 50 per cent of 1000 companies had actually reduced costs, and just 22 per cent increased productivity.[9]

The emotional health of the downsized organization is not all that it should be; it is depressed. Those who are made unemployed and re-enter the workforce elsewhere, do so with a legacy of wounds and wisdoms from their downsizing experiences. They manage their careers more defensively, are cautious about offering more than a moderate degree of commitment to their employer or role, and place far more emphasis on leisure. Once bitten, twice shy.[10, 11]

THE EMOTIONAL REALITIES OF DOWNSIZING

Telling someone they are about to lose their job is not easy, so downsizing is replete with anxiety-reducing euphemisms. An employee can be 'let go', 'put into the mobility pool', 'displaced', 'early retired', 'helped to resign' or placed on permanent 'administrative leave'. General Motors referred to the closure of its UK Luton plant, in 2001, as 'a volume-related production schedule', while Chrysler called its sackings 'a career alternative enhancement pro-gramme'.[12] The conscience-plagued, or simply embarrassed, executive can struggle to give the news face to face. Relabelling provides only modest protection.[13] Some organizations erect a barrier between themselves and the downsizing process, such as hiring an independent specialist, an 'out-placement consultant', to undertake the deed. This reduces the immediate ethical load on the executive, distancing any inflicted damage or pain.

*[handwritten marginalia: * Mgr thought the would do it.]*

The executioner's burden

> We put all, there were blackboards, so we put all the names on the board, and we just sat there, and I can remember, it gave me the creeps, there was a stunned silence, and we felt it was like the Vietnam war or something. We were all that upset, all of us . . . Saying, look what we are doing to all those people! Isn't there any other way? Why are we doing this? It was horrible.[14]

The speaker is referring to a downsizing she managed ten years previously. The event still haunts her. The popular image of downsizing as leaving the implementers, the executioners, unscathed is far from the truth. Many people involved in downsizing, whatever their role, end up feeling disheartened, some even suicidal.[15] The twisted irony of downsizing is that it is often executed by managers who have spent years cultivating trust with the very people they are to lay off, having persuaded them to buy into the corporate culture of care and collaboration. Guilt, feeling a betrayer, while they themselves have survived, is a dominant reaction.[16, 17] The guilt is amplified when the layoff is used as a smokescreen to get rid of unwanted employees, and when the action is bound to hurt families and dependents.

Barry Wright's interviews with downsizers reveal some of the emotional costs. For example, there are downsizers who work extraordinarily long hours to help them to expiate their own guilt and to affirm the value of people they had laid off ('their work should continue to get done'). Often such dedication is at the expense of strain within the downsizers' own families. Being shunned by old colleagues compounds their burden:

> It's very difficult to walk through the halls, I walk through and I break up conversations. You know, oh, here comes X, and there's the disappearance of six or seven people. People don't say 'Hi' to me in the hallway. They've got their heads down. That's tough.[18]

Downsizers' personalities appear to make a difference. Kets de Vries and Balazs divide downsizers into four types: *abrasive*, *dissociative*, *alexithymic*, and *depressive*.[19] Abrasive downsizers are tough, highly intelligent, quick witted, but also impatient, arrogant and lack interpersonal skills. They deal with their guilt by putting the blame on the victim – the 'dead wood', the 'rotten apples'. It served them right, 'To fire them was the best thing I've done for a long time.' Dissociative executives manage by removing themselves psychologically from the source of pain, 'Granted I was there physically, but certainly not emotionally . . . It was like I was acting in a dream!' Alexithymia is a diminished ability to feel, a Greek term for 'no words for moods'. Conducting repeated downsizing leaves some feeling numb, robot-like, their distress expressed in physical symptoms and medical problems. 'I really don't know how I feel; my wife tells me how I feel . . . I have no strong positive or negative feelings'. The depressive downsizers, however, are preoccupied with their guilt and the gloom of the experience. They suffer insomnia, burst into tears at work, and blame themselves for what had happened and the harm they have caused to others.

SURVIVOR SYNDROME

Apart from the executioners, downsizing can have a profound effect on the employees who have been 'spared'. The obvious relief at having retained one's job is tempered in complex ways.[20–25] There is:

- fear of further downsizing and of more radical changes
- increased feelings of insecurity
- guilt at having survived the shake-out while friends and colleagues have fallen by the way
- stress from increased workloads
- unwillingness to do more than the bare essentials
- strained trust in management
- reduced risk-taking and motivation.

The prevalence of such reactions has been termed *survivor syndrome*, or *survivor sickness*. It has been likened to grieving the loss of a loved one, or the effects of a divorce which leaves emotional scars.[26] Parallels have also been drawn with post-Holocaust reactions.[27] Traumatized survivors have felt tense, fearful of persecution, diminished self-esteem, and guilt at having survived.[28, 29]

Shifting the guilt and anger

The emotionalities of survivor syndrome can unfold in different ways.[30] For instance, guilt can soon convert to anger. Anger is often directed at those who instigated the downsizing, the executives who 'explained' or 'sold', it to the organization. O'Neill and Lenn describe such an occurrence:

> Those longest in the company, generally those highest in the company hierarchy, had the most anger. Their anger was directed at two specific types of executive activities: the use of superficial sayings to rationalise the downsizing process and the condemnation of the past.[31]

The 'superficial sayings' were slogans such as: *work smarter, not harder*; *right-size, don't downsize*; *change is your friend*. They felt patronized and insulted by such change-speak, which glossed over the harsh realities of layoffs and corporate restructuring. After years of hard work and loyalty to the company, the implication of 'smarter working' was, in their eyes, that their past working had been 'dumb'; it was trivialized. Downsizing violated the norms of years of effort. The hurt and anger was directed squarely at the way top management had *presented* the change and how it impugned the identities of those affected.

Threats to the psychological contract

A psychological contract is the unwritten set of expectations that exists between people in an organization, employee and employer. It is about mutual expectations on, for instance, trust, dignity and career progression.[32] The traditional psychological contract has been one where, in exchange for job security and career advancement, an employee gives his or her loyalty and commitment to the organization. The shock of downsizing is particularly severe for people who have always worked with such beliefs. The loss of perceived career and job security leaves many as 'unhappy stayers', experiencing similar feelings as those who have been made redundant.[33]

Survivors, whose psychological contracts are threatened, can rebalance them in various ways.[34] Distrust and depressed morale 'justify' being absent, working shorter hours, bad mouthing the company to customers, and quality slips. Survivors can be less supportive of any further changes, suspecting that they will cost them more than they have to gain. The organization begins to psychologically downsize, to emotionally shrink. Fear displaces loyalty, trust and creativity.[35]

Institutionalizing the new psychological contract

The post-downsizing psychological contract is often radically different from the old one. Loyalty to one's task or mission replaces unquestioning loyalty to the organization. Champions of the new contract claim that the old-style psychological contract was oppressive, stifling of individuality and entre-preneurship.[36] On loyalty, one observer trenchantly asserts: 'If you want loyalty go get a dog'.[37] Security is fleeting, tied to the task or project in hand. Success is rewarded with training and development opportunities within the organization to enhance 'employability', not with upward career progression in mind.

A study by Thomas and Dunkerley of downsized middle managers in the UK, explored their experiences of this 'new deal'.[38] Do they suffer the stresses and resentments of unhappy survivors, or do they come to enthusiastically embrace the new psychological contract? Thomas and Dunkerley found evidence of both reactions, but particularly the former. A strong theme was *feeling overworked, under-appreciated and betrayed.* Productivity and quality suffered from the effects of sheer overload. After downsizing, the same amount of work was simply loaded onto fewer workers. A public-service manager explains:

> I find it difficult to find the energy levels demanded of me. I certainly can't do this job up to retirement. We need to have 'rest posts' but there are less and less of these in the NHS [National Health Service] – it is more and more front line. It's more overloaded and there are greater demands. You end up developing a long-term tiredness. (Clinical Manager, NHS Trust)

The researchers also detected a culture of 'presenteeism', fearfulness about leaving their post at the end of the day: 'I don't want to be the first one to leave'. Downsizing left some middle managers feeling betrayed – 'identity-less and misplaced'. Their reconstituted role to 'team leader' was alienating:

> I lost status, lost my job, lost . . . I've worked very, very, hard all my life. I'm not a well-qualified person, you know, I realised early on that if I worked hard and long hours and all this sort of business . . . I could work my way up to a certain level and that's what I did. And I've reached that level and all of a sudden it was just taken away. I was 40 as well and I just thought, what am I going to do now? I had reached the spot at last where I thought I could sort of consolidate, settle down, but it was all knocked out from under my feet. (Team Leader, Utility)

Not everyone was so gloomy and dogged by survivor distress.[39] Some appreciated the closer link between their own efforts and outcomes, and were prepared to 'be seen working hard'; 'the company expects a lot out of me and they get a lot out of me and they reward me well'. For most, however, this felt more like 'working' than 'managing', as they were now disconnected from their link with senior management and their involvement in strategic matters.

NETWORK DESTRUCTION AND HOLES

Another way of examining how differently emotionalities are formed after downsizing is to examine the 'holes' that are left in the organization's formal and informal structure as people are removed from their posts; as desks and offices empty and as long-term relationships are fractured. Structural holes occur where links to unique sources of information or resources are missing.[40, 41] There are always structural holes in organizations but, after downsizing, holes open and close in ways that leave employees little control over the distribution of their relationships. That is, who they can talk to, who has relevant expertise, who are their friends, allies or foes. The political order of the organization is disrupted.

With this in mind, Susskind and Miller recorded the experiences of employees in the corporate office of a large, international, hospitality company, before and after downsizing. Some downsized employees were disadvantaged due to loss of information contacts, resources and friends; others improved their position in the network and gained from the change. Those experiencing increases in structural holes saw the organization in chaos. They became increasingly detached from others, less powerful in their network and saw few benefits from supporting the organizational changes. Those experiencing a closure of structural holes had more to benefit from downsizing. Their social networks were still coherent. But, at the same time, that put them in greater contact with others who were feeling isolation and loss from the downsizing, which negatively affected their own feelings about the organization, especially its trustworthiness.[42]

The image of an organization punctured with holes after downsizing is compelling. The important message, however, is that holes are likely to be more than structural gaps, which may or may not be filled. They will have been repositories for the organization's memory – stories, passions, dramas, visions, tacit knowledge – all of which once breathed life into the organization, a sense of history and expertise. Each person who is laid off leaves a memory gap, which, in many ways, is irreplaceable. The cultural glue of the organization is weakened, perhaps destroyed, and needs long-term repair or renewal.[43]

THE MOTIVATIONAL PARADOX

The downsized organization creates divisions of emotional labour, broadly reflecting the divide between those who have created the change and the survivors. For layoff survivors, being emotionally 'up', or positive, is counter-cultural, the wrong sort of feeling to display.[44] However, it is in top management's interest to be just the opposite, to put on an optimistic face, of the 'change is your friend' sort. Furthermore, they frequently wish to skim over the social–emotional implications of structural holes and get back to business as rapidly as possible.[45] In doing so, however, grieving is short-circuited, deepening resentment and resignation (see Chapter 8). An employee in O'Neill and Lenn's study makes the point:

> Listen, damn it. I stood up in a meeting to say morale was bad, and then was criticized by my boss. 'We don't wash our dirty linen in public.' he said. Well, then, it never gets washed. I'm being criticized for telling the truth. Aren't we supposed to be a company with integrity? I understand what's going on. I'll play along . . .[46]

Such comments underline the *motivational paradox* of downsizing. More work, more flexibility and more creativity is asked of people in social–emotional conditions that are contrary to these ends. Morale and trust are low, anger and insecurity are high.[47, 48] This does not mean that some people will not put in more effort. Insecurity and guilt can impel people to work harder to protect themselves (they believe) from the threat of further downsizing. Survivors can feel undeserved winners of downsizing, so their position needs to be justified, or earned, through increased effort.[49] But these are negative forms of motivation, working harder out of fear or guilt, not from positive engagement with the job. They can lead to a stressful, tense, work culture, of little joy or creativity.

If downsizing has to take place, its emotionalities need to be addressed. Some companies have done so, with a degree of skill and sensitivity. For example, a financial institution in the UK managed to avoid most of the usual signs of distress.[50] They made clear attempts to allay fear and anxiety by open communication, employee participation and ensuring that the process was as fair as possible in everyone's eyes. They offered good redundancy and retirement packages and outplacement services. Those who wanted to leave, but were not laid off, were told, 'stay with us, you are valued, we need you'. Managers were also given special training on 'how to deliver uneasy messages'.

CONCLUSION

Downsizing, through an emotion lens, reveals the fragility of the emotional bonds of an organization. The collapse of social networks takes with it trust, commitment and sense of purpose. Downsizing, as an 'economic necessity', is emotionally corrosive in both the short and long term. It is a shaky basis on which to base economic regeneration.

The economic anxiety that drives executives to downsize in the first place can, ironically, end up generating a new form of depressed enterprise (but disguised as 'crisp, lean and competitive'). Those who have survived are likely to be suspicious and fearful, uneasy about any new economic deal. And the more that firms downsize, the more those in the labour market feel this way. Some of the injuries can be mitigated, as we have seen; but to repair or reconstitute the emotional bonds is a slow, painstaking, task. It requires executives who are convinced that the social and emotional commitments of employees are intrinsic, rather than incidental, to the organization's economic performance.

FURTHER READING

Brockner, J. (1998) 'The effects of work layoffs on survivors: research, theory and practice', in B.M. Staw and L.L. Cummings (eds), *Research in Organizational Behavior*. Greenwich, CT: JAI Press, vol. 10.

Robbins, S.P. (1999) 'Layoff-survivor sickness: a missing topic in organization behavior'. *Journal of Management Education*, 23 (1): 31–4.

Shah, P.P. (2000) 'Network destruction: the structural implications of downsizing'. *Academy of Management Journal*, 43 (1): 101–12.

Wright, B. (1998) '"The executioners' song": listening to downsizers reflect on their experiences', *Canadian Journal of Administrative Sciences*, 15 (4): 339–57.

REFERENCES

1 Fineman, S. (1983) *White Collar Unemployment: Impact and Stress*. Chichester: Wiley. p. 37.

2 Deal, T. and Kennedy, A. (1999) *The New Corporate Cultures*. London: Textere. pp. 73–4.

3 Matheson, J. and Babb, P. (eds) (2002) *Social Trends*. London: The Stationery Office.

4 Cascio, W.F. (1993) 'Downsizing: what do we know? What have we learnt?', *Academy of Management Executive*, 17 (1): 95–104.

5 Deal, T. and Kennedy, A. (1999) *The New Corporate Cultures*. London: Textere. pp. 73–4.

6 Robbins, S.P. (1999) 'Layoff-survivor sickness: a missing topic in organization behavior', *Journal of Management Education*, 23 (1): 31–4.

7 Stamps, D. (1996) 'Corporate anorexia', *Training*, (February): 26.

8 Hamel, G. and Pralahad, C.K. (1994) *Competing for the Future*. Harvard: Harvard Business School Press.

9 Guiniven, J.E. (2001) 'The lessons of survivor literature in communicating decisions to downsize', *Journal of Business and Technical Communication*, 15 (1 January): 53–71.

10 Feldman, D.C. (2000) 'Down but not out: career trajectories of middle-aged and older workers after downsizing.' in R.J. Burke and C. Cooper (eds), *Organizations in Crisis*. Oxford: Blackwell.

11   Fineman, S. (1987) 'Back to employment: wounds and wisdoms', in D. Fryer and S. McKenna (eds), *Unemployed People*. Milton Keynes: Open University.

12   Anonymous (2002), *The Guardian* (23 March), London: 13.

13   Gilson, C. (1992) 'The termination of Eric Clark', in J. Frost, V.F. Mitchell and W. Nord (eds), *Organizational Reality – Reports from the Firing Line*. New York: Harper Collins.

14   Wright, B. (1998) '"The executioner's song": listening to downsizers reflect on their experiences', *Canadian Journal of Administrative Sciences*, 15 (4): 339–57, especially p. 340.

15   Kets de Vries, M.F.R. and Balazs, K. (1997) 'The downside of downsizing', *Human Relations*, 50 (1): 11–50.

16   Gooding, J. (1977) 'The art of firing an executive', in P.J. Frost, V.F. Mitchell and W. Nord (eds), *Organizational Reality: Reports from the Firing Line*. Glenview, Illinois: Scott Foresman.

17   Lamsa, A.-M. and Takla, T. (2000) 'Downsizing and ethics of personnel dismissals – the case of Finnish managers', *Journal of Business Ethics*, 23: 389–99.

18   Wright, B. (1998) '"The executioner's song": listening to downsizers reflect on their experiences', *Canadian Journal of Administrative Sciences*, 15 (4): 347.

19   Kets de Vries, M.F.R. and Balazs, K. (1997) 'The downside of downsizing', *Human Relations*, 50 (1): 11–50, especially pp. 31–7.

20   Cascio, W.F. (1993) 'Downsizing: what do we know? What have we learnt?', *Academy of Management Executive*, 17 (1): 95–104.

21   Robbins, S.P. (1999) 'Layoff-survivor sickness: a missing topic in organization behavior', *Journal of Management Education*, 23 (1): 31–4.

22   Burke, R.J. and Cooper, C. (2000) 'The new organizational reality: transition and renewal', in R.J. Burke and C. Cooper (eds), *The Organization in Crisis*. Oxford: Blackwell.

23   Cascio, W.F. (1998) 'Learning from the experiences of 311 firms that have downsized', in M.K. Gowing, J.D. Kraft and J.C. Quick (eds), *The New Organizational Reality: Downsizing, Restructuring and Revitalization*. Washington, DC: American Psychological Association.

24   Brockner, J. (1998) 'The effects of work layoffs on survivors: research, theory and practice', in B.M. Staw and L.L. Cummings (eds), *Research in Organizational Behavior*. Greenwich, CT: JAI Press, vol. 10.

25   Burke, R.J. and Leiter, M.P. (2000) 'Contemporary organizational realities and professional efficacy: downsizing, reorganization, and transition', in P. Dewe, M.P. Leiter and T. Cox (eds), *Stress, Coping and Health in Organizations*. London: Taylor and Francis. pp. 237–58.

26   Allen, T.D., Freeman, D.M. and Russell, J.E.A. (2001) 'Survivor reaction to organizational downsizing: Does time ease the pain?', *Journal of Occupational and Organizational Psychology*, 74: 145–64.

27   This is not to suggest that downsizing is in any way as devastating as the Holocaust experience.

28 Guiniven, J.E. (2001) 'The lessons of survivor literature in communicating decisions to downsize', *Journal of Business and Technical Communication*, 15 (1 January): 53–71.

29 Noer, D. (1993) *Healing the Wounds: Overcoming the Trauma of Layoffs and Revitalizing Downsized Organizations*. San Francisco: Jossey-Bass.

30 Guiniven, J.E. (2001) 'The lessons of survivor literature in communicating decisions to downsize', *Journal of Business and Technical Communication*, 15 (1 January): 53–71.

31 O'Neill, H.M. and Lenn, D.J. (1995) 'Voices of survivors: words that downsizing CEOs should hear', *Academy of Management Executive*, 9 (4): 23–33, especially p. 25.

32 Rousseau, D. (1995) *Psychological Contracts in Organizations*. Thousand Oaks: Sage.

33 Thornhill, A. and Gibbons, A. (1995) 'The positive management of redundancy survivors: issues and lessons', *British Journal of Management*, 7 (3): 5–12.

34 Kettley, P. (1995) Employee morale during downsizing. Institute for Employment Studies, Report 291, Brighton.

35 Buch, K. and Aldridge, S. (1990) 'OD under conditions of organization decline', *Organization Development Journal*, 9 (1): 1–5.

36 Noer, D. (1993) *Healing the Wounds: Overcoming the Trauma of Layoffs and Revitalizing Downsized Organizations*. San Francisco: Jossey-Bass.

37 Heckscher, C. (1991) *White Collar Blues: Management Loyalties in an Age of Corporate Restructuring*. New York: Basic Books. p. 33.

38 Thomas, R. and Dunkerley, D. (1999) 'Plus ca change . . .? Restructuring and the realities of "new managerial work"'. 5th Critical Perspectives on Accounting Conference, *Ethical Dimensions of Accounting Change* (April), Baruch College, New York: 6–8.

39 Dopson, S. and Stewart, R. (1990) 'What is happening to middle management?', *British Journal of Management*, 1 (1): 3–16.

40 Burt, R.S. (1992) *Structural Holes, the Social Structure of Competition*. Cambridge, MA: Harvard University Press.

41 Shah, P.P. (2000) 'Network destruction: the structural implications of downsizing', *Academy of Management Journal*, 43 (1): 101–12.

42 Susskind, A.M. and Miller, V.D. (1998) 'Downsizing and structural holes', *Communication Research*, 25 (1): 30–6.

43 Deal, T. and Kennedy, A. (1999) *The New Corporate Cultures*. London: Textere. pp. 73–4.

44 Robbins, S.P. (1999) 'Layoff-survivor sickness: a missing topic in organization behaviour', *Journal of Management Education*, 23 (1): 31–4, especially p. 35.

45 Guiniven, J.E. (2001) 'The lessons of survivor literature in communicating decisions to downsize', *Journal of Business and Technical Communication*, 15 (1 January): 53–71.

46 O'Neill, H.M. and Lenn, D.J. (1995) 'Voices of survivors: words that downsizing CEOs should hear', *Academy of Management Executive*, 9 (4): 23–33, especially p. 4.
47 Brockner, J. (1998) 'The effects of work layoffs on survivors: research, theory and practice', in B.M. Staw and L.L. Cummings (eds), *Research in Organizational Behavior*. Greenwich, CT: JAI Press, vol. 10.
48 Spreitzer, G.M. and Mishra, A.M. (2000) 'An empirical examination of a stress-based framework of survivor response to downsizing', in R.J. Burke and C. Cooper (eds), *The Organization in Crisis*. Oxford: Blackwell.
49 Noer, D. (1993) *Healing the Wounds: Overcoming the Trauma of Layoffs and Revitalizing Downsized Organizations*. San Francisco: Jossey-Bass.
50 Baruch, Y. and Hind, P. (2000) '"Survivor syndrome" – a management myth?', *Journal of Management Psychology*, 15 (1): 29–45

Concluding reflections

This book has covered a lot of ground – and could have covered more. Feelings permeate all that we do at work, but feelings and emotions are more than simply 'part of everything'. That understates their influence. They have specific roles and functions, and we have addressed some of them. They are commodities to sell in the marketplace where emotional labour is now a common feature of the employment contract, but with mixed emotional outcomes. They have been promoted, sometimes over-promoted, as key accompaniments to 'intelligent' behavior and success at work. They lie at the core of decision making and ethical conduct, but are often sorely neglected in practice. Leadership and 'followership' spring to life when we see how emotions bond and express the way influence operates. The emotions of leadership reveal much about the way organizations provide precarious, but much sought after, psychological meaning to individuals.

Organizational changes stand or fall on the management of the emotions of those affected, as do major changes from downsizing. Downsizing, however, tends to strip the organization of its emotional assets, which are hard to replace. Virtual organizations have transformed the communication of emotions, but not with the inevitable loss that some critics claim. An emotion perspective also shows where and how organizations can bring a dark cloud over the workplace – in stress, bullying, harassment and violence. These share a common plight: they are most often treated as an individual matter, not an organizational cultural one. Moreover, the emotional and costs are rarely fully counted.

MOVING ON

Beyond these understandings, where does an emotion perspective take us? Ultimately, some suggest, toward a more authentic, more open, more honest workplace, which truly honours emotions. I have some sympathy with these sentiments, but words like 'authenticity' and 'honesty' leave me uneasy. They fail to square with *necessary* emotional hypocrisy that all organizational life feeds upon (see Chapter 2). Authenticity has many faces, not just one. The skilled organizational actor crafts his or her emotional display sensitively, to steer, without undue collision, between the different interpersonal and political demands. Sometimes this brings feeling and emotion into line. Other times not. Emotional honesty, expressing precisely what you feel, is a risky recipe. It can hurt, injure, confuse or overwhelm people. It rattles the 'good enough' agreements that are necessary to complete a task, meet a deadline, or cement a team. The trick is knowing just how much 'honesty' helps or hinders essential organizational processes – such as bonding, deference, collaboration, pride in quality, comfort, authority and efficiency. The socialization of emotion is designed to achieve these very ends.

One strong message from this book is that we usually take these processes for granted, sometimes with dire consequences. In other words, while feeling and emotions are 'there', they are often not acknowledged or valued in workplace design or management. They tend to come after the event, and are readily discounted as worthy experiences or relevant organizational data. This is unfortunate and short sighted.

In several chapters I have spoken about the importance of recognizing the emotional fabric of organizational culture. Organizational culture has become a popular label in management speak ('our production difficulties are a cultural problem', 'there's a punitive culture here', 'this place has a culture of excellence'). It is a term that has become an almost clichéd way of classifying a problem, issue or ethos, with little sense of what follows. Talking about the emotions of culture, therefore, requires some elucidation.

The customs, norms, tacit understandings, ritualized practices (regular meetings, coffee groups, celebrations), status symbols (size of offices, company car, type of personal computer, salary band), all constitute what the workplace signifies, or stands for, in the eyes of the worker. Formally, and blandly, they may be described as 'the work environment' or 'Human Resources Management practices', but as cultural features they are much more than this. They constitute a framework of *affective meaning* for people. Routines, relationships and objects are infused with feeling – excitement, ease, anxiety, boredom, pride, belonging, embarrassment, fear, love, and so forth. When executives, managers, or others, seek to re-form a business, they are also disturbing the emotional culture, the flow of tacit negotiations that give people a 'place' and identity. And when individuals leave or join an organization, emotional understandings are ruffled, sometimes fractured, as the organization attempts to fill structural holes or incorporate newcomers. Performance in the job (and the 'bottom line') depend on all these processes, as does the nature of experience of one's work.

Many such issues are self-resolving. That is, the work culture is self-healing and self-renewing as people re-negotiate their space and place. Emotional meanings are sustained or re-framed to meet important desires, to protect people from unwanted anxieties and to achieve feelings of worthiness. But, as we have seen in this book, it does not always result in happy endings. The social constituency of emotion is a very mixed one, where some individuals have more power and advantage than others, and where emotional concerns and vulnerabilities can be exploited for personal gain. At times, the unhappy endings are a product of an overarching culture of emotional muteness or ignorance. Simply, emotions are not counted by the people who count most other things in the organization.

REFOCUSING

Finally, I have referred, a number of times in the book, to the value of emotional sensitivity in organizational management. If emotions are neglected or not seen, then the managerial lens needs re-focussing. At present it is rare to find this happening, and management education needs to lead the way. While the instrumental benefits (profit, promotion) of emotional intelligence are being extolled, the qualitative gains of social and emotional sensitivity have been neglected.

Emotional sensitivity is the capacity and foresight to read, and work with, emotions, in a pluralistic fashion. That is, to understand that people engage in work for different emotional ends and from different emotional impulses, which are invariably influenced by managerial actions and organizational arrangements. The quality of work-life spins around such considerations, reflected especially in the way emotional injuries are handled, compassion displayed and trust formed. To be sensitive to emotions does not mean transforming the manager into a psychoanalyst. Basically, and pragmatically, it is increasing the manager's awareness of the role and legitimacy of emotions in organizational transactions, and about the organizational benefits that this can bring.

Index